About the author

Alex Butchart is associate professor in the department of psychology, UNISA. A widely published psychologist, he is a long-term activist in democratic public health promotion and was a member of the Goldstone Commission committee.

The Anatomy of Power
European Constructions of the African Body

Alexander Butchart

Zed Books

LONDON AND NEW YORK

The Anatomy of Power: European constructions of the African Body
was first published by Zed Books Ltd, 7 Cynthia Street, London
NI 9JF, UK and Room 400, 175 Fifth Avenue, New York, NY 10010,
USA in 1998.

Distributed exclusively in the USA by St Martin's Press, Inc.,
175 Fifth Avenue, New York, NY 10010, USA.

Cover designed by Andrew Corbett
Set in Monotype Dante by Ewan Smith

A catalogue record for this book is available from the British
Library

US CIP has been applied for from the Library of Congress

ISBN 1-85649-540-X

Transferred to digital printing 2005

Contents

Illustrations

Preface

This study applies some of the theoretical tools developed by Michel Foucault to the problem of the African body as it exists to western socio-medical science[1] in Africa. Foucault argued that all methods of knowing the human body relate to it not as a means of discovery against an object waiting to be known, but as a productive power towards an object that is also its effect. The concept defining this productive relationship between method and object is 'disciplinary power' (Foucault 1977), which consists in the techniques by which human bodies are observed, analysed and fabricated as knowable entities possessed of particular attributes and characteristics. For example, each time it enters the surgery to invite clinical examination by the doctor, or is physically inspected and radiographed in the mine medical examination, the African body is not found but fabricated by these socio-medical micro-powers, not so much their discovery as an invention of their power.

The Anatomy of Power is therefore a genealogical study in that it examines the relations between socio-medical practices as power and the resultant knowledges of the African body: 'The exercise of power perpetually creates knowledge and, conversely, knowledge constantly induces the effects of power' (Foucault, in C. Gordon 1980: 52). The consequence of this is a concern not with what is there but rather with what can be seen, and the study articulates a close historical correspondence between the use of certain methods and the perceived nature of the African body. This makes it possible to analyse changes over time in the identity of the African body as an effect of this productive relationship, rather than a consequence of discovery, the lifting of oppression and ideological distortion, or any other explanatory device drawn from the discourse of progressive humanism that informs conventional analyses of the socio-medical sciences in colonial and most other situations.

The assumptions and aims of the study derive therefore from a plane of cognition independent from that of humanism. Hence it can pose a variety of 'strategic questions' (Armstrong 1987) about particular objects and experiences (such as the body, the mind and subjectivity) which because they form the philosophical bedrock of humanism cannot be problematized from within the humanist framework itself. How is it possible to speak of the human body in general and the African body in particular as distinct corporeal entities? What made possible the perception of an 'African personality' and later 'black consciousness' as the psychological component of identity? How could medicine have first asserted and later denied the fact of racial differences in physiology and disease susceptibility? What conditions of possibility had to be present for the ideas of culture and urbanization to emerge into the socio-medical knowledge of Africa? Flowing from this space of strategic questioning are the three aims of the study.

First, to describe the genealogical method by which this study has been produced, and to articulate how the Foucauldean schema conceptualizes body, power and knowledge. Second, to apply these concepts to analysing how the African body has been analysed in western thought from the Renaissance[2] to the 1990s, and in doing so to identify the power implications of changes in how it has been known and what it has been seen to be. Third, to examine the implications of the study's findings and the Foucauldean method for socio-medical practitioners and scholars of the sociology of medicine.

While most of the source materials for this study concern the socio-medical sciences in South Africa, this does not limit its relevance to that society. Although its generalizability is restricted in respect of the precise details concerning when, how and with what effects the socio-medical sciences emerged, the more general anatomy of power and the bodies that this produces are most certainly applicable to all situations of colonial occupation. Indeed, it is difficult to identify a single example of a colonial or post-colonial society in which the public-health official, the primary-health-care nurse, the hospital doctor, the psychiatrist and many other representatives of the socio-medical sciences are not a ubiquitous presence. It is equally impossible to identify any setting where the population has no knowledge of how to act and react in the ritual of the medical examination by the doctor, inspection by the aid worker, interrogation by the anthropologist or enumeration by the census officer. Wherever such figures and rituals appear, the diagram of power cannot be reduced to a simple equation of power as that which is held and wielded by one group over another, since wherever they appear is also where discipline is at play, fabricating the human body and the social as its visible objects and effects.

However, while this means that colonial power is always more complex and invisible than conventional analyses would suggest, it is also true that its disciplinary underbelly cannot be regarded as evenly distributed in equal circuits operating everywhere with the same intensity and the same results. Rather, it should be thought of as a constantly mutating force field in which socio-medical discipline waxes and wanes in unpredictable cycles and surges. In turn, this implies that while the identity of the African body is always in part an effect of this power, its precise genealogy is situationally specific, demanding that the fine details of its crystallization be established through equally fine-tuned studies of the exact mechanisms by which it is examined and by which its culturally and chronologically specific attributes and characteristics are determined.

Chapter 1 reviews existing historical accounts of the association between the socio-medical sciences and the African body. This shows that despite its prominence in these traditional accounts (which range from Whig histories celebrating medicine to Marxist histories of medicine as repression), there is no history of the African body itself, which is unproblematically assumed to be a given object there to be impinged upon and resist socio-medical practices. By comparing these traditional accounts with the genealogical method, Chapter 1 explicates how genealogical explorations differ from conventional modes of analysis.

Chapter 2 presents a theoretical elaboration of those Foucauldean concepts concerning power, the body and medical knowledge relevant to this study. The emergence of disciplinary power and the correlative constitution by medicine of the human body as a clearly differentiated collection of organs and tissues occurred with some suddenness and only towards the end of the eighteenth century. How was the body seen prior to this great shift? By what languages was the body read, and how did beings believed to exist on and beyond the fringes of the known world confirm these ancient ways of knowing?

An attempt to answer these questions appears in Chapters 3 and 4. Chapter 3 examines texts concerning the body, its properties, and its possible forms produced in the period of Renaissance thought from around 1500 to 1650. During this period human bodies were known not through their direct inspection but through the study of authoritative texts. These texts repeatedly affirmed the resonance of human bodies with astrological and climatic forces, which alongside the legends and virtues attaching to bodies were as much a characteristic of their description as any morphological features. Roughly coinciding with the European colonization of Africa, the age of Renaissance thought gave way from the mid-seventeenth century to the age of Classification.

For the first time, and as examined in Chapter 4, there now commenced 'a meticulous examination of things themselves' (Foucault 1973: 131). Living beings began to be ordered not according to their 'imaginary' characteristics of old, but in terms of their perceptible physical structures. It was therefore at this point that the African body first emerged into western knowledge in something approximating to the distinctively human form we now take for granted, as along with the plants and animals of Africa it was made an object of natural history and installed in the botanical classification system of Linnaeus as 'Afer Niger' under the category 'homo sapiens'.

While the Classical age produced an African body without organs as the object and effect of its taxonomic vision to the body's surface, it was only towards the mid-1800s and with the emergence of 'missionary medicine' that it became possible to speak freely of this body as an object possessed of an interior anatomy. This transformation is examined in Chapter 5, which analyses the medical missionary method and its fabrication of the relationship between African witchcraft and illness as the primary target of an evangelizing project to 'save' Africans by 'weaning' them from 'heathen' superstitions concerning the body and disease.

Because it is both target and effect of the socio-medical practices that sustain and transform it, the human body as an object of disciplinary power can never be considered finished or approaching completion. On the contrary, its contingent status means that it is constantly created and re-created as different components of the socio-medical apparatus negotiate and install different relationships between the body and its disciplinary micro-powers. This is reflected in Chapters 6 to 10, which examine the multiple African bodies fabricated in four distinct domains.

Chapter 6 focuses upon the machinery of mining medicine and its production of the migrant labour force as a closely monitored economy of bodies, disease and deviance. Through the simultaneous deployment of procedures that penetrated deep within the body to fabricate the space of anatomical pathology, and of surveillance techniques directed to the gaps between bodies, this industrious medicine at once individualized the body of the African miner and encased it in a network of rules devoted to the training of healthy conduct and regulation of bodily functions.

The conditions permitting invention of the African mind as an object of psychiatry and psychology are explored in Chapter 7. First within the asylum, and from the 1920s increasingly in the urban spaces of conflict between Europeans and Africans, the psychological sciences had by the 1930s crystallized an 'African personality' as their object and effect. By the 1980s, and reflecting the irony of a progressive humanism that in its quest for liberation produced precisely the authentic African subject as its effect, rejection of the 'African personality' as an ideological myth produced a 'liberatory psychology', which since then has continued to elaborate its repertoire of subjectifying techniques.

Chapter 8 examines public health to show how its technologies produced the African body not through direct inspection, but through problematization of the spaces between bodies and the fabrication of a social body. From the turn of the twentieth century to the mid-1930s, sanitary science produced the social as a series of gaps between bodies and the environment that were seen as a conduit for the transmission of germs and dirt and so required constant policing through prohibitive measures. In the 1930s, these repressive strategies were displaced by positive techniques directed to recruiting Africans into monitoring and managing their own body-boundaries, as the new method of social medicine transformed the socio-physical space of old into a psycho-social one. The chapter continues with an analysis of the emergence of community health in the 1960s, and concludes with the 'socio-ecological' model of the new public health as it lays its lines of surveillance everywhere and throughout the body politic.

Chapter 9 examines what clinical medicine has seen and heard in relation to the African body. Invented in the mid-1930s, the African patient as the objectified effect of a specifically 'Bantu' clinical practice was confirmed until the 1960s, when a new strand entered the 'Bantu clinic' to enable recognition of the African patient's culture, beliefs, emotions and ideas as important components of the clinical encounter. The chapter ends with the 1990s' 'quest for wholeness' and fabrication of the clinical encounter as a socially constructed ritual where doctor and patient are equally agentic participants in the negotiation of illness.

As a postscript, Chapter 10 recursively applies the Foucauldean perspective to analysing the failure of social scientists in Africa to apply Foucault's ideas to the field of socio-medical practice. Closely bound up with the notions of ideology, repression and liberation that dominate conventional critical analyses, this failure is read as an ironic confirmation for the success of disciplinary power in fabricating the African body as an apparently transcendental entity and the socio-medical practitioners who see it as potentially platonic observers.

Itself part of the Foucauldean discourse that makes such an exercise possible, this study cannot be viewed as independent of the domain it analyses. Indeed, precisely because there are no objects of knowledge in the absence of methods for their production, the study is itself a productive component in the discursive context of post-modernism, and it makes no claims to being more correct than existing explorations of the same domain. What is instead hoped is that its analyses of the African body will destabilize what otherwise is experienced as certainty, to induce an appreciation of seemingly trivial practices as invested with a power that in penetrating and rearranging the objects of medical knowledge actively create and regulate the human body.

Like every other subset of bodies produced by socio-medical power everywhere, the African body is not a fixed phenomenon waiting to be distorted by ideological filters or of which medical doctors gradually achieve a more accurate understanding. The human body as a static phenomenon does exist, but only as a product of the modernist discursive regime upon which both Whig histories of scientific progressivism and Marxist histories of liberal humanism rest. Because these accord an ahistorical essentialism to the body they must themselves be considered instruments of disciplinary power, in so far as they operate to obscure the body's contingent status as an end-product of the very force relations they construe as emanating from it.

Notes

1. By the socio-medical sciences is meant all those disciplines (e.g. clinical medicine, public health, psychology, psychiatry, anthropology, sociology and so on) that have at some point been deployed in Africa to manage the relation of Africans to disease, illness and the social context in which these occur.

2. Since the very idea of the African body as we now know it was not a possibility in the Renaissance, it is, strictly speaking, incorrect to write as if there was such an entity in this period. However, and as shown in Chapter 3, there certainly was a class of bodies believed to exist in the geographical region now known as Africa, and it is to this class of bodies that use here of the term 'African body' refers.

CHAPTER I

The African Body in History and Histories of the African Body

The African body appears everywhere in studies of social science and medicine in Africa. For instance:

> The Government and the frontier colonists did all they could and at Kingwilliamstown [*sic*] droves of hungry and dying natives applied daily to Dr. Fitzgerald for help. His fame as a medicine-man spread like wildfire and by August, 1856 he could report enthusiastically on the treatment of 2,278 cases. (Burrows 1958: 182)

As well as appearing in historical studies, the African body is a central focus of current socio-medical practice:

> In Johannesburg a family of surveys has been conducted by the AIDS Virus Research Unit of the Medical Research Council at the National Institute of Virology. These sentinel surveys show that, in STD clinics, 14.6% and 20.4% of black males and females respectively are infected with HIV. This is in comparison to 4.2% and 1.8% of white males and females respectively. (Steinberg 1993: 90)

Despite its ubiquitous presence in historical accounts and contemporary research materials the African body itself is only rarely the subject of historical analysis. Instead, it appears to have been assumed that the African body is possessed of a transcendental ontological status that permits its existence beyond history.

What has therefore been studied in some detail is how representations of the African body in western socio-medical thought have changed over time (e.g. Dietrich 1993; Gilman 1985; Pratt 1992; Seedat 1993), and how its differing treatment within the formal health-care system has reflected the changing social, economic and ideological climate (e.g. De Beer 1984). Because they assume the pre-existence of the African body as an unvarying entity in an external reality round which these historically variable ways of treating it circle, these conventional accounts are not histories of the body, but instead are histories of ideas, images, policies and professions. The present study does not therefore attempt yet another explanation in terms of an historical progression from the past to the present of why sub-branches of the social sciences and medicine devoted to African health and illness appeared, developed and disappeared. In fact, while many of the texts it assembles come from times well before this study commenced, it would be wrong even to think of it as a history in the conventional sense of the term. Rather, it demonstrates how the African body has been created and transformed as an object of knowledge, how its attributes and capacities are contingent upon the methods applied to know it, and therefore how strategies of the state and industry, along with the various socio-medical sciences that assume its existence, are possible.

How can this question of the African body as a distinct object of socio-medical knowledge have been so thoroughly ignored? An answer to this is offered by distinguishing the genealogical method and its histories of the present from the more conventional notion of the history of the past.

Histories of medicine as achievement, function and repression

Existing histories of the socio-medical sciences in South Africa are all histories of the past. That is, they project backwards from the present concepts such as economy, ideology and epidemiology in an attempt to trace how patterns of disease and health-care have altered over time to produce the present situation. These histories can be classified into three broad categories on the basis of how they explain the emergence of the socio-medical disciplines in relation to Africans and the socio-political order more generally.

On the one hand, there are histories of medicine as achievement that portray the discipline's unfolding as one of linear progression driven by factors internal to the medical profession and the scientific method. On the other hand are histories of medicine as repression, that emphasize the place of the socio-medical sciences in relation to Africans as instrumental components of colonialism and capitalism, and tend to interpret the achievements paraded by the first class of histories less as triumphs than as markers of tyranny. In between these two extremes, there is an intermediary class of medical histories that construe the socio-medical sciences as having developed into their present configuration because there was so much disease that required treatment. Following Nettleton (1992: 2), this last class of histories reflects a 'functional approach'.

Histories of medicine as achievement

> And so down the ages these 'mighty medicine men', ... have helped push the boundaries of medical knowledge further forward. Their achievements brought enlightenment and inspiration to succeeding generations, for the work of the present and future is based always on that of the past. (Krige 1939: 72)

In 1939, *The Leech* devoted one entire edition to an historical review of the technological advances underlying the development of medicine in Europe, and how these had enabled the expansion of medical services in Africa. The motivation lay in the idea that a knowledge of the past would limit the possibility of erring in the present: 'Medical history ... prevents us from losing our sense of proportion; its kindly light leads us back to the world of practical realities, and assists us in gaining a proper perspective on health and disease' (Editorial 1939: 7).

Some fifteen years later, the idea that medical history could help retain a 'proper perspective' on the practice and problems of medicine found its first sustained expression[1] in relation to South African medical history with the publication of three books devoted to the topic (Burrows 1958; Hattersley 1955; Menko 1954). Best defined as Whig histories in that they were written for the medical profession, these texts drew upon biographical accounts of people whom their authors considered great doctors to produce heroic accounts of how they had succeeded in establishing western medicine in the barren and hostile context of a new continent and African antipathy toward bio-medicine. 'A record of the development of medicine in a young country depends upon the origins of its people and the sources of its civilization', wrote Burrows (1958: 3). Elaborating this theme, he said of 'the solid achievements of the early pioneers of medical organization' that:

> It was ... they who planted the germ of medical politics and professional union in South Africa; and it was they who were responsible for the emergence of a medical public opinion in the Cape Colony. Without continual pressure of voluntary associations of doctors ... the Colonial Government would probably have delayed its health legislation to the present century ... certainly the profession would have been a great deal poorer in their absence. (Burrows 1958: 367)

In 1959, a Natal newspaper celebrated the centenary of the King William's Town Hospital with a review of its history to 'honour the memory of those who went before, those who by faith, courage and fortitude gave a living example in the greatest of all lessons – man's humanity to man' (*Mercury* 1959: 4). Producing a similar image of western medicine in Africa as the triumphal product of remarkable medical pioneers, the dust jacket to Laidler and Gelfand's (1971) volume superimposed sketches of important doctors upon images of Boer trek wagons to connote the unstoppable march of medicine and 'civilization'. A similar theme characterized Gelfand's (1984) *Christian Doctor and Nurse*, which set out the missionary medical struggle involved in bringing 'God's Medicine' to the African.

In the mid-1970s a second wave of Whig histories that attributed medicine's development less to the agency of particular individuals and more to the inevitable progress of science began to appear (e.g. Brink 1988; James 1975; Malan 1988). Epitomizing this tradition is the dedication to Malan's (1988) *The Quest of Health*, where he portrays a medicine that 'through observation and research' rose 'out of the abyss of tradition, myth, superstition and philosophy into the light of scientific understanding'.

Functional histories of medicine Against the parade of progress that marks histories of medicine as achievement, the cardinal feature of functional histories of medicine is their emphasis upon disease and epidemics, which are viewed as provoking the establishment of medical services and health legislation (e.g. Cartwright 1971; Friedlander 1974; J. F. Murray 1963; H. Phillips 1990; Van Heyningen 1989).

The tenor of these functional histories is illustrated by examining how Phillips (1990) tracked the Spanish influenza pandemic of 1918–19 as it 'struck' South Africa in October 1918. First, the text minutely details the piecemeal reactions of health authorities, private doctors and the public to the influenza epidemic in three major cities. Next, this is used to reveal the inadequacies of the public-health apparatus and to expose the otherwise veiled fabric of society. Finally, the materials are marshalled to argue that in the absence of the epidemic South Africa's first substantive public-health act (the Public Health Act No. 36 of 1919) would probably not have been enacted until much later. Phillips could thus write of November 1918:

> By this time the need for comprehensive public health legislation had been made undeniably clear by the gross failure of the existing organisation to deal with the epidemic. Throughout the country the demand for rapid and concrete action in this direction was clamorous. *The Friend* was one of several newspapers to express this sentiment, pointing out that the calamity of the 'flu 'affords as terrible an object lesson of the need of a Public Health Act administered in the main by central authority as Nature in her most maleficent mood could have devised'. (H. Phillips 1990: 162)

In like fashion, but adding an economic factor into the complex of needs, Murray (1963: 391) argued that the South African Institute for Medical Research grew in response to 'the need for research into diseases which were of vital economic importance to the mining industry'.

Histories of medicine as repression Histories that explain medicine's development in Africa as achievement or as a functional response to overwhelming need do not lend any special focus to the African. Certainly, Africans are present in these stories, but their role is a peripheral one, subordinate to the heroic deeds of white doctors (the achievement approach) or swept up with Europeans in the all-engulfing tide of disease (the functional approach). In sharp contrast, it is primarily upon the African that histories of medicine as repression (which began to appear in the mid-1970s) are focused. For instance, Swanson's (1977) paper on bubonic plague and urban native policy in the Cape Colony between 1900 and 1909, argued how:

> [M]edical officials and other public health authorities at the turn of this century were imbued with the imagery of infectious disease as a societal metaphor, and that this metaphor powerfully interacted with British and South African racial attitudes to influence the policies and shape the institutions of segregation ... Overcrowding, slums, public health and safety, often seen in the light of class and ethnic differences in industrial societies, were in the colonial context perceived largely in terms of colour differences. Conversely, urban race relations came to be widely conceived and dealt with in the imagery of infection and epidemic disease ... In this context the accident of epidemic plague became a dramatic and compelling opportunity for those who were promoting segregationist solutions to medical problems. (Swanson 1977: 387)

Placing equivalent emphasis upon state manipulation of health-care resources in the service of African oppression, the World Health Organization's 1983 volume *Apartheid and Health* stated that 'apartheid has shown itself to be a veritable racist ideology ... And it is this racist ideology which guides all health action in South Africa' (WHO 1983: 6). Extending this theme, a chapter on the origins of South African society and its health system showed how 'The patterns of disease and health care relate directly to the nature of its industrialization and the unequal distribution of resources rather than to any lack of "development" among the black population. Health care policies are directly related to more general government strategies of control through reform' (WHO 1983: 77).

Sharpening the image of medical policy and practices as weapons wielded by the state in its oppression of Africans, Marks and Andersson (1988) delineated South African government responses to typhus epidemics between 1917 and 1950 as revealing 'the concerns of the state and the ruling class in society, both with their own safety and with the reproduction of the labour force' (Marks and Andersson 1988: 259), an interpretation closely echoed in Packard's (1989) analysis of capitalism, racism and tuberculosis.

At the core of these histories of medicine as repression is the idea that the actions of medical practitioners and policy-makers were inevitably imbued with the exploitative interests and ideology of colonial imperialism. Arnold's 1988 volume *Imperial Medicine and Indigenous Societies* was therefore concerned 'not so much with disease and medicine as such as with their instrumentality – what they reveal about the nature and process, the ambitions and methods of an encompassing imperialism' (Arnold 1988: ii). The emphasis in these histories of medicine as repression is therefore upon the equation of socio-medical power with a physical and symbolic force concentrated in the hands of the ruling elite who use it to negate and constrain the authenticity and freedom of those it is turned upon.

> The [South African] health service is the prisoner of this country's political history ... the prisoner of Apartheid. The homelands and their health services are there because of Verwoerd's grandiose vision of partition. The own and general affairs divisions are there because of the tightening of the Apartheid noose under the Botha government. (De Beer 1990: 8)

Historiography, progress and the present

This brief historiography of the socio-medical sciences in Africa demonstrates how explanations for the discipline's emergence are relative to the author's historical context, professional affiliation and political persuasion. This is a far from remarkable observation, the very method of historiography having arisen precisely in response to the observation that histories of the past inevitably reveal as much about the author's historical and political context as they do about the subject matter. But there is a more fundamental point to be taken from this review that renders what are ostensibly politically polarized versions of the past components of a single discursive formation.

This commonality is twofold. First, all three types of history subscribe to an idea of history as one of continuity and progression. For histories of achievement, these developments are internal to the socio-medical professions, involving increasing altruism on the part of doctors and inevitable scientific progression as new medical techniques make possible the abandonment of erroneous beliefs. For functional histories, this human agency and intra-scientific development is subordinate to the external pressure of disease. This forces development of the medical enterprise to mean that its shape today is the product of past disasters and current needs. For histories of medicine as repression, the shape of the enterprise at any given point reflects the outcome of repression and resistance, through which the concentration of medical power in the hands of the state and medical professionals is continually usurped and replaced by a more egalitarian system. In their preoccupation with progress, all three types of history thus reproduce what Foucault described as among 'the most harmful habits in contemporary thought ... the analysis of the present as ... a presence of rupture, or of high point, or of completion or of a returning dawn' (Foucault, in Kritzman 1988: 35).

The second facet of this commonality derives from the first. Because all three historical types privilege accounts of how individuals and groups seized socio-medical power or were systematically debarred from accessing it, they fail to problematize the African body itself by assuming it to exist independently of the socio-medical practices they address. For only if it is taken to have an existence independent of these practices can there be any progress towards more adequately understanding and treating the African body; or from the repressionist perspective, away from its oppression toward its liberation. In terms of the Foucauldean power schema, they all speak in one way or another to the idea of 'sovereign power' (Foucault 1977) alone, the idea that power exists as a commodity or weapon there to be grasped and wielded, fought for and won over. They consequently fail to grasp the significance of such apparently innocent rituals of disciplinary power as the routine clinical examination or school medical inspection: 'Look at the lines of medical surveillance: "What is your complaint?" "How do you feel?" "Please tell me your troubles." See the routine clinical techniques: the rash displayed, the hand applied to the abdomen, the stethoscope placed gently on the chest' (Armstrong 1987: 70).

As Chapter 2 argues, these procedures are the stuff of disciplinary power, repetitive, ritualized and, no matter how repressive the more encompassing socio-political context, strategies to which the entire population at times must yield.

Using the theoretical tension between sovereign and disciplinary power, this study provides a different perspective. It problematizes the African body itself, rather than the legal enactments, professional power-plays and political struggles that constantly envelop and take its existence for granted. It has no interest in whether the South African

Health Act No. 63 of 1977 did or did not represent a move from discrimination towards a progressive politics (WHO 1983: 99). It is unconcerned with whether it really was 'with the arrival of white settlers that our people fell prey to a host of diseases' (WHO 1983: 14); and it has no interest in re-creating the machinations through which the apartheid state suppressed public knowledge concerning the true extent of cholera epidemics in the early 1980s (Marks and Andersson 1988: 257–8). In short, this study does not attempt to reconstruct the past through the conceptual and political lens of the present, but rather to produce a 'history of the present' that examines socio-medical objects, concepts and practices within their own temporal specificity.

The genealogical method and histories of the present In a discussion of the genealogical method, Armstrong (1990) distinguished it from quantitative and qualitative methods. Quantitative methodologies trace the extent in society of a given object of interest such as income, age or disease. Qualitative methods provide a means of demonstrating the subjective impact and meaning that a particular income, a certain age or particular disease have upon and for people and groups. However, by elevating to primacy their objects of study and ignoring their own presence in the analytic field, both approaches eliminate themselves from this field. As a result their objects of enquiry appear as given, their existence and form independent of the methods used to define, describe and explain them. The corollary of this is that changes in how objects of enquiry appear are attributed to forces inherent in the object (society has evolved, a person has developed, the disease has mutated), or to scientific progress that by improving investigative methods (enhanced methods of recording and counting events, microscopes with a higher resolution) reveals what was always there, but before such improvements were hidden by darkness (Armstrong 1990). Either way, observers are saddled with the explanatory problem that whatever they may posit cannot be separated from the contemporary universe of explanation and methodology in which the idea is produced, since a recent explanatory category cannot be used to explain itself.

In response to this problem of explanatory anachronicity Foucault drew upon Nietzsche to formulate the concept of genealogical analysis. The ideas of descent and emergence are central to the notion of genealogy. Descent makes no pretensions to going back in time to restore 'an unbroken continuity' (Foucault, in Bouchard 1977: 146) or establish any particular present as '*the* unique or fundamental or irruptive point in history where everything is begun or completed again' (Foucault, in Kritzman 1988: 35). Instead, descent 'disturbs what was previously considered immobile; it fragments what was thought unified; it shows the heterogeneity of what was imagined consistent within itself' (Foucault, in Bouchard 1977: 147). Methodologically, descent means that genealogy avoids the assumption that any concepts (such as life, the body, consciousness or sexuality) are static, in favour of documenting the profusion of events in which such concepts form and fade and outlining the discursive regimes that make them formalized objects of knowledge and targets for intervention. Hence history, life, the human body, disease, society or the psyche are all legitimate foci of descent, lacking any trans-historical stability and all the effects rather than the origins of the play of disciplinary forces. Applied to the human body, this means that 'It is not that the beautiful totality of the individual is amputated, repressed, altered by our social order, it is rather that the individual is carefully fabricated in it, according to a whole technique of forces and bodies' (Foucault 1977: 217).

Because they do not presuppose their objects' existence, the power mechanisms that co-vary with how the body is known cannot be identified with the works of great doctors or the impact of legal enactments and ideological forces, since all impinge upon and so take for granted the existence of the human body and human interests. Instead, the mechanisms of power discerned by descent are at the extremity of power, 'those points where it becomes capillary' (Foucault, in C. Gordon 1980: 96) – such as 'the single unencumbered gaze of one doctor to an inflamed joint or diseased lung of an individual patient' (Armstrong 1990: 1226). For it is here, as the patient bares the chest to the listening ear of the doctor's stethoscope, that power has its immediate effects in creating the corporeal objects of human experience.

Following from the concept of descent are the data considered germane to genealogical analysis. In this study, descent meant that rather than the biographies and memoirs of great medical personages or government gazettes detailing public-health Acts, the search was for texts describing the actual procedures applied to African bodies, records of the minutiae by which they were handled by doctors and moulded by architecture, and accounts of what was seen when Africans were opened up to anatomical investigation. As well as privileging accounts of the minutiae of socio-medical practice, the genealogical method also differs from conventional historical methods in drawing no distinction between primary and secondary sources. Instead, all sources (diaries, textbooks, transcriptions of spoken interviews etc.) are considered primary for their own period of authorship. This is because all texts are chronologically specific in that they can only draw upon the conceptual repertoire available to their authors at the time of production. For example, since it enters African socio-medical discourse only in the late 1800s, it is impossible to speak of a distinctive African anatomy and physiology before then.

If descent disturbs a sense of continuity from the past to the present by fragmenting what was considered immutable, then emergence, or the entry into discursive existence of particular objects of knowledge, upsets assumptions that seek the origins of things in neatly ordered ensembles of indexical events: 'Historians have been accustomed to a history which takes in only the summits, the great events' (Foucault, in C. Gordon 1980: 37). Against 'great events', emergence casts the effective forces of history as continuous responses to haphazard conflicts, an unending play of dominations, subjugations and struggles, for which the formal centres of power in any society are simply concentrations of disciplinary power within this generalized force field. The human body is thereby constantly appearing and vanishing, changing and continuously being renegotiated as the crystallization of disciplinary power in the shape of medical procedures 'discovers' new objects and domains of illness (Armstrong 1985: 112).

Genealogy inverts the approach of conventional history, enabling us to examine power from the assumption that it works not only through repression and inhibition, but also as a creative[2] force that fabricates not only the human objects of social reality, but the social itself: 'Power produces; it produces reality; it produces domains of objects and rituals of truth. The individual and the knowledge that may be gained of him belong to this production' (Foucault 1977: 192). Hence, as Nettleton (1992: 124) comments, where conventional histories of the past find continuity, absolutes, stability and noble origins, the genealogical analysis finds discontinuity, no absolutes, instability and mundane events.

History will teach us nothing

As this chapter was being written in late 1994, South Africa was celebrating its first 100 days of democratic government. Among the human sciences history had been propelled to prominence as academics, politicians and ordinary people strived to transcend the politics of oppression embedded in four centuries of colonial and apartheid rule. Underlying history's perceived importance was the belief that through a critical review of the past it was possible to learn from it and avoid repeating earlier patterns interpreted from the vantage point of the present as corrupt and evil. For instance, a 1993 history of South African public health initiatives had this to say: 'As South Africa undergoes rapid social, economic, and political change, the rich heritage of public health and primary health care that has long been overlooked is being rediscovered ... The article ... critically assesses what South African public health professionals could learn from the past while planning for the future' (Yach and Tollman 1993: 1043).

Concerning the psycho-social sciences, critical observers such as Hayes (1993) were equally confident in their claims that careful scrutiny of the past would enhance the probability of a better present.

> The history of psychology's complicity with apartheid and oppression cannot simply be wished away. This does not mean either that we have to stay stuck in the shame or guilt of the past. The complex task of transforming psychological theory and practice in terms of a more social liberatory discipline, requires a thorough analysis of the past, so that the lessons of that antipathetic time ... can be properly learnt, and not repeated ... A self-conscious remembering of our history will facilitate an understanding of what *constraints* and what *spaces* are available to us. (Hayes 1993: 12)

From the Foucauldean perspective, appeals to history as a teacher in how to tame power in the present are futile in that they are always also components of disciplinary power. Their fault is that they address sovereign power only, repeating the error of Parisian students in 1968 who believed that following De Gaulle's flight from France the state would vanish. To their bewilderment, the state continued without its head. 'Their mistake was to believe that power could be seized from the person who apparently held it; but power simply ran through their fingers' (Armstrong 1985: 113). The body itself is at once object, effect and a conduit of power, the fist raised in defiance of the soldier a sign of the beginnings of a self-existence for the nascent individual. Hence Foucault's famous claim that 'we need to cut off the king's head: in political theory this still has to be done' (Foucault, in C. Gordon 1980: 121). Sovereign power exists, it inscribes pain, torture and deprivation on the surface of the skin and in the workings of the body. But this body, its abuses scrupulously documented by the custodians of human rights and civil liberty (e.g. Silove 1990; Swartz and Levett 1989; Zwi 1987), is always also a fabrication of their practices. For from far below the tumult of sovereign force there arises disciplinary power which is everywhere, not because it embraces everything, but because it comes from everywhere. Sovereign power cannot easily be grasped by everyone but, as shown in Chapter 2, disciplinary power is within the grip of us all.

Notes

1. The first published examinations of medical history in South Africa would appear to be those of Laidler (1937, 1938, 1939), in which he examined

such things as the 'Proclamations' governing the practice of physician or surgeon, and the first use of anaesthetics in the Cape of the early nineteenth century.

2. Use of the terms 'creative' and 'productive' in relation to disciplinary power is intended to show only that this is a power which fabricates objects. It does not imply (as the almost unambiguously positive connotation lent to such terms in their common usage would suggest) that its functioning is 'good' or, for that matter, 'evil'.

CHAPTER 2

Power, Knowledge and the Body

The field of Foucauldean scholarship consists of two broad categories of work. The first is colloquially known as the 'Foucault industry'. It contains studies that engage in academic reflections upon Foucault's work, often attempting to plumb the philosophical origins of what Foucault thought, or else offering a critique of his theories by comparing these with those of other theorists and philosophers of the social and the subject (e.g. Hinkle 1986; Lemert and Gillan 1982; Paternek 1987; Rorty 1986). The second category of Foucauldean scholarship is made up of studies that do not so much reflect upon the tools of Foucauldean thought as apply them to particular problems, such as the chronic patient (Arney and Bergen 1983), the profession and practice of obstetrics (Arney 1982), 'the mouth with teeth and the profession of dentistry' (Nettleton 1992: vi), the emergence and functioning of the psychological sciences in Britain (Rose 1985), and the relationship between medicine, the individual and the social more generally (Armstrong 1983; Arney and Bergen 1984). To date only Megan Vaughan's *Curing Their Ills: Colonial Power and African Illness* (1991) approaches a Foucauldean analysis of western medical practices in relation to the African, although, in her own words, this 'stopped short of a full scale constructionist approach', and committed 'what, for the social constructionist, is the cardinal sin of assuming some material reality to which medical constructs ... refer' (Vaughan 1991: 7).

It is squarely within the second category of work that the present study belongs, and the theoretical materials reviewed here are restricted to those aspects of Foucault's work pertinent to the study's concern with western socio-medical practice and the African body. Given the diverse qualities of Foucault's work, it must moreover be emphasized that the methodological apparatus derived from it cannot be thought of as illustrating *the* Foucauldean method. As both Nettleton (1992) and Vaughan (1991) have cautioned, and as attested to by the divergency in their own readings of Foucault, a range of methodologies could and have been derived from the Foucault schema.

The individual as invention

As shown in Chapter 1, conventional histories of the socio-medical sciences in Africa presuppose a human subject along the lines suggested by the model of classical philosophy, endowed with a consciousness which power is then thought to seize upon. Standing at the centre of these studies (whether as dominator or dominated, observer or observed) is the knowing, seeing, feeling and acting person, for this is always the point from which these analyses are constrained to begin.

The human body and the person are also prominent in the Foucault schema. Not, however, as points of departure for the human and socio-medical sciences, but instead as the very opposite, as the result of these sciences and therefore the very locus of insertion of their knowledge. 'The individual is not a pre-given entity which is seized on by the exercise of power. The individual, with his identity and characteristics, is the product of a relation of power exercised over bodies, multiplicities, desires, forces' (Foucault, in C. Gordon 1980: 74). In short, Foucault inverts the human body by viewing it not as the origin of force or source of answers, but as the effect of forces and a problem demanding explanation. How is it possible to conceive of the body? How was it possible that until the end of the eighteenth century the body did not exist in the sense we know today? The human body and subjectivity as problems requiring explanation rather than objects awaiting scientific or philosophical elaboration are therefore at the core of Foucauldean theory and its genealogical method, described by Foucault as:

> A form of history which can account for the constitution of knowledges, discourses, domains of objects etc., without having to make reference to a subject which is either transcendental in relation to the field of events or runs in its empty sameness throughout the course of history (Foucault, in Gordon 1980: 117).

This refusal to accept the presence of a transcendental, unchanging subject as an explanatory device has led certain theorists to define Foucault as the 'author of a philosophy of history based on discontinuity' (Kritzman 1988: 99). However, far from a Foucauldean explanatory fiction, the contingent and historically variable subject is in fact a discovery of the genealogical method, and the attendant notion of discontinuity a problem requiring resolution and not an answer.

The discovery of discontinuity and the episteme   The preface to Foucault's great genealogical study *The Order of Things* began with a passage from Borges that quoted a '"certain Chinese encyclopaedia"' (Foucault 1973:

xv). An unexpected coupling of ordinary and extraordinary things, the passage produced in Foucault a laughter that shattered

> all the familiar landmarks of my thought – *our* thought, the thought that bears the stamp of our age and our geography – breaking up all the ordered surfaces and all the planes with which we are accustomed to tame the wild profusion of existing things, and continuing long afterwards to disturb and threaten with collapse our age-old distinction between the Same and Other. This passage quotes a 'certain Chinese encyclopaedia' in which it is written that 'animals are divided into (a) belonging to the Emperor, (b) embalmed, (c) tame, (d) sucking pigs, (e) sirens, (f) fabulous, (g) stray dogs, (h) included in the present classification, (i) frenzied, (j) innumerable, (k) drawn with a very fine camelhair brush, (l) *et cetera*, (m) having just broken the water pitcher, (n) that from a long way off look like flies'. In the wonderment of this taxonomy, the thing we apprehend in one great leap, the thing that, by means of the fable, is demonstrated as the exotic charm of another system of thought, is the limitation of our own, the stark impossibility of thinking *that*. (Foucault 1973: xv)

Foucault's concern in presenting this passage was to induce in readers a sense that the forms of knowledge peculiar to our contemporary way of knowing are limited by what he called the 'conditions of possibility', or 'episteme' from which they emerge and which they reproduce. For on trying to think out of this epistemic space we are tugged back in by a subterranean current, an unthinkable force that prevents us from considering the 'Chinese encyclopaedia' as anything other than a quaint taxonomic game.

Foucault attempted various definitions of episteme, and consistent with the metaphor of a subterranean force they all referred to an organizing stratum buried well below the level of epistemology, paradigm or philosophy. For instance, an episteme is the 'total set of relations that unite, at a given period, the discursive practices that give rise to epistemological figures, sciences and possibly formalised systems' (Foucault 1972: 191). Or, an episteme consists in:

> [T]he fundamental codes of a culture – those governing its language, its schemas of perception, its exchanges, its techniques, its values, the hierarchy of its practices – [which] establish for every man, from the very first, the empirical orders with which he will be dealing and within which he will be at home. (Foucault 1973: xx)

Given these definitions' obscurity it is perhaps more useful to clarify what Foucault meant by the term by briefly outlining the contours of the three epistemes he identified: one dominated Renaissance thought, one covered the Classical period, and the last and most recent is that which has governed Modernist thought in the nineteenth and twentieth centuries.

Each episteme was synonymous with a great swathe in history, and the gaps between them contiguous with the 'massive disjunctions in knowing that their change implied' (Armstrong 1987: 13). These Foucault delineated by comparing how Language, Life and Labour were cognitively ordered within each episteme. Take the question of 'life' for instance. In the Renaissance, it was not, strictly speaking, even possible to think of living things as possessed of 'life', since it was only with the Modernist episteme that biological science became possible and 'life' could be seen as immanent in a living thing's biological constitution. By contrast, living things in the Renaissance were animated by the great cosmic web of which they were mere nodes, and from which they gathered the legends and virtues that were an intrinsic part of their description. With advent of the Classical episteme at around the mid-seventeenth century, the natural world was transformed by a new way of seeing that ordered living things according to their perceptible physical structures. Within the Classificatory age, the 'imaginary' characteristics of plants, animals and people (which previously were paraded for edification and entertainment in the circular procession of the show) were jettisoned, and in place of the show living things were grouped according to their perceptible physical resemblances and arranged for scrutiny by natural scientists in the abstract space of charts and tables, such as exemplified by the botanical taxonomy of Linnaeus, or the complex disease classification of Sydenham. A second disjunction occurred towards the end of the eighteenth century, when the taxonomic gaze of Classification to the surface of living things was replaced by a deep gaze that analysed internal structure and its relationship to function. Functions (such as emotion, instinct and metabolism) are, of course, invisible, yet their identification to thought marked the emergence into science of the phenomenon of life, which in its turn became the principal object of the new biology.

Just as the natural history of the Classificatory age gave way to the Modernist science of biology, so the analysis of wealth was replaced by economics, and the study of general grammar by linguistics.

> These three new knowledges were a part of a complete reorganization of knowledge in the late eighteenth century; but, more significantly, these three new sciences of Life, Labour, and Language defined a new central object for the modern episteme, namely what Foucault calls 'Man'; and with the advent of Man arose the specific studies of man in the form of the human sciences. (Armstrong 1987: 62–3)

Epistemic archaeology therefore reveals that, when not projected back into time by conventional histories of the past, a point is reached on the genealogical descent down a continuous present where not only the human subject as the throne of consciousness vanishes but also the very idea of life as an immanent of the body's organization. As a consequence, this same epistemic space and the disjunction between epistemes cannot be explained through recourse to the human subject as a given and the human body as a constant. Hence Foucault's concern to make clear that discontinuity was not an explanation but a problem.

> In *Les Mots et les choses* I set out ... from this self-evident discontinuity and tried to ask myself the question: is this discontinuity really a discontinuity? Or, to be precise, what was the transformation needed to pass from one type of knowledge to another type of knowledge? For me, this is not at all a way of declaring the discontinuity of History; on the contrary, it is a way of posing discontinuity as a problem and above all a problem to be resolved. (Foucault, in Kritzman 1988: 100)

In revealing how the human sciences became possible only in the late eighteenth century, *The Order of Things* (1973) had already begun to suggest the historical contingency of biology and human anatomy. It was, however, in *The Birth of the Clinic: An Archaeology of Medical Perception* (1976) that the genealogical method found specific application to the problem of human anatomy, for it was here that Foucault first traced how the concrete individual of conventional history was invented as an object of positive knowledge and opened up to the language of rationality (Foucault 1976: xiv).

The gaze and the problem of human anatomy 'The gaze' is a term that appears frequently in this and other Foucauldean studies of power and medical knowledge. It refers both to how things have appeared to medicine and to the techniques by which medicine has made things appear, in coming to have a particular knowledge of the human body. As such, the gaze is not merely some cognitive or perceptual skill waiting to be grasped by the doctor and cultivated through medical training. On the contrary, while it certainly is through training in the socio-medical sciences that the gaze is reproduced, it is the gaze as technique that makes possible the very idea of a bodily interior and the doctor as its observer, and it is the gaze as limit that circumscribes how the doctor is taught, how the doctor practises and hence what the doctor can see.

> The great biological image of a progressive maturation of science still underpins a good many historical analyses; it does not seem to me to be

> pertinent to history. In ... medicine ... up to the end of the eighteenth century one has a certain type of discourse whose gradual transformation, within a period of twenty-five or thirty years, broke not only with the 'true' propositions which it had hitherto been possible to formulate but also, more profoundly, with the ways of speaking and seeing, the whole ensemble of practices which served as supports for medical knowledge. These are not simply new discoveries, there is a whole new 'regime' in discourse and forms of knowledge. (Foucault, in C. Gordon 1980: 112)

To illustrate this crucial point concerning the temporal specificity of the gaze and how it produces the doctor and in turn the human body as its objects and effects, Foucault began the *Birth of the Clinic* by juxtaposing two contrasting images of what was seen by two physicians, one writing in the 1700s the other in the 1800s. First, Pomme's eighteenth-century description of the treatment of a female hysteric, which relied upon ideas of nervous pathology and derived its description of the body from the study of texts. Assuming the cause of hysteria to be dryness and 'desiccation' of an 'overheated' nervous system, treatment involved 'making her take "baths, ten or twelve hours a day, for ten whole months"' (Foucault 1976: ix), with the result that:

> 'membranous tissues like pieces of damp parchment ... peel away with some slight discomfort, and these were passed daily with the urine; the right ureter also peeled away and came out whole in the same way'. The same thing occurred with the intestines, which at another stage, 'peeled off their internal tunics, which we saw emerge from the rectum. The oesophagus, the arterial trachea, and the tongue also peeled in due course; and the patient had rejected different pieces either by vomiting or expectoration'. (Pomme, in Foucault 1976: ix)

Second, and written less than a hundred years after Pomme's description, was Bayle's nineteenth-century account of the anatomical detail of the brain, produced through direct inspection of the body, and relying upon the idea of anatomical pathology:

> 'Their outer surface, which is next to the arachnoidian layer of the dura mater, adheres to this layer, sometimes very lightly, when they can be separated easily, sometimes very firmly and tightly, in which case it can be very difficult to detach them. Their internal surface is only contiguous with the arachnoid, and is in no way joined to it ... The false membranes are often transparent, especially when they are very thin; but usually they are white, grey, or red in colour, and occasionally, yellow, brown, or black. This matter often displays different shades in different parts of the same membrane. The thickness of these accidental productions varies greatly; sometimes they are so tenuous that they might be compared to a spider's web'. (Bayle, in Foucault 1976: ix–x)

This juxtaposition reveals the gaze itself, since had they witnessed the same event neither physician could have seen what the other saw.

Arising from our contemporary embedment in a world seen according to *Gray's Anatomy*, the inclination is to dismiss Pomme's description as fanciful or mistaken, for unlike Bayle's account of the brain it fails to confirm the contemporary belief in the truth of disease as residing within the body itself. But the real error is to assume that the earlier vision could be mistaken. For, and as confirmed by their convergence with the epistemic shifts identified in *The Order of Things* (Foucault 1973), these two visions of the body simply reflected and reproduced two incommensurable worlds. To cast the first vision as mistaken is therefore to create the illusion that the body of modern medicine has always existed as the only body there ever was, and of death and disease as always having inhabited this same anatomical space.

> In the history of medicine, this ... illusion functions as a retrospective justification: if the old beliefs had for so long such prohibitive power, it was because doctors had to feel, in the depths of their scientific appetite, the repressed need to open up corpses. There lies the point of error, and the silent reason why it was so constantly made: the day it was admitted that lesions explained symptoms, and that the clinic was founded on pathological anatomy, it became necessary to invoke a transfigured history, in which the opening up of corpses, at least in the name of scientific requirements, preceded a finally positive observation of patients; the need to know the dead must have already existed when the concern to understand the living appeared. So a dismal conjuration of dissection, an anatomical church militant and suffering, whose hidden spirit made the clinic possible before itself surfacing into the regular, authorized, diurnal practice of autopsy, was imagined out of nothing. (Foucault 1976: 125–6)

To identify this history as one that had been imaginatively conjured out of nothing through its fiction of the body as an unvarying entity independent of anatomical practice, required that Foucault demonstrate the alternative, that in fact it was only in the actual practice of the doctor to the patient that the anatomized body of the individual could have emerged at all.

Spatialization

> The exact superposition of the 'body' of the disease and the body of the sick man is no more than a historical, temporary datum. Their encounter is self-evident only for us, or, rather, we are only just beginning to detach ourselves from it. The space of *configuration* of the disease and the space of *localization* of the illness in the body have been superimposed, in medical experience, for only a short period of time – the period that coincides with

> nineteenth-century medicine and the privileges accorded to pathological anatomy. (Foucault 1976: 3–4)

Following Armstrong (1995), the concept of spatialization is a device for analysing the play of the gaze at any given point in the history of the present, and refers to the triumvirate of cognition, perception and practice that configure disease and determine the space and location of illness. The cognitive component refers to what Foucault called 'primary spatialization', and addresses the conceptual ordering of the elements of illness, such as sign, symptom and lesion. The perceptual component corresponds to 'secondary spatialization', and refers to the location of illness in relation to the body of the patient. The practical component was called by Foucault 'tertiary spatialization' and consists in the concrete practices, techniques and institutional arrangements that constitute health-care activity.

To illustrate the notion of spatialization and how it dissolves the certainty of the solid and visible body laid down in the anatomical atlas, it is useful to trace how changes in the spatialization of illness made possible the displacement of 'bedside medicine' by 'hospital' or 'clinical' medicine (cf. Ackernecht 1967). For it was with this respatialization of illness that the body of the disease and the body of the patient first came to inhabit the same space, to invent the anatomized body of the individual as the cardinal object and effect of what remains the dominant model of western medicine.

For bedside medicine, primary spatialization made illness coterminous with the symptoms reported by the patient, so a headache or abdominal pain was the illness. This was therefore a medicine for which there was no lesion, and secondary spatialization thus located illness to a point beyond the body where it hovered until coinciding with the body to induce the symptoms experienced by the patient. Because all diseases would in the course of their autonomous progression move through and out of the body, the physician's diagnostic task involved capturing this mobility by closely monitoring the sequence of symptoms. 'Presence in an organ is never absolutely necessary to define a disease: thus disease may travel from one point of localization to another … while remaining identical in nature' (Foucault 1976: 10). In this way diseases could be classified after a 'botanical model' into the families, genera and species that composed 'God's garden of pathology'. Within this garden illnesses sharing similar symptoms were evidence that they shared a common root. For instance, because paralysis, apoplexy (stroke) and syncope (fainting) all result in the abolition of voluntary movement, they were manifestations of the same disease: 'when they become dense enough, these similarities cross the threshold of mere kinship and accede to the unity of essence' (Foucault 1976: 7). Since diseases themselves determined when and where they would appear and disappear, tertiary spatialization demanded that doctors avoid extracting patients from the natural locus of the disease, and treatment was ideally accomplished at the bedside of the patient by the physician whose task was to wait and watch as the disease ran its autonomous course through time and the body. 'The natural locus of disease is the natural locus of life – the family: gentle, spontaneous care, expressive of love and a common desire for cure, assists in its struggle against the illness, and allows the illness itself to attain its own truth' (p. 17). Primary, secondary and tertiary spatialization thus maintained a medical space in which the body of the patient was a subsidiary problem, and even a barrier to proper diagnosis.

> In order to know the truth of the pathological fact, the doctor must abstract the patient: 'He who describes a disease must take care to distinguish the symptoms that necessarily accompany it, and which are proper to it, from those that are only accidental and fortuitous, such as those that depend on the temperament and age of the patient'. (Foucault 1976: 8)

Where bedside medicine had subtracted the patient and the interior of the body, the tertiary respatialization of illness marking the late-eighteenth-century rise of hospital medicine crystallized a gaze for which the individual body of the patient and its interior were cardinal. Emphasizing the significance to this shift of tertiary spatialization and underlining the primacy of hospital practice to the invention of the body, Foucault argued that the hospital 'is the point of origin of the most radical questionings. It ... was on the basis of this tertiary spatialization that the whole of medical experience was overturned and defined for its most concrete perceptions, new dimensions, and a new foundation'. (Foucault 1976: 16)

The great desecration of hospital medicine was to move the body of the sick man from the home as the temple of life and shrine of disease, to the neutral domain of the hospital (initially regarded as a 'temple of death'), and there to subject it to the practice of physical examination. These practices denied the truth of a medicine directed to essential diseases located beyond the body by crowding them together in a space where their purity was corrupted through 'cross-breeding'. Hence they provoked in their beginnings a marked resistance, as instanced by one physician who noted that it would require a very skilful doctor: '"to avoid the danger of the false experience that seems to result from the artificial diseases to which he devotes himself in the hospitals. In fact, no hospital disease is a pure disease"' (cited in Foucault 1976: 17).

Highlighting the power of practice to overturn the truth of one age and replace it with the next, the sheer repetition of hospital medicine had by the early 1800s imprinted the reality of a new anatomy on the social conscience, and by 1858 it was possible to publish the first edition of *Gray's Anatomy*. The origins of this new anatomy lay at a point following the French Revolution when Parisian hospitals underwent an institutional transformation whereby medical research and teaching began to be conducted in 'teaching hospitals'. This shift in tertiary spatialization inserted the bodies of the sick into a space of systematic observation where patient could be compared with patient and disease with disease. This relocated the locus of medical education from authoritative texts to the new classroom of the ward round, in which doctors took instruction from the very bodies of the patients they surveyed.

Here one would learn not what the old masters thought they knew, 'but that form of truth open to all that is manifested in everyday practice: "Practice will be linked to theoretical precepts. Pupils will be practised in chemical experiments, anatomical dissections, surgical operations, and in the use of machinery. Read little, see much and do much"' (Foucault 1976: 70).

The body now isolated to close inspection by sight, touch and smell, the cognitive order of illness could be reconfigured into a three-dimensional framework involving symptom, sign and pathology. As under bedside medicine, the symptom remained an index of how patients experienced illness. But added to this was now the sign. The sign being 'an intimation of disease elicited by the attentive physician' (Armstrong 1995: 3) – such as the pulse that betrays the invisible strength and rhythm of the circulation – neither it nor the symptom was the illness. Together, though, they triangulated the position and nature of the underlying lesion within the body that was the disease. A new relationship between surface and depth was therefore established by this clinico-pathological correlation, to dispel the earlier notion of disease as an autonomous and mobile entity. Disease was instead located to a fixed point within the body, demanding innovative perceptual techniques that would allow doctors to see into its three-dimensional interior. The installation of hospital medicine thus necessitated invention of the classical techniques of clinical examination (percussion, palpation, auscultation and inspection), each a means of extending the doctor's sensory apparatus and making transparent the opaque depths of the body to see the lesion within.

The secondary spatialization of illness to the interior of the body turned death into a tactic of seeing life. For bedside medicine, disease had departed the body with the patient's demise, and so it was futile to search the corpse for traces of its nature. Accordingly, while dissection did occur, its aim was not to observe the body's interior but rather illustrate the schemata set out in authoritative texts about its 'humoural' systems, 'members' and 'virtues' (see Chapter 3). In contrast, the post-mortem was an essential component of hospital medicine, for it enabled the exact nature of the hidden lesion to be incontrovertibly identified.

> Life, disease, and death now form a technical and conceptual trinity. The continuity of the age-old beliefs that placed the threat of disease in life and of the approaching presence of death in disease is broken; in its place is articulated a triangular figure the summit of which is defined by death. It is from the height of death that one can see and analyse organic dependences and pathological sequences. Instead of being ... the night in which life disappeared, in which even the disease becomes blurred, it is now endowed with that great power of elucidation that dominates and reveals both the space of the organism and the time of the disease ... It is no longer that of a living eye, but the gaze of an eye that has seen death – a great white eye that unties the knot of life. (Foucault 1976: 144)

Where bedside medicine had abstracted the body of the patient from medical space, hospital medicine fabricated a gaze for which it was the body itself that was ill, and therefore the body itself that had to be known in all its fleshy and intimate detail: through the probing fingers to the abdomen; the listening ear of the doctor to the chest of the living, and the penetrating scalpel of the anatomist to the bodies of the dead.

Either side of this shift from bedside to hospital medicine are the very different objects and effects of very different spatializations. As demonstrated in the following chapters, there is good reason to conclude that it is never in what is seen or who does the seeing that the forces governing these shifts reside, but rather in the principle of spatialization and the gaze itself. 'The order of the solid, visible body is only one way – in all likelihood neither the first, nor the most fundamental – in which one spatializes disease. There have been, and will be, other distributions of illness' (Foucault 1976: 3). But without any historically unchanging human anatomy and subject to know and be known, how can there be any knowledge of the body and the person at all? Foucault's answer to this problem was *Discipline and Punish* (1977), which placed knowledge in a productive relationship to power by demonstrating that 'It is not the activity of the subject of knowledge that produces a corpus of knowledge, useful or resistant to power, but power–knowledge, the processes and struggles that traverse it and of which it is made up, that determines the forms and possible domains of knowledge' (Foucault 1977: 28).

Power and the body

When writing *The Birth of the Clinic* and *The Order of Things* Foucault had yet to conceptualize a link between power and the great disjunctions in knowing that these analyses had revealed. With *Discipline and Punish* this missing piece of the puzzle was found and inserted to complete the diagram of power and knowledge with which the adjective Foucauldean has become synonymous.

'When I think back now, I ask myself what else it was that I was talking about, in *Madness and Civilization* or *The Birth of the Clinic*, if not power? Yet I'm perfectly aware that I scarcely ever used the word and never had such a field of analyses at my disposal then' (Foucault, in C. Gordon 1980: 229). By analysing transformations from the middle ages to the early twentieth century in the control exercised over people, *Discipline and Punish* (1977) identified a framework in which the emergence of particular ways of knowing the body could be correlated with changes in how these control strategies operated. The late-eighteenth-century discovery of pathological anatomy by which diseases were localized to the body's interior as it lay in the strictly ordered space of the hospital could now be seen as contemporaneous with analogous changes in the regime of criminal punishment. From being subjected to torture, pillorying and public display, the criminal started to be incarcerated and subject to continuous surveillance in the closed and cellular space of the prison. Changes in two disparate and opposing domains of practice thus converged around the common pole of isolating the body as the object and effect of an increasingly sustained, intimate and penetrating surveillance.

Foucault defined this moment not as one of humanist enlightenment, but rather as one where power was reconfigured, the point at which what could now be known as sovereign power gave way to what from here on would be seen as the practice of disciplinary power.

Sovereignty and the spectacle of power Symbolized by the majestic visibility of the king, it is easy to appreciate the mechanics of sovereign power, since in addition to its dramatic prominence it is to sovereign power that conventional analyses of control continue to speak when they refer to power as if it were something that is 'acquired, seized or shared, something that one holds on to or allows to slip away' (Foucault 1979: 94). Functioning through being visible to those on whom it had its effects, the force of sovereign power was epitomized in Foucault's famous description of the public torture and execution of Damiens the regicide.

> On 2 March 1757 Damiens the regicide was condemned 'to make the *amende honorable* before the main door of the Church of Paris', where he was to be 'taken and conveyed in a cart, wearing nothing but a shirt, holding a torch of burning wax weighing two pounds'; then, 'in the said cart, to the Place de Greve, where, on a scaffold that will be erected there, the flesh will be torn from his breasts, arms, thighs and calves with red-hot pincers, his right hand, holding the knife with which he committed the said parricide, burnt with sulphur, and, on those places where the flesh will be torn away, poured molten lead, boiling oil, burning resin, wax and sulphur melted together and then his body drawn and quartered by four horses and his limbs and body consumed by fire, reduced to ashes and his ashes thrown to the winds'. (Foucault 1977: 3)

Analogous with the less bloody but equally ostentatious displays of monarchial might enacted in rituals, palaces, processions and public displays signifying the royal presence, such ceremonies of torture realized a power that constituted the public as an extension of the monarchial body with the king as its head. 'In a society like that of the seventeenth century, the King's body wasn't a metaphor, but a political reality. Its physical presence was necessary for the functioning of the monarchy' (Foucault, in C. Gordon 1980: 55). Abstracted as a relationship of visibility, sovereign power was a massive and capricious force dependent for its functioning upon the visibility of itself. It was, accordingly, a regime where the only 'individuals' it produced were those (famous and infamous) inscribed on the conscience of the public through privilege, ritual, heroics and ceremony. Because sovereignty depended on its being seen by the unseen eyes of the crowd it moreover demanded that this presence be constantly renewed. 'The public execution, however hasty and everyday, belongs to a whole series of great rituals in which power is eclipsed and restored (coronations, entry of the king into a conquered city, the submission of rebellious subjects)' (Foucault 1977: 48). As shown in Chapter 3 where the knowledge implications of this sovereign power are explored, its principle of exertion over bodies to bend them into an homogenous mass was mirrored in its constitution of living things as formed from the outside by the equally capricious forces of God, the planets and the climate.

Against sovereign power (but never instead of it, since the two powers continue to coexist), there occurred towards the end of the 1700s a displacement in power's point of application. For it was then that the visibility of sovereign power in the dramatic theatres of punishment started to have effects opposite to its intended consequences. Instead of uniting the masses in sympathy with the king against offenders, the scaffold spectacle began to create a solidarity between the condemned and the watching crowd against the king (Foucault 1977: 63). The moment the effectiveness of these techniques started to fade was when the scenic model of sovereignty became displaced by the secretive device of the prison, and marked not the rise of a new humanism in justice, but rather the switch to a more efficient practice of social control, 'a tendency toward a more finely tuned justice ... a closer penal mapping of the body' (Foucault 1977: 78). Appearing as a complex tissue of events, 'often minor processes, of different origin and scattered location, which overlap, repeat or imitate one another' (p. 139), this moment was the shift to disciplinary power that was shared by the new gaze of pathological anatomy as it magnified the once irrelevant interior of the body. For, just as the medical gaze made individual anatomy into its new point of application, so the regime of criminal punishment began to install the novel practice of the penitentiary and its solitary inmates.

Through its physical assault upon the body, sovereign power had made the body into a screen for broadcasting monarchial might by the inscription of pain. For the penitentiary, it was not the body's surface that mattered, but rather its interior, its rhythms of sleep and waking, eating and hunger, social intercourse, and tolerance for solitude. The great theatres of pain were gone, and in their place

> a new 'economy' of the power to punish, to assure its better distribution, so that it should be neither too concentrated at certain privileged points, nor too divided between opposing authorities, so that it should be distributed in homogenous circuits capable of operating everywhere, in a continuous way, down to the finest grain of the social body. (Foucault 1977: 80)

By the late eighteenth century the body of the ordinary person had thus replaced the body of the king as the effect of power, as rituals for restoring monarchial integrity were displaced by remedies and therapeutic devices deployed towards the bodies of everyone.

Panopticism and disciplinary power Collectively known as disciplinary power, devices directed to ordering and analysing the bodies of everyone found condensed expression in Bentham's 1843 design for an ideal prison, the Panopticon. Disciplinary power inverted the scenic principle of sovereignty, for its functioning demanded not the visibility of itself but of its target, 'and that target was the individual body which became at the same time both object and effect of the disciplinary gaze' (Armstrong 1983: 4). Hence the mid-nineteenth-century possibility for Bentham to conceive of the Panopticon and Panopticism as 'a way of obtaining from power "in hitherto unexampled quantity ... a great and new form of government"' (Foucault 1977: 206).

The Panopticon was a circular building divided into cells and built as a ring around an observational tower at its centre. Each cell had two windows: an outer one illuminating the inmate, and a shuttered inner one allowing a guard in the central tower to observe the inmates, but not the inmates to observe the guard. Side walls to each cell prevented the inmate from communication with other inmates, and so each inmate was 'seen but does not see; he is the object of information, never a subject of communication' (Foucault 1977: 200). Each cell was thus like a small theatre in which the solitary actor was perfectly individualized and constantly visible, yet never certain of actually being watched and so perpetually subject to the gaze of the guard. 'In short, the principle of the dungeon is reversed; daylight and the overseer's gaze capture the inmate more effectively than darkness, which afforded after all a sort of protection' (Foucault, in C. Gordon 1980: 147). The Panopticon therefore made the operation of power continuous by inducing in the inmate a state of conscious and permanent visibility that assured the automatic functioning of power (Foucault 1977: 201). Initially conceived of as a prison, the Panopticon was also a principle of power through surveillance, and so could extend beyond convicts to the lunatic, the schoolchild, the patient, the worker and the entire population.

With the swarming of such techniques for monitoring and manipulating the gestures, capabilities, behaviours, illnesses and ideas of everyone, the political axis of individualization underlying sovereignty found its final reversal, to allow the spread of discipline. Individualization under sovereign power had been 'ascending', such that the closer bodies were to the king the more they were marked off by ceremony. In the disciplinary regime individualization is 'descending', for as power increases its anonymity and functionality, so those on whom it is exercised are more strongly individualized. Not by ceremony, but by surveillance, and not by commemorative accounts with ancestry as their referents, but by comparative measures against a 'norm'.

> The moment that saw the transition from historico-ritual mechanisms for the formation of individuality to the scientifico-disciplinary mechanisms, when the normal took over from the ancestral, and measurement from

status, thus substituting for the individuality of the memorable man that of the calculable man, that moment when the sciences of man became possible is the moment when a new technology of power and a new political anatomy of the body were implemented. (Foucault 1977: 193)

While maximized where new innovations in architecture laid down particular places for particular individuals, the exercise of discipline was not restricted to concrete domains, and its manifestations appeared wherever the techniques of bodily surveillance emerged to prominence in the eighteenth and nineteenth centuries. In schools, pupils began to be tested to ascertain their scholastic proficiency; in the army, the new routine of drill and parade-ground inspections operated to create a disciplined soldier, and in workshops, schools and hospitals the timetable – long used in monastic communities to prevent idleness – was widely introduced to subject bodies to temporal ordering through the establishment of rhythms and regulated cycles of repetition. These were just some of the 'means of correct training' necessary to a power that replaced the homogenizing effect of the crowd under the regime of sovereignty with a collection of separate individualities.

The means of correct training Inherent in the Panopticon's arrangement of lights, lines of sight and barriers, were the three instruments by which discipline jumped the walls of the prison to infiltrate the most intimate elements of the social and the individual.

The first of these instruments was *hierarchical observation*. This refers to the principle of concretizing inconspicuous surveillance in the way that built space is configured around the problem of who can see and who can be seen. For instance, how should the tents of a military camp or dwellings in a housing estate be arranged so that each occupant comes to be part of a network of gazes that supervise one another? Or, what is the optimal layout in the classroom that will ensure scholars know they are being seen while allowing the watching teacher to remain the discrete observer? Or, when the number of bodies to be supervised becomes too great to be seen by a single eye, how to install further observational relays? Each time such questions are asked it is to the instrument of hierarchical observation that they speak.

The second instrument of disciplinary surveillance is *normalizing judgement*, by which individuals can be assessed and measured through their comparison with others. As the term implies, normalizing judgement refers to all those procedures (even that as simple as having people stand in line according to their height), which in creating a field of comparison between different individuals allows the generation of a norm with which to grade the capacity, attributes or performance of the subjects. It therefore contains within it an element of correction and the correlative concept of deviance, which together permit disciplinary power to fabricate and embrace 'the whole indefinite domain of the non-conforming' (Foucault 1977: 179).

> The workshop, the school, the army were subject to a whole micro-penalty of time (latenesses, absences, interruptions of tasks), of activity (inattention, negligence, lack of zeal), of behaviour (impoliteness, disobedience), of speech (idle chatter, insolence), of the body ('incorrect' attitudes, irregular gestures, lack of cleanliness), of sexuality (impurity, indecency). (Foucault 1977: 178)

Against the bloody spurts of public torture through which sovereign power renewed itself, the steady pulse of discipline is the subdued practice of *the examination*. A synthesis of hierarchical surveillance and normalizing judgement, in the examination 'are combined the ceremony of power and the form of the experiment, the deployment of force and the establishment of truth. At the heart of the procedures of discipline, it manifests the subjection of those who are perceived as objects and the objectification of those who are subjected' (Foucault 1977: 184–5).

Functioning in three crucial ways, the examination is that 'tiny operational schema', so widely spread from psychiatry to education, and from the diagnosis of disease to the hiring of labour, that every member of the population must at some time participate in its ritual and so be recruited into the wider disciplinary network that this most nodal form of surveillance enables.

The examination is analogous to a cell of the Panopticon, and is therefore a functional site that transforms the economy of visibility into the exercise of power. For in the examination it is not the examiner that emerges to visibility, but the subject being examined, who once a participant in this minute ritual of surveillance carries for ever 'the fact of constantly being seen, of being always able to be seen that maintains the disciplined individual in his subjection' (Foucault 1977: 187). Second, intrinsic to the examination is the procedure of recording, the power of inscription by which the identity and attributes of the individuals it fabricates are traced in a network of writing (or computer databases) that captures and fixes them in a permanent analytic space. The examination thus functions to produce the individual and the collective, for through their aggregation the records of individuals may be sorted and seriated to fix the individual as a calculable entity within the tabular order of an arithmetic collectivity. Third, in fusing the power of surveillance with its documentary techniques of notation, registration and filing, the examination 'makes each individual a case ... a case which at one and the same time constitutes an object of knowledge and hold for a branch of power' (p. 191).

Limited only by these parameters, the flexibility of the examination makes it the quintessential disciplinary device, a compact and portable Panopticon that requires no walls, towers or guards for its successful operation, and which through its properties of recording can interlink every point in the disciplinary regime to every other, so making the distribution of power continuous and autonomous of any 'control centre'.

To summarize this analysis of power, the spectacle of punishment and the ritual of the examination invoke the principles of two very different diagrams of power, and with them two equally distinct domains of possible objects and effects.

1. Where sovereignty exerts control through violence and restraint, discipline does so through surveillance alone.
2. Where sovereign power requires the visibility of itself, the unseen force of discipline makes visible the individual as object, effect and target of power.
3. Where sovereign power emanates from a central point, disciplinary power is relational and distributed into each body and every gap between bodies.
4. Where sovereign power is sporadically eclipsed and restored, discipline functions constantly and automatically through recruitment of the individual and the social as its relays.
5. Where sovereign power destroys and conceals beneath its weight, disciplinary power creates and illuminates its points of articulation in the objects, effects and knowledges it sustains.

Despite these clear distinctions between sovereignty and discipline, their operation is never mutually exclusive. As demonstrated in the substantive chapters of this study, the shift from sovereignty to discipline has been one of emphasis. For while the late-nineteenth-century demise of the public execution as a legal means of justice in many parts of Africa marked the point where sovereignty formally bowed to discipline, this inversion in the relationship of visibility between colonial power and the African body enabled a new complex of calculable sovereignty to emerge. In this, the analytic gaze of discipline produced as visible objects those individuals and groups on whom the dramatic spectacles of sovereignty could then be selectively visited: in the shape of the missionary doctor's theatres of healing aimed at demonstrating the power of 'God's medicine' to the watching witch doctors; in the form of the heat chamber as a spectacle of the mining industry's might over the body of the African; and in the technique of the psychological test and its isolation of the African as a 'dangerous individual' to be targeted by the tactics of violent repression.

Discipline as power and the disciplined society How should this theory of power be read, especially in Africa, where every day sees the mob against the spectacular might of the army or police, where conventional history over even the last decade is punctuated by burning barricades, brutal acts of state violence and waves of 'ethnic cleansing'? Certainly, this speaks to societies that are not 'disciplined' in the sense of consisting in people who mechanically obey the dictates of the state and meekly conform to their politically and economically allocated place in the social order. But, and precisely because this notion of a 'disciplined' society reflects the idea that certain groups could hold power and exert it over others, this has no bearing upon whether African societies are or are not disciplinary societies. As is made abundantly clear in the following chapters, most African societies have since at least the turn of the twentieth century been constructed and organized in ways that starkly reflect the programmatic structure of the Panopticon, confirming that while not 'disciplined' they most definitely are disciplinary societies.

What then is to be made of the resistance to colonialism that constituted so great a part of the African past? Surely, in refuting the tactics of repression and subjectification aimed at inducing acceptance of their place as the 'dominated', black Africans have given the lie to discipline? Such critique assumes that resistance is contrary to disciplinary power, that where there is resistance there is no power, or at least a sufficient weakening to let the 'authentic' person emerge from beneath its crushing weight. But this too is mistaken, for not only do such arguments speak to sovereign power alone – which can and must be resisted – but also to the idea of 'freedom', which in its modern guise is itself a product of disciplinary power. For freedom today means the freedom of the individual, but since it is the individual who is a product of disciplinary power, the struggle to defend the 'rights of man' is itself as no more than another facet of discipline. Far from being a threat to the disciplinary regime, resistance is precisely that through which it ceaselessly expands and reproduces itself: 'Disciplinary power ... provokes and works through resistance: an up-raised hand to avert the gaze of surveillance marks the beginning of a self-existence for the nascent individual' (Armstrong 1987: 69).

Analysing power: methodological requirements

Flowing from the Foucauldean analysis of power into its sovereign and disciplinary manifestations are a number of methodological requirements.

The first requirement is that analyses avoid thinking of power as having a fixed form, for it is only through variations of the practices outlined above that it condenses into the political diagrams of sovereignty and discipline. Hence 'it is necessary to be a nominalist: power is not a stricture, or a certain force with which people are endowed; it is a name given to a complex strategic relation in a given society' (Foucault, in C. Gordon 1980: 27).

Second, because power creates itself in concrete practices, analyses should address power not at its formal centres in society (which are simply points of concentration within a generalized force field) but 'at its extremities ... those points where it becomes capillary' (Foucault, in C. Gordon 1980: 96), such as where the pincers are applied to tear the flesh, or, in a disciplinary regime, the gaze of the psychiatrist to the electroencephalogram of the patient. The Foucauldean analysis is always ascending, moving from these capillary points of application to the more general mechanisms (like the monarchy, the economy, the state or the liberation struggle) that require the human objects and subjects that power invents.

The third requirement holds that since power is not the product but the producer of human interests, desires and motives, analyses must not concern themselves with power at the level of conscious decision or intention: 'It should refrain from posing the labyrinthine and unanswerable question: "Who then has power and what has he in mind?" ... Instead, it is a case of studying power at the point where its intention, if it has one, is completely invested in its real and effective practices' (p. 97). The emphasis upon 'real and effective practices' is important also to underline the point that the Foucauldean analysis of power avoids linguistic reductionism. When it does use the term 'discourse' (as in parts of this study) what is referred to is not the meaning of the body created through language and dialogue alone, but also the concrete practices of the socio-medical sciences (such as the way the doctor's hands palpate the body, or how built space conditions hygienic habits).

The final methodological observation addresses the question of ideology which, because it forms so central a theme in the conventional discourse around colonialism and the socio-medical sciences in Africa, is more fully addressed in the Postscript (Chapter 10). Suffice here to note that in the Foucault schema power is never to be thought of as ideological.

It is both much more and much less than ideology ... It is the production of effective instruments for the formation and accumulation of knowledge – methods of observation, techniques of registration, apparatuses of control. All this means that power ... cannot but evolve, organise and put into circulation a knowledge, or rather apparatuses of knowledge, which are not ideological constructs. (Foucault, in C. Gordon 1980: 102)

A trans-humanist frame of analysis

This review of Foucauldean theory establishes an analytic framework by filtering the ideas set forth in *The Order of Things* (1973) and *The Birth of the Clinic* (1976) through the concepts of power and knowledge articulated in *Discipline and Punish* (1977). The result is a theoretical and methodological apparatus able to problematize the existence and transformations of the human body as an object and effect of socio-medical power by disrupting all humanist assumptions concerning the idea of it as a transcendental, unchanging entity, and, reciprocally, of knowledge as something that progressively accrues to enhance steadily the truth of what we know.

Instead, a continuous present is set in place in which the body is always contingent upon the force relations that concretize themselves in the procedures deployed to know it and the bodies of socio-medical knowledge that result. Substitute for the Panopticon as prison the hospital or clinic; replace the unseen but all-seeing guard with the doctor or nurse; see the silent, mystifying experience of the medical examination as the side walls prohibiting communication among the inmates, and construe the ever-expanding archives of disease statistics and patient files as the raw material from which the ambient infra-penalties of normalizing judgement silently form themselves. The seemingly unambiguous object language of textbook medicine metamorphoses, as do the actions of the researcher, clinician and health administrator, into the components of a finely wrought disciplinary regime, geared to the surveillance and subtle modulation of the interior and the exterior of the body, of the relations between different bodies, and of the social itself.

Turning now from this abstract and general anatomy of power, Chapter 3 commences its application to the production of a specifically African anatomy of power, by entering a present where how the body was understood and became an effect of power confirmed the existence of bodies in Africa which in their shape and form are today unimaginable to conventional historians, except as bizarre and grotesquely prejudiced distortions of the 'truth' as it appears in *Gray's Anatomy*.

CHAPTER 3

Renaissance Body Myths and the Spectacle of Strangeness

Consider the following descriptions of the inhabitants of 'Ethiopia'. The first appeared in a late-sixteenth-century version of Isidore of Seville's sixth- and seventh-century *Etymologies*[1] under the heading 'On Men and Monsters' (Sharpe/Isidore 1964: 38):

> 12. Just as among individual races there are certain members who are monsters, so also among mankind as a whole, certain races are monsters, like the giants, the Cynocephali, the Cyclopes, and others ...

> 17. It is believed that the Blemmyae in Libya are born as headless trunks, that they have both eyes and mouth in their chests; and that there are others, born without necks, having eyes in their shoulders ...

> 20. The Artabitae in Ethiopia are reported to walk on all fours like beasts, and none of them passes the fortieth year of age ...

> 23. The race Sciopedes is said to exist in Ethiopia, with only one leg but marvelous speed withal: the Greeks call them SKIOPEDES because in the summertime they stretch out on their backs, covering themselves with the shadows of their huge feet.

> 24. The Antipodes in Libya have their soles turned around behind their legs, and have eight toes on their soles. (Sharpe/Isidore 1964: 51–3)

Two centuries later, in the first edition of *Systema Naturae* by the natural historian Linnaeus (1735), there appeared the following classification of 'homo sapiens' into six varieties:

> a. Wild man – four-footed, mute, hairy.

> b. Europaeus albus – white, sanguine, muscular, long blond hair, blue eyes, gentle, ingenious, inventive, governed by law.

> c. Americanus rubesceus – liberty-loving, copper-coloured, choleric, obstinate, governed by customs.

> d. Asiaticus Luridus – yellowish, melancholic, dark hair and eyes, proud, avaricious, greedy, governed by opinion.

e. Afer Niger – black, phlegmatic, black frizzled hair, silk-like skin, ape-like nose, thick lips, the breasts of women distended, crafty, lazy, governed by caprice.

f. Monstra – divided into two categories, namely those so by nature, such as dwarfs and giants, and those so by custom, such as eunuchs. (Linnaeus 1735, in Dietrich 1993: 264)

The difference between these two lists lay in what was missing from that of Linnaeus. All but gone from his classification (relegated to the tail end under the heading 'monstra') were the legendary qualities that constituted the very stuff of Isidore's marvellous bestiary. These removed, all that remained was a mechanical listing of the essential characteristics of each human type, presented in uniform order to enable their comparison. Between Isidore and Linnaeus: 'the whole of animal semantics has disappeared, like a dead and useless limb. The words that had been interwoven in the very being of the beast have been unravelled and removed: and the living being, in its anatomy, its form, its habits … appears as though stripped naked' (Foucault 1973: 129).

Drawing upon resurrected Greek and Roman myths and legends, Isidore's description was clearly the more fantastic, and perhaps induces a sense of wonder in the contemporary reader at how anyone could believe such a patently absurd set of fictions. By contrast, Linnaeus' description may create a sense that, although distorted by a heavy veil of prejudice, it showed at least some traces of the direct observation of actual bodies.

Such an evaluation speaks to 'what the historians say' (Foucault 1973: 125), where they ascribe the displacement of myth by classification to a curiosity and desire that caused eighteenth-century scholars 'if not to discover the sciences of life, at least to give them a hitherto unsuspected scope and precision' (p. 125). On the one hand (say the historians), this was made possible by the new privileges accorded to observation in the seventeenth and eighteenth centuries. For instance, the invention of the microscope and its enhancement of observational acuity, or the then recently attained privilege of the physical sciences, which in permitting analysis of the laws of movement and light through theory, experimentation and observation, offered a model of rationality with which to analyse the adjacent realm of living beings and strip away the veneer of myths that clouded their 'true' apprehension. On the other hand, a variety of new interests (such as an economic attitude towards agriculture) incited a curiosity directed towards exotic plants, animals and peoples. Which were useful, and which could be domesticated for European use?

But, wrote Foucault, running through such conventional analyses is a thread of progress that for histories of the present is as mythic as the legends it devalues, itself the application of a modernist category that is anachronistic to these obsolete knowledges. This category is 'life' itself, and the idea that life is immanent in living things.

> Historians want to write histories of biology in the eighteenth century; but they do not realize that biology did not exist then, and that the pattern of knowledge that has been familiar to us for a hundred and fifty years is not valid for a previous period. And that, if biology was unknown, there was a very simple reason for it: that life did not exist. (Foucault 1973: 127–8)

What is meant by this claim that before the birth of biology 'life did not exist'? How can it be argued that to accept such an assertion can contribute to understanding the African body as the object and effect of power? This and the following chapter on the African bodies of knowledge produced from around the 1400s to the turn of the nineteenth century attempt to answer these questions, and so contextualize the subsequent emergence of disciplinary modernism by highlighting its discontinuity with the Renaissance and Classical epistemes that preceded it.

The body as prose and the renaissance episteme

> The mother in a woman is a singular member, disposed as a bladder, and kind has ordained that member to take and receive the humour seminall ... The mother hangeth between the spleen and the bladder, but somewhat higher than the bladder, the bottom of hollowness is extended into the navell, and is the place of the first Fragma, of conception called Embrion, because of carnal copulation. (Batman 1582: 62)

Until the middle of the 1600s, a scholar like Batman who explored the qualities of the human body could be secure in the truth of assertions such as this because its investigation proceeded not through the use of a cold cadaver and a scalpel, but rather parchment, a pen and the 'book wheel'. Indeed, the book from which Batman reproduced his description of 'the mother' – Bartholomew Anglicus' *On the Properties of Things*, 'first set forth in 1360' (Batman 1582: 1) – was perhaps itself penned using a 'book wheel', for, as Batman's introduction informed the reader it drew upon such authorities as Aristotle, Pliny, Hippocrates, Isidore of Seville, Cicero, Galen, Theophrastus and Zeno.

The 'book wheel' (see Grafton 1992: 117–18) typified the 'circular system of authentication' (Greenblatt 1992: 35) that prevailed in Renaissance thought and dictated that the absence of anything new in a text was a sign not of its intellectual sterility but of its truth. Like a scaled down Ferris wheel, the circumference of the 'book wheel' was partitioned into shelves each containing a number of volumes which could be opened and read without removing them from the shelves. To turn the device, an elaborate system of cranks, cogs and gears was activated by a foot pedal. Whenever a new compartment on the 'book wheel' was to be selected, depressing the pedal and engaging the machinery would result in the chosen texts whirring into place before the reader's eyes. Since all knowledge already existed in the pages of authoritative texts,[2] the 'book wheel' thus allowed users to move throughout the library (and, by extension, the universe) while remaining seated at the desk in the calm posture appropriate to scholarly contemplation. By spinning from text to text, authority could be compared with authority, and the object of interest confirmed as a component of knowledge by assembling all that had been seen and heard, and everything that was recounted of it, 'either by nature or by men, by the language of the world, or by tradition' (Foucault 1973: 40).

Moving closer to the 'book wheel', we may peer over the shoulder of the Renaissance scholar to read what he read, and, more importantly, to see what he saw in the way the words and sections of his text were physically arranged on the page. Perhaps the text was Batman's (1582) rendition of *On the Properties of Things*. Examining the 'catalogue' of the matters dealt with, we see that it was not arranged according to the order of the alphabet,[3] but instead that it juxtaposed seemingly unrelated topics, such as the following sequence of matters: 'man's fasting spittle kills serpents; the harmony of the elemental humours; carnall lust; corruptions of the flesh; man's body is spirit, humour and members'. But this arrangement was far from random, for like the 'book wheel' that was perfectly closed in its circularity upon itself, the way words were linked together and the 'matters' arranged in the space of the printed page reconstituted the very order of the universe. Within this episteme 'the names of things were lodged in the things they designated' (Foucault 1973: 36), and it was therefore the encyclopedist's ideal 'to spatialize acquired knowledge both in accordance with the cosmic, unchanging, and perfect form of the circle and in accordance with the sublunary, perishable, multiple, and divided form of the tree' (Foucault 1973: 38). Arranged according to just this principle, the *Nuremberg Chronicle* (Schedel 1493), for instance, arranged all of history into seven ages, each age a different section of the text, and each analogous to the first week in which God created the universe. Every thing was connected to every other thing in a complete cosmic web, the organizing principle of which was resemblance as it repeated and replicated itself through the play of the four 'similitudes'.

The first of the similitudes was 'convenience', which assured that like things would tend to occur in juxtaposition with one another, and that things which were adjacent would through their mere proximity tend to become similar. 'Convenience' thus linked the world together in the form of an endless chain where at each point of contact there began and ended a link that resembled the one before it and the one after it (Foucault 1973: 18–19). 'Emulation' referred to a force of resemblance by which things imitated one another in the absence of the physical proximity required by 'convenience'. For instance, the human face emulated the sky and man's wisdom that of God, and through emulation things widely dispersed throughout the universe were able to resonate with and answer one another. 'Analogy' was a mode of connection between things that induced resemblances not only between visible and substantial things, but between entire patterns of relationships. Thus, the human body was analogous to the universe, for the pulse beat in the veins as the stars circled the sky, and the seven orifices of the head were to the face what the seven planets were to the sky (Foucault 1973: 21–3). Completing the similitudes were the 'sympathies', a capricious force of resemblance and assimilation emanating from the sameness of the invisible virtues of things. Sympathy attracted what was heavy to the heaviness of the earth, and it was the sun's warmth and light that attracted fire into the air. Preventing, however, the merging of everything into an undifferentiated mass was the antithesis of sympathy, 'antipathy'. This maintained the isolation of things by enclosing each within its own impenetrable difference. So, the olive and the vine 'hated' the cabbage, just as Nature had ordained that the rat and the crocodile should be eternal enemies (pp. 23–4).

Folded upon itself in a chain of relentless duplication, the similitudes that maintained the Renaissance universe were visible on the surface of things as 'signatures' of the invisible analogies that linked them. The signature of bravery, for example, was the presence of large and well-developed extremities to the limbs (which marked the affinity between the lion and the gladiator), and it was the task of the scholar to scrutinize every thing so as to decode its 'signature' and establish its rightful place in the order of things. The Renaissance episteme was therefore a mode of knowing in which the connection between the eye that looked and the properties of the beings it saw

> was that being itself, within the whole semantic network that connected it to the world. The division, so evident to us, between what we see, what others have observed and handed down, and what others imagine or naively believe, the great tripartition ... into Observation, Document and Fable did

not exist, because ... signs were then part of things themselves. (Foucault 1973: 129)

In this age of authority and kingdom of resemblance things were undivided from words, and to know something was to collate the entire semantic complex through which it existed, as had Pliny where he stated in the preface to Book One of his *Natural History* that 'by perusing about 2,000 volumes, very few of which ... are ever handled by students, we have collected in 36 volumes 20,000 noteworthy facts obtained from 100 authors' (Pliny 1938: 13).

Was Foucault correct in asserting that under the Renaissance episteme 'life did not exist' because it was not immanent in living things? If so, then the genealogical method must identify texts that: (1) reveal the absence of life in living things such as the human body; (2) localize the source of animation to forces other than those chemical, organic and physical processes we now take for granted as emergents of the body and the determinants of life; (3) demonstrate how the practice of doctors was constitutive of the living body without life; and (4) explicate how the bodies conceived of by Renaissance knowledge as existing in Africa were contingent upon this episteme.

Lifeless bodies of the living

> The soul, *anima*, was so called by the pagans because they took it to be wind. Whence also 'wind' is anemos in Greek, because we seem to live by taking in air with our mouths, but this is most likely false since the soul arises long before air can be taken in by the mouth, and is already alive in its mother's womb. (Sharpe/Isidore 1964: 38)

The soul withdrawn, the Renaissance body as its temporary corporeal container collapsed into a heap of blood, bones and skin, like a heavenly glove-puppet from which the celestial hand has been removed. 'When the soul departs, what is left is no longer an animal, and that none of the parts remain what they were before, excepting in mere configuration' (Barnes/Aristotle 1984: 997). All the arteries pulsing blood, the ventricles coursing humours and the lungs bellowing air were in themselves bereft of the power of life, empty skeins until breathed into by the 'vital virtue'. The Renaissance episteme's lifeless bodies of the living were repeatedly confirmed through the practice of dissection, since because the animate body was merely the temporary vessel of the soul, to search for the mechanisms of life in the dead body was unthinkable. As an exercise in medical education, the practice of dissection was therefore akin to other forms of textual illustration (e.g. 'trees', 'wheels' and 'wound men' representing the theory of temperament and diagramming humoural systems) in that it aimed to help scholars achieve a grasp of organizing schemes rather than to enable naturalistic description of the body itself.

> The goal of physiological or anatomical study was, in many instances, a better understanding of texts ... The academic environment in which the dissection of a human cadaver was regularized integrated the occasional presentation of the body itself as the object of study with frequent and habitual attention to learned texts on the subject. (Siraisi 1990: 80–2)

If life was not an immanent of the body's functioning, then how was it possible to explain the living body? The Renaissance solution to this question was to treat the body as a complex jigsaw of outward signatures (such as the shape and positioning of bones and features) that encoded the invisible web of analogies by which the living was spatialized in the sympathetic interplay of everything.

> These links proceed so strictly that they appear as a rope stretched from the first cause as far as the lowest and smallest of things, by a reciprocal and continuous connection; in such wise that the superior virtue, spreading its beams, reaches so far that if we touch one extremity of that cord it will make tremble and move all the rest. (Porta 1650, in Foucault 1973: 19)

And so to Purchas, for whom the human body 'is a microcosme, and created after the rest, as an Epitome of the whole Universe, and truest Mappe of the World, a summarie and compendious other world' (Purchas 1619: 25–6). Just as the universe was explicable in terms of 'Man', so 'Man' was explicable in terms of the universe.

> O Man, Know thy selfe, and know all things ... Thou hast thy Body, a Booke of Nature, and carriest a little Modell of the greater World continually about thee. In thy composition, thou seest the foure Elements; the elementarie qualities in thy complexions; all the ranks and classes of creatures in thy growth. Is not the Haire as grasse? the flesh as Earth? the Bones as Mineralls? the Veines as rivers? the liver a Sea? Are not the lungs and Heart Correspondent to the ayrie and fierie elements? the Braines, to the clouds and Meteors ... the Eyes, to starres, or those two Eyes of Heaven, the greater lights? and the circular frame of the Head, to the globositie of the heauens? (Purchas 1619: 29–31)

To explain how the similitudes could produce so perfect a symmetry between the body and the universe required a medium that could invest both the animate and the inanimate with the properties and form proper to themselves. Following Anglicus (Steele/Anglicus 1893) this medium consisted in the 'substances' common to all things by which they retained and reproduced their proper place and function in the universe.

> True it is that after the noble and expert doctrine of wise and well learned philosophers ... we know that the properties of things follow and ensue their substance. Herefore it is that after the order and distinction of substances, the order and the distinction of the properties of things shall be and ensue. (Steele/Anglicus 1893: 11)

Explanations of the living body privileged this elemental force. Subdivided into four, the elements in turn explained the principal properties of every thing.

> Elements are four, and so there are four qualities of elements, of which every body is composed and made as of matter. The four elements are Earth, Water, Fire, and Air ... Four be called the first and principal properties, that is hot, cold, dry, and moist: they are called the first qualities because they slide first from the elements into the things that be made of elements. (Steele/Anglicus 1893: 23)

Reading the Renaissance human body thus involved tracing the transmutations of the elements in its 'members' (arms, legs, organs and collections of organs), and following their minglings through the different 'offices' conferred upon each member and group of members by the cosmic template. Quoting Batman (1582), 'Avicen says that members are bodies made of the first meddlying of humours'. Each member 'is ordained to some special office', and each office was ordained by the soul. 'Because the soul has diverse virtues, so are diverse members needed' (Batman 1582). Batman divided the body through classification of its members into those that 'make ready', 'purge', 'cleanse', 'defend', and 'bear about'. Similarly, De Liuzzi's *Anatomy* (cited in Siraisi 1990: 107–8) segmented the body according to how the vital, animal, and natural virtues were localized. 'Animal' virtues (such as motion, sensation and thinking) produced 'animal members' – the skull and its contents. 'Spiritual' or 'vital' virtues (breathing, the pulse, the heartbeat) produced 'spiritual members' – the thorax and its contents. 'Natural' virtues (growth, nutrition, reproduction, excretion) produced 'natural members' – the abdomen and its constituent organs.

Animating this corporeal microcosm was the 'vital spirit', 'by whose benefits and continual moving, both wits and virtues in beasts are ruled to work and do their deeds' (Steele/Anglicus 1893: 26). The 'vital spirit' was heated by the liver to form a smoke. This smoke was then 'made subtle' by the liver's veins until it became 'the natural spirit'. In turn, this moved the blood and brought the heart together, by which it was 'more pured, and turned into a more subtle kind' (Steele/Anglicus 1893: 27). This was the 'vital spirit' and by it 'The soul is joined to the body ... And therefore if these spirits be impared, or let of their working in any kind, the accord of the body and soul is resolved, the reasonable spirit is let of all its works in the body' (p. 28).

This, then, was the human body of Renaissance thought, a complex interplay of invisible elements, virtues and spirits that united it to the irreducible 'soul' and inscribed their signatures in the body's members. Far from an intellectual abstraction, it was precisely this body that was produced through the concrete practices of the Renaissance doctor.

Doctoring the Renaissance body Since it existed as the finely balanced space where the elements coincided, the living human body of Renaissance thought was a particularly resonant link in the great web of reciprocal and continuous cosmic connection. Hence the necessity that the Renaissance doctor be conversant with all the scholastic disciplines, and hence the manner of diagnosing and treating the sick.

> 1. Some ask why the study of medicine is not included among the other liberal disciplines. It is because whereas they embrace individual subjects, medicine embraces them all. The physician ought to know literature, grammatica, to be able to understand or to explain what he reads.
>
> 2. Likewise also rhetoric, that he may delineate in true arguments the things he discusses; dialectic also so that he may study the causes and cures of infirmities in the light of reason. Similarly also arithmetic, in view of the temporal relationships involved in the paroxysms of diseases and in diurnal cycles.
>
> 3. It is no different with respect to geometry because of the properties of regions and the locations of places. He should teach what must be observed in them by everyone ...
>
> 4. Finally also, he ought to know astronomy, by which he should study the motions of the stars and the changes of the seasons, for as a certain physician said, our bodies are also changed with their courses. (Sharpe/Isidore 1964: 64)

As a reflection of every thing within the universe, every thing could influence the body's working. Diagnosis therefore required deciphering the signatures of this resonance from the texture, colour and smell of bodily excrements (faeces, phlegm and urine); the rhythm of the heart-beat and pulse; the texture and colour of the skin; the appearance of the face; and the sick man's telling of his illness. To complete the puzzle, this complex of signs was mapped on to the macrocosm through the horoscope, astrolabe, inspection of the weather and knowledge of the climate. The comparison drawn by Crollius between apoplexy and tempests thus extended the correspondence identified by Purchas (1619: 30) of 'the Braines to the clouds and Meteors':

> The storm begins when the air becomes heavy and agitated, the apoplectic attack at the moment when our thoughts become heavy and disturbed; then the clouds pile up, the belly swells, the thunder explodes and the bladder bursts; the lightning flashes and the eyes glitter with a terrible brightness, the rain falls, the mouth foams, the thunderbolt is unleashed and the spirits burst open breaches in the skin; but then the sky becomes clear again, and in the sick man reason regains ascendancy. (Crollius, 1624, in Foucault 1973: 23)

In other cases, the cause of illness (which was almost always humoural imbalance) might lie not in the weather but in astrological events, discernible through scrutiny of the sick man's horoscope. Likewise, corruption of the air through which illness was spread would be ascribed to unfavourable planetary conjunctions (Siraisi 1990: 187). Yet other afflictions arose simply through the contact of things, as with 'mourning roses which have been used at obsequies', whose adjacency to death left those who smelt them 'sad and moribund' (Porta 1650, in Foucault 1973: 23).

If the play of sympathies caused infirmity, so too the opposite, and by identifying positive sympathies between plants or minerals and afflicted members of the body remedies could be established and applied. Because the seeds of aconite are tiny dark spheres set in white, skin-like coverings that resemble the eyelids, they were good for treating diseases of the eye. Similarly, the affinity between walnuts and the human head was signalled by the fact that their shells (like the pericranium) enclosed the nut itself, 'which is exactly like the human brain in appearance' (Crollius 1624, in Foucault 1973: 27). Thus, the shells helped heal skull wounds, and the nuts repaired sickness to the brain.

The soul, elements, humours, spirits, affinities and sympathies – all invisible and ephemeral, yet there for all to see in the prose of the Renaissance body. All only words, yet words that were contiguous with the forces they designated and so were those forces. It is therefore incorrect to speak of the Renaissance body as if it was anything other than these semantic constellations. Correspondingly, it is correct to say of the monstrous and marvellous beings set around it at the edges of this episteme that they were just as real as it was.

Monstrous men

It is perhaps ironic that this analysis of the Renaissance body should
have commenced at the centre of the Renaissance episteme. For it was
at its edges, where the cords of similitude were most tautly stretched,
that its power to produce bodies of prose was most clearly evidenced in
the variety of the monstrous men that crystallized along this periphery.

> Ethiopia, blue men's land, had first that name of colour of men. For the
> sun is nigh, and roasteth and toasteth them. And so the colour of men
> showeth the strength of the star, for there is continual heat ... In this land
> be many nations with divers faces wonderly and horribly shapen ... Also
> there be great cockatrices and great dragons, and precious stones be taken
> out of their brains ... The men of Ethiopia have their name of a black river,
> and that river is of the same kind as Nilus ... Some oft curse the sun bitterly
> ... for his heat grieveth them full sore ... Troglodites dig them dens and
> caves ... and they eat serpents and all that may be got. (Steele/Anglicus
> 1893: 74–5)

Bizarre as they were, the possibility of knowing and representing these
'wonderly and horribly shapen' bodies lay in the omnipresent play of
the similitudes. For, as d'Ailly said in his *Imago Mundi* (printed *c.*1480–83,
and cited in V. J. Flint 1992: 25–7), to know all of the earth's inhabitants
was to proceed as would a doctor understanding the sick man. First,
deduce the disposition of the planets and stars in relation to the area of
the earth in question. Which planet was it 'governed' by? Where was it
in relation to the sun? Then, infer from this how the humours would
be constellated, and whether the 'vital spirit' so produced would induce
activity or torpor. Third, examine the presence of seas, rivers or deserts
to discern the terrestrial conveniences at play. With this cosmic template
complete, sketch the shapes of men, monsters and marvels that, if it be
inhabited, must and can only be there.

Epitomizing this system of knowing and representing the earth's
inhabitants was the Macrobian 'zone map' (see Friedman 1981). These
maps reflected the world's division into horizontal layers according to
temperature and natural harmony. Of these zones, only the middle
climatic zone (Europe) was sufficiently temperate and balanced to
sustain bodies in their familiar human form, because, as Hippocrates
had argued: 'Growth and freedom from wildness are most fostered
when nothing is forcibly predominant, but equality in every respect
prevails ... For the seasons which modify a physical frame differ; if the
differences be great, the more too are the differences in shape' (Hippocrates, in Friedman 1981: 52).

Contingent upon the interplay of these external forces that created and conditioned its form and functioning, the boundaries of the Renaissance body were tenuous and indistinct, so that when located in zones lacking 'equality' it might deliquesce and distort. Hence the correctness of Al-Kindi's statement concerning the 'Zanj' of North Africa:

> His country being very hot, the heavenly bodies exert their influence and draw the humours to the upper part. Hence his bulging eyes, his drooping lips, his big, flat, nose, the flaccidity of his head resulting from the abundance of humours drawn to the top of his body. Thus the mixture in his brain is no longer in balance, and the soul cannot exert its full influence upon him; his discernment is altered, and the acts of the intelligence desert him. (Al-Kindi, in Devisse 1979: 218)

In Mandeville, whose *Travels*[4] (Seymour/Mandeville 1967) exemplified Foucault's description of the Renaissance as 'the age of the theatre' (Foucault 1973, p. 131), it was emulation that moulded men and monsters. Owing to their adjacency to Jerusalem and therefore God, the centres of Christian power were places of pleasant climate inhabited by people of beauty, gentleness and wealth. 'Mancy', for instance, was a 'good and great country', and its inhabitants 'ben fulle faire folk, but thei ben alle pale ... and men clepen that land Albanye because the folk ben white' (Seymour/Mandeville 1967: 149). Distant from these centres, extremes dominated to form 'fulle cursed peple' (Seymour/Mandeville 1967: 143), and 'wylde men that ben hidouse to loken on' (p. 198). Planetary and other cosmic forces shaped the destiny of nations, the proclivity of their peoples for exploration, and their bodies. 'India' was a land of numberless people, because living under the slowing and nearly motionless 'climate' of Saturn they 'han of no kynde nor will for to move ne stere to seche strange places', and so never 'gon out of here owne contree' (p. 119). By contrast, Europe lay within the 'climate' of the moon, which because it orbited the earth faster than other planets and moved the waves conferred upon those within its aura the will 'to meve lightly and for to go dyuerse weyes and to sechen strange thinges and other dyuersitees of the world' (p. 120). An island of the 'Great See Ocean' was so hot that traders' 'ballokkes hangen doun to here knees for the gret dissolucoun of the body', a difficulty avoided by the 'natives' through binding and anointing the testicles (p. 120).

Whether considering these secular texts of scholars and travel writers such as Mandeville, or the more theologically inclined 'T-O' maps and 'mappa-mundi' (see V. J. Flint 1992; Friedman 1981), the answer was always the same. As the distance from the centre of the Renaissance world increased, so did the mutability of power and with it the body.

For instance, at the centre of the circular Hereford map made around 1300 by an English canon (see V. J. Flint 1992: 12) was Jerusalem. Just below Jerusalem converged three inland seas which took the form of a rough 'T' that symbolized Christ on the cross and divided the land into three unequal continents: to the left, Europe, at the top Asia and on the right Africa. Following biblical tradition, each continent was associated with one of Noah's sons: Asia with Shem, Africa with Ham, and Europe with Japhet. Superimposed upon this land mass were illustrations depicting the wonders to be found at the point of their insertion. Moving from Jerusalem towards the circumference there occurred increasing numbers of bizarre beings, with their greatest frequency in narrow bands along the edge of the world where there clustered the monsters produced by the fiends of hell copulating with Ham's son, Membroth, which: 'engendred on hem dyuerse folk, as monstres and folk disfigured, summe withouten hedes, summe with grete eres, summe with on eye, summe geauntes, sum with hors feet, and many other of dyuerse schapp ayenst kynde' (Seymour/Mandeville 1967: 160–1)[5]

The spectacle of strangeness and the Cape of Good Hope The Renaissance was an episteme in which the strangeness of living beings 'was a spectacle: it was featured in fairs, in tournaments, in fictitious or real combats, in reconstitutions of legends in which the bestiary displayed its ageless fables' (Foucault 1973: 131). Due to a tradition of knowing things not through direct inspection but through collation of the words and myths that were synonymous with them, the effects of this fascination with the marvellous were nowhere more apparent than in the practice of exploration and reports of the 'new worlds' brought back by voyagers to the Americas, Asia and Africa.

In *The Imaginative Landscape of Christopher Columbus* the medievalist Valerie Flint (1992) analysed the books that composed his library and which Columbus may have studied in preparation for the 1492 voyage to what we now know as the Americas. By comparing these books with what Columbus reported seeing (which included the Hispaniola Indians as 'well made men' alongside descriptions of other humans that were hairless, had tails and the heads of dogs), Flint concluded that: 'This old world held great power ... Thus, though some of it could later ... be described as fanciful, it was so real at the time that it had a decisive impact upon the establishment of "objective reality"' (V. J. Flint 1992: xxi). 'Discovered' by Vasco da Gama between 1497 and 1499, the Cape of Good Hope was no exception to this power of the fabulous, the accounts of voyagers from then until well into the 1600s repeatedly confirming its indigenous inhabitants as the embodiment of

Renaissance mythography. Far from puncturing this self-sealing semantic universe, the great voyages of exploration that commenced in the late 1400s were at the start analogous to the role of dissection in Renaissance medicine, serving less to enable naturalistic description of the un-expected peoples encountered than to embellish the ancient texts that had populated the unknown corners of the world with headless monsters and cannibals. As V. J. Flint (1992: 23) noted, it was as though the further back the boundaries of geographical knowledge were driven, the more zealous were the makers of maps and authors of travelogues in their attempts to create a sense of the marvellous.

What historians consider to be the first account of the Cape of Good Hope's inhabitants was recorded by da Gama during his voyage between 1497 and 1499.

> The inhabitants of this country are tawny-coloured. Their food is confined to the flesh of seals, whales and gazelles, and the roots of herbs. They are dressed in skins, and wear sheaths over their virile members. They are armed with poles of olive wood to which a horn, browned in the fore, is attached. Their numerous dogs resemble those of Portugal, and bark like them. (da Gama, in Ravenstein 1898: 6)

Remarkable in its restraint, this bland portrait was produced in the course of a voyage propelled by the very power of Renaissance mytho-logy, for da Gama had been commissioned to find the fabled land of Prester John, said to be an earthly paradise that harboured precious jewels and minerals, the fountain of eternal youth, and nearly all the marvellous and monstrous creatures ever described.[6] Thus, some fifty years later Sebastian Munster's *Cosmographiae* of 1550 could include a map of Africa showing a 'monoculi' on the coast where Cameroon is today, Prester John's kingdom in the region of modern-day Ethiopia, and the 'Caput bone Spei' as inhabited only by wild beasts. Commenting upon the region, he wrote:

> Only the coastline of this region has been explored, since it is very hot and so sandy that nobody could ever live there. It is mainly situated between the tropic of Capricorn and the tropic of Cancer, which is the hottest area and neither human beings nor animals can live there, only dragons, snakes and other dangerous animals. And if there were to be found people there, then they must be like animals, living underground and not coming together in the way that others do. (Munster 1550)

For Linschoten, it was the hardy myth of the cannibal that was pressed into the service of his 1596 account which said of the 'Kaffers' between Mozambique and the Cape of Good Hope that:

> Some of them are cannibals ... They cut off the penis of their prisoners but let them go afterwards. They bring the dried pieces of flesh to their king as proof of bravery. They go before the King in the presence of the highest dignitaries of the village, put one penis after another in their mouth and spit them out in front of the king. (Linschoten 1596, in Hirschberg 1967: 38)

In addition to its high dramatic value, the figure of the cannibal perhaps reflected in symbolic form a fear that the body boundaries of the European (who came from a climate of harmony and balance) would deliquesce and be absorbed into the bodies of those who against all reason existed where the theories of Renaissance medicine and geography said they could not. For the spectacle of the Cape as home to cannibal hordes was repeated like a litany in the reports of many other Renaissance explorers (for these texts in English translation, see Raven-Hart 1967). As if it were the land 'beyond the Valley Perilous' – where Mandeville had talked of a people that 'han no clothinge but of skynnes of bestes that thei hangene upon them. And thei eten more gladly of mannes flesch than any other flesch' (Seymour/Mandeville 1967: 205) – Downton could in 1610 describe the inhabitants of the Cape as:

> very brutish and savage, as stupid as can be and without intelligence, black and mis-shapen, with no hair on their heads, their eyes always running. They cover their privy parts with the hairy skins of beasts and their backs with an entire large skin which they tie below the chin, leaving the tail hanging so that from a distance one might say that they had tails. The women have very long breasts, and dress like the men. They eat human flesh and entirely raw animals, with the intestines and guts without washing them, as do dogs. (Downton 1610, in Raven-Hart 1967: 47)

Sharpening the notion of body boundary dissolution and recalling an isle in Mandeville where the bodies of female virgins contained serpents which stung men's penises and killed them (Seymour/Mandeville 1967: 206), Tavernier could in 1649 describe 'the women of the kaffers [as] ... so hot blooded that when they have their menses and make water, if a European passes over it he at once gets a head-ache and fever, and even sometimes the plague' (Tavernier, in Raven-Hart 1967: 181). De Beaulieu, writing around 1620, perhaps echoed the Mandevillian myth of Ethiopia where men and women lay together in the rivers or buried in the sand to avoid the heat (Seymour/Mandeville 1967: 120) when he recorded how

> some of our men met them with their wives and children at the place where they had gone to pass the night, where they had no shelter other

than bushes and some skins stretched on two crossed sticks, with another in the middle to thrust into the ground like a parasol, under which their wives and children set themselves, buried to the waist in sand. (De Beaulieu 1620, in Raven-Hart 1967: 101)

The Cape was not only a repository of the bestial and bizarre, but also of the more wondrous things befitting a region that for some explorers was the land of Prester John.

In this Land of Prester John ther was seene by our Men Lyons and monkeyes, Babownns a multid, with divers other Strange beastes as Antilops and many other deformed creattures verie strange to be Sene ... The Bay of Soldania and all about the Cape is so healtfull and frutfull as might grow a Paradise of the World; it well agrees with English bodies ... The Countrey is mixed, Mountaines, Plaines, Medowes, Streames, the woods as if they were artifically planted for order. (Best 1612, in Raven-Hart 1967: 59)

Although such visions of the Cape as a land of plenty were not uncommon, it was time and again accounts of its human inhabitants that took centre stage, as exemplified by the section on the Cape of Good Hope in Herbert's popular and much reprinted *Travels into Africa and Asia* (Herbert 1638, in Hirschberg 1967).

The Natives being propagated from *Cham*, both in their Visages and Natures seem to inherit his malediction. Their colour is ugly black, are strongly limbd, desperate, crafty and injurious. Their heads are long; their haire, woolly and crisp, no apparell in any place shewing more variety ... Their noses are flat, crusht so in their infancie; great lips, description cannot make them greater; quick, crafty eyes; and about their necks (in imitation of the Dutch *Commandores* chains) have guts and raw puddings, serving both for food and complement, eating and speaking both together ... Solinus calls the tawny *Africans, Agriophagi* (or Panther and Lyon-eaters) we now call them *Icthio* and *Anthropophagi* ... These Savages eat men alive or dead Which when they faile of, dead Whales, Seales, Pengwins, grease or raw Puddings diet them. Safety is scarce among themselves, for when the frost of old age benums their vigour, unapting them to provide their owne food; they either eat them, or leave them destitute of defence upon some Mountain pittied by none. (Herbert 1638, in Hirschberg 1967: 16–17)

The African body that was the object and effect of Herbert's late Renaissance report was clearly more substantial than the purely imaginative monsters such as the 'Blemmyae' and 'Cynocephali' described by Isidore of Seville and popularized by Mandeville. For, while travellers continued to weave myth and legend into their accounts of the African body until the mid-1600s, they none the less created an increasingly stable corporeal form that was more than and thus autonomous of the words that described it. This transformation begs the question as to what effects the practice of exploration must have had upon the Renaissance episteme. More specifically, to what extent did these practices constitute the conditions of possibility for the emergence of a Classificatory gaze to the surface of the African body?

The eye of the explorer and the rise of Classification

The practice of exploration involved the respatialization of knowledge formation from the library to the zone of situated observation in Africa and other unknown regions of the world.

Even as the practice of exploration served to confirm the ancient myths and legends of Renaissance thought, so it operated to install a new vision of the universe and a new way of seeing the human body. Analogous with the movement of the patient from the home to the hospital that fabricated a deep anatomy to demand the invention of new devices for seeing into it (such as the stethoscope), this respatialization of exploration required the deployment of new observational techniques able to regularize what was seen and how such observations were recorded.

As early as 1575 there began to appear a new kind of text devoted not to describing the marvels of the world, but to calibrating the eye of the explorer as itself an object of knowledge and target of power. Among these was *The Traveiler of Jerome Turler* (1575). 'A notable discourse on the manner, and order of traveiling oversea, or into strange and forrein countreys', this advocated that the traveller 'make down suche things in strange countries as they shall have neede to use in the common trade of life' (Turler 1575: 3). In 1578, Bourne's 'tresure for traveillers' problematized the act of seeing by warning how 'banketting, and play, and gaine, and dauncing and dalying with women' would so distract the traveller as to dampen his observational acuity, demanding their strict avoidance. Meirus' (1587) 'speciall instructions for gentlemen, merchants, students, souldiers, mariners, and c.' aimed at enrolling every explorer in the 'catalogue of Homer' as 'seers of many Regions and of the manners of many nations':

> If in our peregrinations and travels, we shal observe and note in our tables
> those things which do occurre and seeme worthie of regard, we shall make
> our journies and voyages in great measure, pleasant and delectable unto us:
> not thinking that our diligence can search and mark any thing in any place
> … but to discourse and recorde any thing, rather than to passe the way, and

spend the time in idelnesse: and with by all this means, this commoditie is reaped, that whatsoever the eye seeth, is the easier and the better remembered, if it once be written. (Meirus 1587: 22)

As for Meirus, so in Lipsius (1592), who asserted that nothing was more likely to ensure wisdom and sound direction 'than the sight, consideration and knowledge, of sundry rites, manners, pollycies and governments'.

All instructing the eye of the explorer in somewhat broad and global terms, these textual teachers of observation represented the nascent beginnings of a new way of knowing, the rise of a Classificatory gaze directed in its seeing not by the semantic force of myth and legend but by the very bodies of people and things themselves. They therefore exemplify what Foucault described as having come surreptitiously into being between the age of the theatre and that of the catalogue: 'not the desire for knowledge, but a new way of connecting things both to the eye and to discourse. A new way of making history' (Foucault 1973: 131).

> The documents of this new history are not other words, texts, or records, but unencumbered spaces in which things are juxtaposed: herbariums, collections, gardens; the locus of this history is a non-temporal rectangle in which, stripped of all commentary, of all enveloping language, creatures present themselves one beside another, their surfaces visible, grouped according to their common features, and thus already virtually analysed, and bearers of nothing but their own individual names. (Foucault 1973: 131)

Epitomizing the taxonomic space in which this new knowledge would form itself was the observational grid devised in 1666 by the Royal Society and directed to systematizing the information recorded by the 'labours of the ingenious in many considerable parts of the world' (Royal Society 1665–66). Under its 'general heads for the natural history of a country' were instructions for the classification of flora, fauna and geology, and a special section on how to see 'both Natives and Strangers':

> And in particular their Stature, Shape, Colour, Features, Strength, Agility, Beauty (or the want of it), Complexion, Hair, Dyet, Inclination, and Customs that seem not due to Education. As to their Women (besides other things) may be observed their Fruitfulness, or Barrenness; their hard or easy labour, etc. And both in Women and Men must be taken notice of what diseases they are subject to. (Royal Society 1665–66)

'Between 1550 and 1650 Western thinkers ceased to believe that they could find all truths in ancient books' (Grafton 1992: 1). On the one side of this massive disjunction in knowing was the 'book wheel' and the great compilations of documents and signs enabled by its use; on the other side was the empty observational template of the Royal Society that created a gaze to the strictly transected surface of the body. It was precisely this transformation in the underlying base of knowledge that made possible the African body as an object of positive knowledge, and the Cape of Good Hope a site for the formation of a sovereign power directed to its surface.

Notes

1. Sharpe (1964) stated that the first three printed editions containing Isidore's works on medicine appeared in Paris (1580), Madrid (1590) and Cologne (1617).

2. As Bentham's Panopticon is to disciplinary power in the Modernist episteme, so the 'book wheel' was to the Renaissance episteme. In the former, it is the bodies of all who are rendered visible to the omnipresent gaze; in the latter it was to see better the texts of ancient wisdom containing the legends, virtues and fables characteristic of things that technology was bent.

3. Foucault (1973: 38) noted that except in regard to the study of languages – since the alphabet is its raw material – use of the alphabet as a means of creating encyclopedic order appeared only in the second half of the seventeenth century, suggesting therefore that it was only then that linguistic signs became disengaged from things themselves and hence imbued with the power to order things.

4. Historians tell us that the frequency with which *Mandeville's Travels* was reprinted, translated and used as a source for subsequent texts points to it being among the more popular of Renaissance travelogues:

> Mandeville's influence on the literature of the sixteenth century was profound. Many of his stories and most of his monsters, as depicted by his artists, found their way into the *Nuremberg Chronicle* and Munster's *Cosmographia* (1544). Like the *Nuremberg Chronicle*, Munster's book was extremely popular, there having been as many as forty-seven editions in seven languages before 1650. (Letts 1949: 38)

While not the province of this study to debate whether what Mandeville wrote was really taken to be the truth or not, the historian Newton argued that because it was written into a vacuum of comparative information by which to disentangle 'the true wonders from the false, both made an equal appeal and had an equal aspect of reality' (Newton 1950: 160).

> For most contemporary readers the book had to rest on its own foundations, and as the marvels which Mandeville sets down as sober facts can be capped and even outrivalled by other writers ... the reading public of the fourteenth and fifteenth centuries probably swallowed their Mandeville whole. Bale,

who published his *Catalogue of British Writers* in 1548, had no doubt about the authenticity of the 'Travels', and his contemporary Leland (who died in 1552) goes even further, for he placed Mandeville above Marco Polo, Columbus and Cortez and other travellers. (Letts 1949: 34)

5. Speaking to the endless cycle of telling and retelling by which the epistemic base of Renaissance knowledge folded in upon itself, Letts (1949) suggests that Mandeville's *Travels* can just as well be read as a textual annotation of the Hereford 'mappa mundi', for the one is in effect supplemental to the other: 'Detach some thirty-five or forty pictures from the Map, reproduce them separately, and they become a set of illustrations for Mandeville, so apt for their purpose that all that is necessary is to fit them into their places in the text' (Letts 1949: 106).

6. The myth of Prester John dates to the twelfth century when there appeared the Latin text of a letter addressed to the Byzantine emperor Manuel Comnenus and purportedly written by Prester John. Eager to discover his wondrous realm, European monarchs and travellers mounted many an expedition to search for it. Some travellers succeeded in returning, such as an Englishman by the name of Edward Webbe, who in 1590 reported that he had visited the court of Prester John and seen there a monster. Kept chained to prevent its devouring human beings, the monster was fed human flesh only after executions. Its geographical location variously conceived, the realm of Prester John was initially in or near India, and later in Abyssinia (see Malefijt 1968: 115–16).

CHAPTER 4

A Body without Volume: the African as Target of Sovereignty and Object of Taxonomy

Contemporaneous with the emergence into travel writing of a discursive strand that problematized the act of observation, the Cape of Good Hope was in 1652 established as a 'refreshment station' for ships *en route* to the East Indies, and in 1671 raised to a government to formalize its colonial status. This new context of situated interaction between Europeans and Africans emerged to visibility as continuous settlement coincided with a massive surge in the production of formal and informal texts that recorded European perceptions of the Africans. For instance, in 1655 Heeck wrote:

> Behind the Table Mountain we came into a village of the inhabitants, called *Hottento* and *Hottento: Broqua* because they thus sing of themselves for a little bread … Their clothing is nothing but the skins of wild beasts and seals, the men wearing one skin only, not longer than to their waist, and the women 2, 3, or more skins, somewhat longer, and all also covering their privities with a small skin. The men are tolerably tall and well built, and exceptionally fast runners, but by nature cruel, sly and rascally: the women are quite short of stature and very ugly … They … plait some little shells in their hair, smearing this, as also their whole body, with every sort of fat that they can get, and from this they stink exceptionally foully (as do most of the black peoples in general), and otherwise they would be yellow rather than black because of the cold climate of this land … In hair and all else they resemble the Caffers of *Guinea*, *Angola* and *Monzembicque*, their neighbours; but since (as aforesaid) they live far further to the southwards, they are nothing like so black of skin, and somewhat better built. In a word, it is almost impossible, and quite unbelievable by those who have never seen such people, to realize their wild, strange, and altogether beast-like manners. (Heeck 1655, in Raven-Hart 1971: 34–8)

Despite its appeal to the bizarre by invoking the 'wild, strange, and altogether beast-like manners' of the Hottentots, the African body of this account was distant from the fabulous creatures of Renaissance imagining such as the 'Cynocephali' of Isidore's *Etymologies* (Sharpe/Isidore 1964) and Herbert's 'Icthio' or 'Anthropophagi' of 1638 (in Hirschberg 1967). Where such accounts had constituted the African body through recourse to tradition and mythology, this did so in a language of the senses: through the voice as it was heard by the ear, through the eye as it scanned the body, and through the nose as it received the stench of fat applied to the skin.

The problem of the African body as a surface

This chapter concerns the 180 years between 1650 and 1830 when as an object of knowledge and target for power the African body[1] shed its fabulous qualities and for the first time emerged as a collection of overtly perceptible external organs – noses, teeth, hands, the skin, the hair, the feet, the genitalia, the breasts and so on. What force relations had to be present for a knowledge that allowed the African body as a surface of skin and topography of corporeal proportions to replace the densely woven tissues of myth which for so long had sustained its fabulous properties? Or, to state the problem from a Modernist perspective that takes the anatomized body for granted, how could this regime not see the African as a three-dimensional anatomical interior possessed of organs such as the heart, the lungs, the spleen, the kidney or the brain? For to search the record of this time for any account of a systematic gaze that saw beneath the African skin is to toil under a delusion, since the African quite simply failed to exist as a body with volume.

It is true that in his 1686 *Account of the Cape of Good Hope* Ten Rhyne mentioned that 'a surgeon of my acquaintance lately dissected a Hottentot woman who had been strangled'. But what was seen marked this report as no more than an exercise in the Renaissance preoccupation with the exotic, since

> He observed these finger-shaped prolongations of the *Nymphae* falling down from the private parts, two nipples in one breast, and various stones in the pancreas. What is more, the Governor, whose word can be absolutely relied upon, added the following: 'I too owned a remarkable stone. It was cut from the middle of a man's testicle, and, on account of its diamond-like brilliance I had it set in a ring. But I made a present of it to the King of the Negroes, a superstitious fellow, who displayed a profound belief in its power as an amulet.' (Ten Rhyne 1970/1686: 115)

It is also true that a century later, Sparrman, professor of physic at

Stockholm and inspector of the Swedish Royal Society's cabinet of natural history, could expiate his curiosity concerning the appearance of 'negro flesh' by undertaking to oversee the cure of a slave with an ulcer in the leg.

> A young Madagascar slave, who had an inveterate ulcer in his leg two inches broad, and of three years standing, was sent to the warm bath under my care ... Being curious to examine a negro's flesh, I had for some weeks before we set off, undertaken to look after the sore myself. In general the discharge from it was very trifling. The raw flesh looked exactly of the same colour with that of an European. After the proud-flesh was suppressed, the ulcer began to heal, by throwing out fresh fibres in the same manner as ours do, with something whiteish on the side of the skin, which otherwise was of a dark colour. (Sparrman 1786: Vol. 1, 143)

But these two instances, even if they are to be counted as such, were exceptions which proved this regime to be one ruled by a constellation of power for which the African body as a surface – without internal organs, tissues and systems – was all that existed to the European gaze.

While it would have to wait until the 1800s to begin being invested with an anatomical interior, what did change across the 200 years explored in this chapter was the nature of this surface. Initially, the African body was merely a random collection of external organs, while later and towards the end of this regime it began to be defined as much by these elements as by the pattern of relationships between them. Thus, the 'build of the Kaffirs or Hottentots' seen by Dapper in 1668 was little more than a listing of separate surface features.

> In build and shape of the body the Hottentots ... are on the average people of medium stature, but slender, with ill-formed bodies and insignificant appearance, and yellowish in colour ... The forehead is reasonably broad, but wrinkled; the eyes beautifully black, and as clear and pure as those of the hawk. But men, women and children all have flattened noses, more marked in some than in others; and in addition their lips are almost always thick, especially the upper, which is turned up and out. The mouth is well shaped and of normal size and proportions, with teeth beautifully clean and white, like ivory, and hard, so that the bite is firm. The neck is moderately long, shoulders narrow, and arms rather long but quite slender and lean at the wrists ... The belly with almost all of them is lean and slender and the buttocks protrude, with the result that the body, when stripped or lightly clad, is not evenly balanced. (Dapper 1970/1668: 43–5)

In Barrow (1801), writing 133 years later, the gaze to the body surface was more systematizing, with the result that the body of the Hottentot it fabricated was no longer a mere enumeration and evaluation of external features, but a morphological structure reflecting the composition of the pieces in their relation to one another.

> The person of a Hottentot while young is by no means void of symmetry. They are clean-limbed, well-proportioned, and erect. Their joints, hands, and feet are remarkably small. No protuberance of muscle to indicate strength; but a body delicately formed as that of a woman marks the inactive and effeminate mind of a Hottentot ... The colour of the eye is a deep chestnut: they are very long and narrow and removed to a great distance from each other; and the eyelids at the extremity next the nose, instead of forming an angle, as in Europeans, are rounded into each other exactly like those of the Chinese ... The cheek-bones are high and prominent, and with the narrow-pointed chin form nearly a triangle. Their teeth are beautifully white. The colour of the skin is that of a yellowish brown or faded leaf, but very different from the faded hue of a person in the jaundice, which it has been said to resemble. The hair is of a very singular nature: it does not cover the whole surface of the scalp, but grows in small tufts at certain distances from each other, and, when kept short, has the appearance and feel of a hard shoebrush, with this difference, that it is curled and twisted into small round lumps about the size of a marrowfat-pea. (Barrow 1801: 157)

This is the problem of the African body as a surface, a collection or assemblage of external organs without an interior anatomy to unify them.

For conventional twentieth-century historians such as Pratt (1985) and Dietrich (1993), how the African body of this period was seen negated its 'authentic fullness', and was 'bound up with the socio-political, economic, and cultural events of [the] ... time and shaped by visual traditions and aesthetic ideologies' (Dietrich 1993: 4–5). Or, where Pratt commented upon a fragment of Barrow's (1801: 283–4) account of the Bushmen, such descriptions

> [C]ould serve as a paradigmatic case of the ways in which ideology normalizes, codifies, and reifies ... As Catherine Belsey puts it in her lucid study *Critical Practice*, 'the task of ideology is to present the position of the subject as fixed and unchangeable, an element in a given system of differences which is human nature and the world of human experience, and to show possible action as an endless repetition of "normal" familiar action'. (Pratt 1985: 120–1)

Against this Modernist perspective, and while agreeing that the African body of the seventeenth and eighteenth centuries was contingent upon that time, the Foucauldean answer to the problem of this body as a surface is somewhat different.

First, it recognizes this body without volume as the outcome of a power quite distinct from that of the late twentieth century that assumes the interior of the body and individual subjectivity. This was the diagram of sovereign power, for when abstracted as a relationship of observation the requirement that sovereignty be visible to those over whom it is exercised has the reciprocal effect of preventing its subjects from crossing the threshold of visibility into the domain of describable individuality. From this perspective, the question is therefore not why the African body of the seventeenth and eighteenth centuries was never more than the sum of its external features, but how this corporeal topography could have crystallized at all.

The second component to the conditions of its existence must therefore be located in some productive counterpoint to the limiting effects on visibility imposed by the exercise of sovereignty. This appeared with the new space of seeing that opened up with emergence of the Classificatory episteme and its attendant discipline of 'natural history'. Preoccupied with the 'meticulous examination of things themselves', this was a method of seeing that restricted itself to the description and analysis of visible surfaces only. Natural history was thus a discipline of seeing that deflected the lines of observation away from the thickness of the body, dovetailing with the demands of sovereign power in much the same way as the deep gaze of pathological anatomy does with disciplinary power.

This interpenetration of sovereign power and Classificatory knowledge meant that disease was never coterminous with the individual body. Quite the reverse was true, sickness serving to map not the nature of the body but rather the characteristics of the places in which it occurred. First, the great strategies of quarantine which, preoccupied with keeping the sick from the healthy, divided geographical space into places that had to be kept separate to prevent the movement of infected bodies between them (cf. Armstrong, 1993). For instance, an outbreak of smallpox in 1748 was seen to have radiated from the linen of infected sailors. Hottentots employed to wash these items were rapidly infected, and to prevent the disease from spreading, the Hottentots 'contrived to draw lines round the infected part of their country, which were so strictly guarded, that if any person attempted to break through them, in order to fly from the infection, he was immediately shot dead' (Mead 1748: 10).

Similarly, in 1796 La Vaillant described how to prevent the spread of smallpox:

[T]he Company's surgeons are always sent to examine with the utmost care such ships as arrive in the roads. On the least appearance of infection, the crew are rigorously interdicted from having any communication with the town or its inhabitants; and an embargo is laid on the goods, no part of which, however small, is suffered to be brought on shore. (La Vaillant 1796: Vol. 1, 24)

Second, the analysis of endemic diseases such as 'colds, catarrh and fluxions of the chest' (Mentzel 1921/1785: Part 2, 255), which illuminated the characteristics of the extra-corporeal space from which they impinged upon the body. In Kolben (1731), as in Mentzel (1970/1785), La Vaillant (1796: Vol. 1, 22–4) and Stavorinus (1798: 567), the probability of such diseases waxed and waned with the changing of the air:

While the South-East winds blow, the Air is serene and very wholesome; and that in the Time of the North-West winds the Air is heavy and unwholesome ... For the Summer-Air, when the wind is still, becomes corrupt and sickly. The ... Reeds they call *Sea Trumpets*, and the Sea-Grass driven ashore, rot and fill the Air with most offensive stenches ... The Air is darken'd with swarms of Flies, Gnats, and C, which are exceedingly troublesome: And 'tis ragingly hot. When the Wind rises again, the Air becomes again serene and wholesome: Offensive stenches are no longer felt in it. The Inhabitants recover quickly of their Disorders; and flies and Gnats are immediately driven out of the Region. (Kolben 1731: Vol. 2, 326–7)

Correlated with this medical gaze that illuminated not bodies but places, airs and climates, was a control regime that epitomized the diagram of sovereign power. Within it the body of the African was certainly visible – not as an object of surveillance, but instead as a relay in the bloody rituals of punishment by which a sovereignty, momentarily injured by the crime of the offender, reconstituted itself through spectacular shows of the monarch's physical might, 'who seizes upon the body of the condemned man and displays it marked, beaten, broken' (Foucault 1977: 49).

The power of punishment and the sight of sovereignty

Whenever an execution takes place, a military display is made in the following manner. After the guard for the day has been changed, the remaining available men – about 99 in number – are assembled in the market place and divided into 3 companies of 33 men each. Two of these companies, are armed with muskets, the third, which is carefully selected from the best physical specimens, is armed with long pikes (about 7yds. long). The pikemen are drawn up between the files of infantry. The battalion marches in this formation to the Governor's house ... The Secretary to the Council of Justice then mounts the 'Katt', and reads out the sentence of the condemned. The troops now march to the place of execution, with band playing and form a ring with their pikes in such a way that each man can grasp his own pike and the end of his neighbour's pike at the same time. The musketeers take up a position immediately outside this ring formed with the pikes, with orders to keep the area enclosed free of encroachment. The executioner, with his assistants, under strong guard, now brings up the criminals ... Next comes the court messenger, bareheaded, carrying a silver-tipped staff of office. He is escorted by the sergeant, corporal and 12 grenadiers of the guard, and represents the majesty of the law. A clergyman ... offers a short prayer and the executioner does his work. (Mentzel 1921/ 1785: Part 2, 72–3)

In this 1785 description of the ritual prescribed for public executions in the Cape of Good Hope occurred all the elements of drama that composed the sovereign theatres of punishment by which this power renewed itself to the eyes of the anonymous onlookers. Confirming the African body without volume as the outcome of this force field that propelled the lines of visibility away from the bodies of all towards the 'majesty of justice', dissolution of this body as a surface was roughly coterminous with the legal abandonment of public execution in South Africa. The last occasion on which sovereignty was seen in its marking of the criminal's body thus occurred in Grahamstown in 1861,[2] some ten years after the emergence of missionary medicine (see Chapter 5) had begun to surround the African body with a new strategy of attention that in apprehending its anatomical interior marked the beginnings of a shift from unalloyed sovereignty to a nascent disciplinary power.

Prior to this point, and with the effect of strictly limiting the field of corporeal observation to maintain an unencumbered space for sovereignty's ostentatious displays, the castle, the ceremonials, the looming machinery of the gallows, the wheel and the whipping post served as constant indicators of its ubiquitous presence. Among the devices for its display was the 'New Castle Good Hope' built in 1666, which as a concrete spectacle of the sovereign's hold over other bodies was illuminated in the following verse.

> Thus more the kingdoms are extended;
> Thus more and more are black and yellow spread,
> Thus from the ground a wall of stone is raised,
> On which the thundering brass can no impression make.
> For Hottentoos the walls were always earthen,
> But now we come with stone to boast before all men,
> And terrify not only Europeans, but also
> Asians, Americans and savage Africans.
> Thus holy Christendom is glorified;

> Establishing its seats amidst the savage heathens.
> We praise the Great Director, and say with one another:
> 'Augustus's dominion, nor Conquering Alexander,
> Nor Caesar's mighty genius, has ever had the glory
> To lay a corner stone at earth's extremist end!' (Anon 1666,
> in Leibbrandt 1901: 170)

If the castle was a constant sign of the sovereign presence to the 'savage heathens' set about it, then it was through the public execution as a theatre of punishment that the surface of the body was inducted into this same service as a screen on which the wrath of the king was inscribed for all to see. In a 1772 extract of the 'Colonial Office Journal' the sentence for nine Hottentots involved in murdering a Dutch 'burgher' was

> [T]o be brought to the place where criminal sentences are usually carried into execution here, and being there delivered over to the executioner, the first Kleyne Booy bound to a cross, and broken thereon alive, from under upwards, with the *coup de grace*, as also the second Kleyne Jantje Links, to be punished on the gallows, with the rope, until death ensues, and thereupon their dead bodies dragged to the *Bytengeregt*, and there that of the first laid upon a wheel, and that of the second being again hung upon the gallows, thus to remain a prey to the air and to the birds of the heavens; and, further, the remaining seven, ... one after the other, bound to a post and severely flogged with rods upon the bare back; and then the 3d, 4th, 5th, and 6th to have the sinew of the heel cut asunder, and be banished for life to the public works, at the Honorable Company's slave lodge. (Moodie 1960: Part III, 17)

Punishments were carefully calibrated to fit the nature of the injury inflicted on the monarchial body: blasphemers were bored through the tongue; fighting with knives was punished by lashing and being forced to stand with the knife driven through the hand into the post; and sheep stealers were flogged with rods and made 'to stand as a public spectacle with a sheep's skin upon their head and shoulders' (Moodie 1960: Part I, 382–3). Similarly, a 1782 'resolutien' prescribing the rates of pay for a Cape executioner listed no less than fifteen permutations of torture to the body surface.

Breaking limbs	Rds[3]	12
Pinching with red-hot tongs	"	4
Burning	"	12
Decapitating	"	8
Hanging	"	8
Strangling	"	6

Scorching	"	2
Quartering and hanging up the pieces	"	6
Transporting body to 'outside place' of execution	"	3
Torturing	"	10
Chopping off the hand	"	4
Scourging	"	3
Branding with red-hot iron	"	1
Placing a rope around the neck under the gallows	"	2
Putting in the pillory	"	2

(De Kock 1950: 167)

While it was only in 1861 that public execution was legally outlawed to confirm the subordination of sovereignty to disciplinary power, it was towards the late 1700s that, at least for some observers, the spectacle of sovereign pain began to have effects opposite to its intended function of subordinating the masses to the might of the king. Hence Sparrman's comment of 1786 on encountering the gallows:

Heus Viator! Here we stopped a little to contemplate the uncertainty of human life. Above half a score wheels placed round it, presented us with the most horrid subjects for this purpose; the inevitable consequences, and at the same time the most flagrant proofs of slavery and tyranny; monsters, that never fail to generate each other, together with crimes and misdemeanours of every kind, as soon as either of them is once introduced into any country. The gallows itself, the largest I ever saw, was indeed of itself a sufficiently wide door to eternity; but was by no means too large for the purpose of a tyrannical government, that in so small as town as *Cape*, could find seven victims to be hanged in chains. (Sparrman 1786: Vol. 1, 52–3)

The display of its power to punish was not the only way that sovereignty invented itself to the eyes of its subjects. Complementing these violent strategies of majestic visibility were the less bloody but equally spectacular tactics by which the power of monarchial might was fabricated in the course of those more placid rituals where the African was approached by the European for purposes of observation and enquiry. Highlighting how the economy of sovereign visibility invested even the act of observing the African was the procedure adopted by the French naturalist La Vaillant, who in 1796 described his preparations for the contemplation of an 'interesting horde' of Africans he had chanced upon during his 'travels into the interior parts of Africa'.

After arranging my hair, I dressed myself in the most magnificent manner I

could. Among my hunting frocks I had one of a dark brown colour, orna-
mented with steel buttons, cut facet-wise; this I made my dress of ceremony;
as the rays of the sun, falling upon the different facets, would by their
reflection form a splendour very proper for exciting the admiration of these
savages ... When I was within two hundred yards of the horde, I discharged
both my shot, and ordered my four hunters to do the same ... [A]nd this
was to the whole horde the signal for a general shout of joy. I shall not
make any reflections upon this affecting scene: the tender reader will share
in the emotions of my heart. (La Vaillant 1796: Vol. 2, 18–21)

While captivating of the attention, it would be tedious to catalogue
more strategies for the manufacture of sovereign visibility, the point of
their presentation being to establish this regime as dominated not by a
gaze to the African body, but by precisely the reverse: the gaze of the
African to the sovereign might of colonial power as it was produced
through the rituals of the European. Leaving La Vaillant examining the
'savages' as they 'examined [him] ... with the utmost attention, even to
the minutest part of my dress' (La Vaillant 1796: Vol. 2, 21), this chapter
now analyses how the African body was made known in the slender
space of Classificatory observation that was all which remained for its
formation as an object of knowledge.

Natural history: the African body as surface, structure and character

Of all possible perceptual strategies for apprehending the nature of
living things, it was no coincidence that natural history should have
surfaced in the middle of the seventeenth century as the knowledge
side of the sovereign-power coin. For in the concern of the Classificatory age to order and distribute things on the basis of their perceptible
physical structures, the world of nature it invented emerged as a world
of excess, a teeming plenitude of minute variations between things.
For them to be seen and described in a way that reflected their natural
ordering thus demanded an observational technology able to shut down
this confused wealth of representation.

> In order to establish the identities and differences existing between all natural
> entities, it would be necessary to take into account every feature that might
> have been listed in a given description. Such an endless task would push the
> advent of natural history back into an inaccessible never-never land, unless
> there existed techniques that would avoid this difficulty of making so many
> comparisons. (Foucault 1973: 139)

Hence the affinity between the science of natural history and sovereign power, for as the latter was concerned with maintaining the visibility of the king, so the former offered itself as a technology for systematically restricting the space of what could be seen.

> Natural history did not become possible because men looked harder and more closely. One might say, strictly speaking, that the Classical age used its ingenuity, if not to see as little as possible, at least to restrict deliberately the area of its experience. Observation, from the seventeenth century onward, is a perceptible knowledge furnished with a series of systematically negative conditions. (Foucault 1973: 132)

Accordingly, where conventional histories consider seventeenth- and eighteenth-century representations of the African body to be fictions produced by accretions of ideology upon an ahistorical body, it is no surprise that for the history of the present this body was the very real outcome of a perceptual process premised not on a strategy of accretion but on one of depletion.

First, the stripping away of all the obscure similitudes that for the Renaissance episteme had been the truth of the African body's fabulous identity. Second, installation of the theories of structure and character as filters of the visible, by which natural history secured the African body as a morphology in its taxonomic grid. In the same way as it was not the outcome of ideological distortion, neither was this African body the product of a better way of seeing that replaced Renaissance mythology, but merely the object and effect of a new way of seeing, 'a new field of visibility being constituted in all density' (Foucault 1973: 132).

Seeing the body surface itself: the invention of fantasy and death of imagination For bodies to be revealed to the Classificatory eye demanded that the old Renaissance techniques of knowing be identified and eliminated to create a clear epistemic space for the installation of a taxonomic gaze. The first signs of this nascent transformation in relation to the African body appeared with the fabrication of fantasy as itself an object of knowledge, for only with its isolation could the play of imagination give way to the technology of examination. This occurred between 1650 and 1750, during which time the old ways of knowing and the fabulous attributes that had invested the African body were themselves elevated into the field of classificatory visibility, analysed and discarded.

By the 1660s accounts describing Africans at the Cape of Good Hope had stabilized into a consistent structure closely resembling the observational categories laid down in the Royal Society's instructions for the classification of 'natives and strangers' (see Chapter 3, page 51). For instance, and in all respects formally identical to those of contemporary writers, Dapper's 1668 account of *Kaffraria or Land of the Kaffirs, also named Hottentots* (Dapper 1970/1668) was divided into eighteen sections under the following heads: 'The build of the Kaffirs or Hottentots; clothing of the men; clothing of the women; ornamentation; weapons; food; industry; subsistence; marriage; death; punishments of theft; incest; punishment of homicide and assault; dwellings; language; trade; government, and religion.' However, while this grid operated to regiment what was recorded of the bodies, manners and customs it invented, its properties as a screen for the delimitation of how things should be seen was restricted by its coarseness, for it permitted the entry of 'hearsay' into the constitution of its objects. Indeed, Dapper's descriptions were all hearsay, derived 'as far as these have come to knowledge from some reports recently sent over by men who have dwelt in these parts for some time' (Dapper 1970/1668: 7).

Albeit in rapidly fading form, this failure to filter out hearsay briefly sustained the African as an object of Renaissance myth and similitude. In 1686 Ten Rhyne could thus note that the build, character and 'temper' of the Hottentots 'afford a clear proof that even a mild climate can produce monstrous dispositions' (Ten Rhyne 1970/1686: 125).

> They have the temper of wild animals (I am quoting the words of Florus) and bodies more than human. But it has been found by experience that as their ardour is at first fiercer than that of men, so it dwindles till it is feebler than that of women. The bodies of a mountain folk bred amidst moist clouds have a resemblance to their native snows: they warm at once to the battle, fall immediately into a sweat, and are dissolved by a slight effort, as if by the sun. But the flinty rocks and shuddering woods match their real fierceness. For the Hottentots hang about the mountains, scouring every part of them by night and day. (Ten Rhyne 1970/1686: 133)

By 1695 the antipathy of the Classificatory gaze to all knowledge not derived through direct observation was further confirmed in Grevenbroek's astonishment 'that Rumour, never bearing a clear report, should have acquired such strength in her course and proved so tenacious of falsehood that those half truths spread abroad about our Africans should have reached even your ears' (Grevenbroek 1970/1695: 173). Despite this protestation, his 'rough sketch, embodying matters of hearsay as well as information gathered from reliable witnesses, written records, authentic documents and my personal observations' (p. 299), could still assert of the Hottentots:

> Those who live near our Cape are of middle height; but the inhabitants of the remote parts of the region are shaggy fellows, with taller and sturdier

frames, and with frizzy hair. Among them has been seen a king, Longurio, twelve foot high, with hair all over his body thicker than a water spaniel's. (Grevenbroek 1970/1695: 175)

In 1731 an English translation of Kolben's *The Present State of the Cape of Good Hope, or, A Particular Account of the Several Nations of the Hottentots* was published. A turning point of some significance, Kolben's text marked a new intensification in the ingenuity of the Classificatory gaze to identify barriers to its meticulous observation of things themselves. In it, the minimal commentary provided by earlier writers upon the problems of hearsay and rumour was substantially expanded, the translator's preface to this edition offering an eight-page essay concerning 'some Reflections on History and Historical writers' (Medley, in Kolben 1731: Vol. 1, ii). This recognized three classes of barriers 'to Pursuit of Historical Truth … *Ignorance* … *Knavery*, and the *Constitutions* of writers' (p. iii). Noting that other authors had already said enough on ignorance and knavery as sources that 'plague the World with mutilated Fact and Historical Fiction' (p. vii), this concentrated on 'how Truth may be injur'd by the *Melancholic*, the *Phlegmatic*, the *Choleric*, and the *Sanguine* Tempers of Men' (p. viii). Writers of Sanguine temper were prone to over-emphasizing the virtues of what they liked; the Choleric to making everything they disliked infinitely worse, and the Melancholic to reporting 'Shadows for Substances, and airy Suspicions for the best grounded Truths in the World' (p. ix). The Phlegmatic, however, excelled 'all others in Accounts of Fact' (p. xv), precisely because they saw only to the surface of things.

> The *Phlegmatic* have no Eyes, indeed, for the *Inside* of Things; but they have excellent ones for the *Outside*; and give a Detail of a Thousand Particulars there which escape Men of other Complexions … They are neither ravish'd with beauty, nor frighted at Deformity; neither elated with Success, nor depress'd with Misfortune. They are subject to none of those Flurries of Imagination that transport and bewilder other Men. (Medley, in Kolben 1731: Vol. 1, xv–xvi).

Not surprisingly, it was 'of the Class of *Phlegm*' (p. xvi) that Medley reckoned Kolben to be.

The second reason for singling out Kolben's text as a turning point in the solidification of the taxonomic gaze to the African body occurs in the text itself. Here, appearing wherever what was seen by the eye contradicted what rumour had claimed or temper had fantasized, was the imaginative error and its attendant Classificatory correction. In his account of 'the Shape, Stature and Features of the *Hottentots*', Kolben could thus write: ·

They are by no Means so Hideous as the Press has hitherto made them ...
What a frightful Picture has *Anderton* drawn of this People in his Travels!
After saying, the Features of the *Hottentots* are monstrously ugly, he adds,
their Faces are shrivell'd. Yes, those of Old People ... But the Face of a
young *Hottentot* is as smooth and plump as that of any Youth in *Africa*, or
even in *Europe*. For a general Description of the Persons of the *Hottentots*,
they are not so small of Stature as we have been told, most of the Men
being from 5 to 6 Foot high. The Women are a great deal less. Both sexes
are very erect and well made, keeping a due Medium between Gross and
Meagre. Their Heads being generally large, their Eyes are so in Proportion.
The Noses of both Sexes are flatted, & their Lips thick. Their Teeth are
white as Ivory. And their Cheeks have Something of a Cherry; but, by
Reason of their continual Dawbings, it is not easily discern'd. Their Hair is
like that of *Negroes*, short, and black as jet. The Men have large broad Feet:
The Women have them very small and tender. Neither Men nor Women
cut the Nails of their Fingers or Toes. (Kolben 1731: Vol. 1, 52–3)

Dapper was shown by Kolben to be 'out' where he reported the Hottentots as eating whale fat, and of the reports 'by several Authors' that the
Hottentots are 'black from their Birth' he noted: 'What a mistake is
Here! ... I have seen a great many new-born Children of the *Hottentots*,
and always found them of a bright olive' (Kolben 1731: Vol. 1, 54).

While the truth of the African as constituted in Kolben's account
would last out the next fifty years, its appearance coincided with the
recognition by natural history of a new class of barriers to its taxonomic
task. Until Kolben, the primary difficulty had been stilling the play of
imagination to clear the perception so that it could be imprinted upon
by the surface of things themselves. The very success of this strategy
of attention, however, brought with it the new problem of excess. For,
as Medley had noted, the down side to nature as revealed by 'the
exactest Relaters of the World of what they See' (in Kolben 1731: Vol.
1, xvi) was its 'dullness' and 'tediousness' since: 'they relate every Thing
they see and hear, with most religious exactness, not omitting the
smallest or most indifferent Matter or Circumstance, they remember,
tho' it be of neither Use nor Entertainment, nor any Thing at all to the
Purpose' (p. xv). Accordingly, the next refinement in Classificatory
perception occurred with elaboration of the theories of structure and
character as mechanisms by which to sift from the newly apprehended
mass of the visible only those few things which could be analysed,
recognized by all, and hence given a name that everyone would understand.

Screening the seen: the African body as structure and character As the
period in which it finally became a formal discipline, the years between

1735 and 1760 were of some significance to natural history. In 1735 Linnaeus published his famous system of botanical classification *Systema Naturae*, in 1751 his *Philosophia Botanica*, and in 1753 his *Species Plantarum*. Buffon's *Histoire Naturelle* appeared in 1749 and Adanson's *Famille des Plantes* in 1763 (cf. Foucault 1973; Pratt 1992: 25). While differing in aspects of the debate over classificatory method, these authors shared a concern with providing to natural history a theory and technique of seeing and describing that would at last enable it to engage with its proper object. This object was known as the structure of any living thing, and was

> the extension of which all natural beings are constituted – an extension affected by four variables. And by four variables only: the form of the elements, the quantity of those elements, the manner in which they are distributed in space in relation to each other, and the relative magnitude of each element. As Linnaeus said, in a passage of capital importance, 'every note should be a product of number, of form, of proportion, of situation'. (Foucault 1973: 134)

In the theory of structure was thus articulated the ideal object of natural history, the effect of a gaze strictly screened to admit the visual alone and then only certain components of what was seen. Now, the earlier system of screening by which hearsay had been excluded was extended to eliminate taste, smell and even touch, leaving sight with an almost exclusive privilege. As Buffon noted, 'the method of examination will be directed towards form, magnitude, the different parts, their number, their position, and the very substance of the thing' (in Foucault 1973: 135). The theory of structure enabled a new precision to be entered into the act of describing what was seen. First, number and magnitude could be quantified through counting or measuring. Second, the specification of form and arrangement could be done through the qualitative method of identification with geometrical figures and the strictly clarified use of analogies.

Alongside structure as the natural history method of seeing by which its possible objects were restricted to surfaces and lines, the theory of character was a device of secondary sifting. Given the practical impossibility of classifying things by taking into account every feature listed in a given description, the theory of character prescribed that a particular structure be selected as the locus of identities and differences. For instance, the structural locus advocated by Linnaeus for the comparison and classification of plants was the pattern formed by their organs of reproduction – the stamens, fruits, seeds and so on. Thus, 'the character should be composed of "the most careful description of fructification of the first species. All the other species of the genus are compared with the first, all discordant notes being eliminated; finally, after this process, the character emerges"' (Foucault 1973: 140). In outline, this was the taxonomic gaze through which the body of the African as invented by Kolben was, towards the close of the eighteenth century, consigned to the now extensive cabinet of accounts of the curious: 'Kolbe's "Caput Bonae Spei" was from the beginning received with great favour and was eagerly devoured by lovers of the marvellous. At that time no one found cause to doubt its accuracy or to pick holes in it' (Mentzel 1921/1785: Part 1, 21). In its place were the tentative outlines of a new African body as a structure which began to crystallize in the first formal natural history of the Cape, Sparrman's (1786) *A Voyage to the Cape of Good Hope*.

Sponsored by no less than 'the late Archiater LINNAEUS [who] ... in his own name drew up a petition for the voyage to be made' (Sparrman 1786: Vol. 1, xii), Sparrman observed that his description – 'never relying on the relations of others ... he sees every thing with his own eyes, and trusts only to the report of his own senses' (p. vi) – would disappoint the reader expecting 'accounts ... of a most entertaining and wonderful import':

> Nature has presented herself to me in various shapes, ever worthy of admiration, often enchanting, and sometimes terrible, and clothed with horror. But at the same time I must apprise the reader, that a great many prodigies and uncommon appearances, about which I have frequently been asked by many, who have been brought to entertain these conceits by perusing the descriptions of others, are not to be found in my journal. Men with one leg, indeed, Cyclops, Syrens, Troglodytes, and the like imaginary beings have almost entirely disappeared in this enlightened age. At the same time, however, many have been hitherto induced to give credit to tales almost as marvellous, with which authors, who have before me visited and described the Hottentots, have seasoned their relations ... So that the reader must not be surprized to find my narrative frequently differ much from those of various of my predecessors. (Sparrman 1786: Vol. 1, xv–xvi)

Where earlier accounts had set the African body in a broader space of sensationalist descriptions concerning ways of eating, hunting, copulating, childbirth, punishment and so on, the African body fabricated by Sparrman appeared alongside the carefully measured and minutely detailed descriptions of animals and plants, which, indeed, were invested with a substantially greater degree of visibility, thus locating the body of the African to the very edge of taxonomic space.[4] Nevertheless, and albeit only faintly, Sparrman's description of the Hottentot body revealed its inscription in the new perceptual strategies of structure and character, where, through their proportions and relationships, the body's external organs began to form some impression of a distinctive arrangement, a 'characteristic mark':

> With regard to their persons they are as tall as most Europeans; and as for their being in general more slender, this proceeds from their being more stinted and curtailed in their food ... But that they have small hands and feet compared with the other parts of their bodies, has been remarked by no one before, and may, perhaps, be looked upon as a characteristic mark of this nation. The root of the nose is for the most part very low, by which means the distance of the eyes from each other appears to be greater than in Europeans. The tip of the nose likewise is pretty flat. The iris is scarcely ever of a light colour, but has a dark brown cast, which sometimes approaches to black. Their skin is of a yellowish brown hue, which something resembles that of an European who has the jaundice in a high degree; however, this colour is not in the least observable in the whites of the eyes. One does not find such thick lips among the *Hottentots* as among their neighbours the *Negroes*, the *Caffres*, and the *Mozambiques*. In fine, their mouths are of a middling size, and almost always furnished with a set of the finest teeth that can be seen; and, taken together with the rest of their features, as well as their shape, carriage, and every motion, in short, their *tout ensemble*, indicates health and content, or at least an air of *sans souci*. (Sparrman 1786: Vol. 1, 180–1)

Five years later the apotheosis of the African as object and effect of the taxonomic gaze appeared in Barrow's (1801) *An Account of Travels into the Interior of Southern Africa*. Here the hesitancy evident in Sparrman to invent the African body as structure and identify from this its distinguishing character gave way to a textbook precision in the discernment of number, magnitude, form and arrangement. The effect of this was the African body as a geometrized morphology that at the same time bore within it a sufficiency of isolated structures to permit the establishment of its character:

> The great curvature of the spine inwards, and extended posteriors, are characteristic of the whole Hottentot race; but in some of the small Bosjesmans they are carried to a most extravagant degree. If the letter S be considered as one expression of a line of beauty to which degrees of approximation are admissible, these women are entitled to the first rank in point of form. A section of the body, from the breast to the knee, forms really the shape of the above letter. The projection of the posterior part of the body, in one subject, measured five inches and a half from a line touching the spine. (Barrow 1801: 281)

Elsewhere, in the Hottentot, as in the Bushman, it was not the curvature of the spine but the shape of the eye that was selected as the locus of pertinent identities and differences. 'The upper lid of this organ, as in that of the Chinese, is rounded into the lower on the side next the nose, and forms not an angle, as is the case in the eye of an European' (Barrow 1801: 278). The women of the Hottentots were readily distinguished from those of other nations by their 'protruded nymphae'.

> The longest that was measured somewhat exceeded five inches ... Their color is that of livid blue, inclining to a reddish tint, not unlike the excrescence on the beak of a turkey, which indeed may serve to convey a tolerable good idea of the whole appearance both as to color, shape, and size. The interior lips or nymphae in European subjects which are corrugated or plaited, lose entirely that part of their character when brought out in the Hottentot, and become perfectly smooth. (Barrow 1801: 279)

A more problematic task of comparison was presented by the corporeal structure of 'the Kaffer'. Where the spine, the eye and the nymphae were identifying singularities on the Hottentot body, that of the 'Kaffer' was more difficult to place, owing to the closeness with which the form of the head approximated to that of the European.

> Though black, or very nearly so, they have not one line of the African negro in the composition of their persons. The comparative anatomist might be a little perplexed in placing the skull of a Kaffer in the chain, so ingeniously put together by him, comprehending all the links from the most perfect European to the Ourang-Outang, and thence through all the monkey-tribe. The head of a Kaffer is not elongated: the frontal and the occipital bones form nearly a semicircle; and a line from the forehead to the chin drawn over the nose is convex like that of most Europeans. In short, had not nature bestowed upon him the dark colouring principle that anatomists have discovered to be owing to a certain gelatinous fluid lying between the epidermis and the cuticle, he might have ranked among the first of Europeans. (Barrow 1801: 205–6)

From theatres of punishment to theatres of healing

It is here that this chapter must end, where the eye of Barrow fabricated the African as object and effect of a taxonomic gaze to the surface of the body, while at the same time threatening to become more than skin-deep as it outlined the interior lips of the 'nymphae', delineated the occipital bones of the skull, and engaged with the 'gelatinous fluid lying between the epidermis and the cuticle'. For, some twenty-five years later, the classificatory gaze of natural history itself began to be made visible to a new strategy of attention which recognized 'Man himself' as a central concern of its surveillance. Writing in 1827, Thompson observed:

> The majority of travellers who penetrated into the interior of the country in former times, were men enthusiastically and almost exclusively devoted to scientific pursuits. Discoveries in natural history were their paramount objects. Man himself, whether social or savage, was secondary, in their researches, to a new plant or animal. (G. Thompson 1827: vi)

This emergence of 'Man' marked the point of epistemic disjunction where Classification gave way to Modernity and natural history to the new science of biology through which the taxonomic ordering of morphologies would be complemented[5] by the penetrating analysis of structure and its relationship to function. In this new epistemic space, 'the internal laws of the organism were to replace differential characters as the object of the natural sciences' (Foucault 1973: 145), and within medicine there could emerge the deep gaze of pathological anatomy and its concern to establish how the organs of the body are ordered, the mechanics of the cell, the nature of the tissues of the skin, and the dynamics by which pathology localizes itself to a distinct point within the body.

It was this disjunction in knowing that made possible the mid-nineteenth-century articulation of the African body in a new power regime, as alongside the older spectacles of sovereignty there began to appear the minute rituals of disciplinary power by which the interior of the African body was fabricated as a visible, analysable and useful space for the installation and reticulation of power. Thus, Chapter 5 examines the unfolding of the African body as an object and effect of missionary medicine, which as the first socio-medical discipline to emerge into this anatomy of power bore within its practices elements from the diagrams of both sovereignty and disciplinary power – its theatres of healing standing where in the earlier regime had loomed the theatres of punishment; the hands of the doctor and his instruments of treatment where before had been the tools of the torturer; and the act of healing the infirm African body supplanting the inscription of pain upon its surface as a strategy of sovereign visibility.

Notes

1. To highlight the variability of the taxonomic gaze itself by holding constant the object that was its effect, this chapter focuses on the body of the Hottentot only, while acknowledging that alongside the Hottentots many other 'tribes' of Africans were delineated on the basis of their perceptible physical characteristics.

2. In South Africa, the statutory abolition of capital punishment in public occurred only eight years later, with the passing of Act 3 of 1869.

3. 'Rds.' was an abbreviation for 'Riksdaalders'.

4. Foucault commented on this phenomenon by noting that 'in so far as there are a great many constituent organs visible in a plant that are not so in animals, taxonomic knowledge based upon immediately perceptible variables was richer and more coherent in the botanical order than in the zoological' (1973: 137).

5. It is important to reflect briefly upon the resilience of taxonomy as a strategy of perception and a tactic of power. For, with Barrow's articulation of the skull of the African into the great grid of classification, we see the nascent beginnings of a new sovereignty that through the course of the nineteenth and twentieth centuries would continue to operate upon the typology of bodies produced through the interplay of structure and character. Thus, a 1958 volume of 'race studies' – written for the teaching of standard-six high school pupils – installed precisely the same human body as that seen by Barrow where it depicted for all to see the instruments of ethnographic observation and classification: an 18-point 'scale for comparing colour of skin'; thirty samples of human hair systematically arrayed in a metal box labelled 'scale for comparing hair'; sixteen artificial eyes that composed the 'scale for comparing eye colours'; and a set of three 'instruments for measuring the skull' (Bruwer et al. 1958: 14–17). Although it is true that with the beginnings of the nineteenth century a new regime of power that worked less upon the body's surface than through its interior would begin to materialize, this switch in power must be recognized as one that did not so much displace as complement the sovereignty of taxonomy and the dividing practices it made possible.

CHAPTER 5

Missionary Medicine, Moral Sanitation and Fabrication of the Heathen Heart

Chapter 4 has shown how the Classificatory age produced the African body as a one-dimensional specimen consisting in the geometric measurements of facial and bodily surfaces by which these bodies were compared to one another, grouped according to their perceptible resemblances, and arrayed on a hierarchical chain of being from man to ape. Exemplifying the power implications of this knowledge that fabricated the body as a flat surface without volume was the taxonomy of terror which accompanied it, from the spectacles of public torture and execution that inscribed their pain upon the body, to the *cordon sanitaires* that kept separate the geographical spaces occupied by disease through violent prohibition of the movement of bodies between them.

As argued in Chapter 2, the Classificatory age was by the end of the eighteenth century beginning to give way in Europe to the new regime of disciplinary power and the three-dimensional body as an anatomical container of disease which the gaze of hospital medicine produced as its object and effect. Among the consequences of this respatialization of illness to the deep interior of an individual anatomy was problematization of the boundary zone between the interior space of anatomy and the external space of the environment. As Armstrong (1993) has shown, this occurred through the installation of lines of hygienic surveillance directed to monitoring the passage of substances between the inside of the body and the outside:

> Air, water and food originated in this external environment but had to pass into the body; equally, all those substances such as faeces, urine, sweat, semen, etc., which departed the body had to cross into the world of places. Thus the focus of late nineteenth-century public health became the zone which separated anatomical space from environmental space, and its regime of hygiene developed as the monitoring of matter which crossed between these two great spaces. (Armstrong 1993: 396)

Finding rapid expansion through crowded Victorian cities, these techniques marked the mid-1800s as the dawn of a disciplinary regime in which, for the first time, it became possible through sanitary science to 'dissect the mass and recognise separable and calculable individuality in the form of anatomical space in the crowd' (Armstrong 1993: 405).

Far from restricted to the formal centres of imperial power, these power transformations provoked an equally dramatic mutation within the margins of colonial expansion. Contemporaneous with the expansion in Europe of sanitary science through the previously unanalysed mass of the crowd, so Africa grew 'dark' with the barbarism of its native inhabitants as Victorian explorers, missionaries and scientists flooded it with a light refracted through the gaze of a new power targeted to the analysis and abolition of 'savage customs' in the name of 'civilization' (Brantlinger 1985: 166). Where conquest had previously operated through the exercise of sovereign force directed to domination through demonstrations of the power to inflict pain and kill, it could now be conceived of as a 'humanitarian' and productive endeavour aimed at liberating Africans from the 'chains of grossest ignorance' that made them 'prey to the most savage superstition' (Buxton 1840, in Brantlinger 1985: 173).

Analogous to how sanitary science in Europe individualized the body by delineating the boundaries between it and environmental space, this new colonial power constellation emerged in the formation of missionary medicine as a device of 'moral sanitation' directed to the boundary between the African body and a surrounding space of customs, rites and superstitions. Where in Europe environmental space was seen as a reservoir of dangerous substances whose passage into the body could cause disease, so in Africa it became possible to think of the 'moral' space surrounding the African body as harbouring every variety of vice and superstition calculated to corrode its vitality and render it susceptible to sickness. Similarly, as the regime of sanitary science demanded that prohibitions be set in place to prevent the contamination of environmental space by bodily wastes, so missionary medicine gave rise to methods that could protect this moral space from further corruption by disabling the influence of the 'witch doctor' as this was circulated through the beliefs and the behaviour of ordinary Africans.

The tactics through which missionary medicine installed an anatomical space in the diagram of colonial power marked it as far from a purely disciplinary regime. While possible only in the cognitive context of a clinical gaze that spatialized sickness to the body's deep interior, missionary medicine drew at the same time upon the sovereign power of the spectacle, to crystallize in the shape of the dramatic theatres of healing that until well into the twentieth century typified this practice of moral sanitation.

Creation of the African with a soul and a body of organs

> In performing most severe surgical operations they sit, both men and women, as if they had no feeling ... The spirit of God alone can affect their hearts. (Livingstone 1841, in Schapera 1959: 40)

No one can be certain who it was or how they may have chanced upon the surprising powers invested in the simple act of medically examining and treating the infirm African body. Perhaps it was Theodorius van der Kemp, who some twentieth-century historians claim to have been among the first medical missionaries in Africa (Burrows 1958; Gelfand 1984), while for British readers in the mid-nineteenth century it was without doubt David Livingstone. An 1858 book review in the *British Medical Journal* exalted:

> The triumph of DR LIVINGSTONE in having been the first European – indeed we may say the first human being – that has ever made his way across Africa ... The various savage tribes whose territories he had to traverse were dumb to the voice of the missionary, but were capable of appreciating the good services of the medical man. A knowledge of the healing art is acknowledged by Dr Livingstone to be indispensable to those who would penetrate the wilds of this vast continent ... This is indeed a high testimony to the benevolent and all powerful character of our profession. (Anon. 1858: 52)

Important as they are to presenting an accurate history of the past, concerns about the identity of the first medical missionary are of less significance to this genealogical study than identifying when it became possible to speak freely of the African with a soul and a body that could somehow be impacted upon by the practice of medicine. For only then can it be concluded that there was in fact a mutation occurring in the anatomy of power – away from its dependence on the unalloyed tactics of terror enabled by the Classificatory episteme, towards a new way of functioning that played less upon the bodies of Africans than into and through them.

This leads into the late 1840s and 1850s. For it was here that just such a shift towards a nascent regime of medical practice and knowledge as disciplinary power was revealed in a swarming of anecdotes, teaching texts and institutions concerned with mapping a set of relationships between medical practice and the African with a body of organs and a soul. In an 1842 letter David Livingstone recounted an incident that occurred in the course of his surveying the African 'tribes' around Kuruman, and which seemed 'to indicate that even the darkest minds feels [*sic*] the need of a something [*sic*] to speak peace to their troubled thoughts' (Livingstone 1842, in Schapera 1961: 20).

> On one occasion Sekomi, having sat by me in the hut for some time in deep thought ... said, 'I wish you could change my heart. Give me medicine to change it, for it is proud, proud and angry, angry always'. I lifted up the Testament and was about to tell him of the only way in which the heart can be changed, but he interrupted me by saying, 'Nay, I wish to have it changed by medicine, to drink it [and] have it changed at once' ... He then rose and went away. (Livingstone 1842, in Schapera 1961: 20)

Compare this to a similar observation made by Dr J. P. Fitzgerald who, unlike the missionary David Livingstone, was a secular practitioner recruited to participate in Sir George Grey's campaign to 'civilize' South Africa's eastern frontier around Grahamstown and King William's Town. Following his arrival in King William's Town, Fitzgerald had ridden through the country on horseback to 'take stock' of the situation, and reported of the Africans he encountered:

> I have performed some minor operations amongst them and not even a semblance of an objection is ever raised ... They tell me that through every part of Kaffir Land wherever I may go I will be well received with affection and kindness ... Before ten years pass over many a savage heart will be won to the British Govt. (Fitzgerald 1856, in Cory Library: Folder 1, 9)

These are doubtless but two of countless medical experiences with 'natives' (whether in China, India, Africa or elsewhere) that struck their European interlocutors as surprising enough to report upon. What was it about the gaze of their authors that rendered such seemingly trivial incidents important enough to record in writing?

The answer lies in the notion that such anecdotes at once discovered and were productive of the conditions of possibility for a new form of power. For in these reports appeared an eye that saw not only the surface, but into the very heart of the African body, a way of seeing that through the techniques of surgery penetrated deep within it to constitute as its object and effect the African as an anatomized body. Or, more accurately, their innovation was to invent the African as a body of organs and a soul, between which and the surrounding space of African tradition there lay a gap in which to discern the workings of custom and belief upon the individual body. This gap was made visible by the device of illness itself, which in its occurrence, its manifestations on the body, and attempts to treat it, signalled the perverse play of

African tradition and invited the purifying counterpoint of Christian medicine. Hence the Bishop of Bloemfontein's authoritative statement on 'the sacredness of the medical calling': 'The body [is] ... the instrument of the soul, by means of which that soul is brought into relations with its surroundings, and is, moreover, trained and disciplined for its own perfection' (Hicks 1896: 87). It thus became possible to conceive of this three-dimensional corporeal space (extended by the soul into the social) as the central object for a new strategy of colonial power premised upon its existence. This was the 'medical missionary method'.

Moral sanitation and the medical missionary method

In his 1849 *Medical Missions. An Address to Students*, Miller aimed 'to shew how we might profitably blend ... cure of the body with care of the soul' (Miller 1849: 4). Proof of this lay in the diseased body of 'the heathen' itself:

> Are the hearts of the distant heathen less impressible than our own? ... Spiritually, they are dying and dead. Morally, their very virtues are vice. Intellectually, they are uncultivated, feeble and depraved. Socially, they are little removed above the beasts that perish. Their bodies are peculiarly the prey of sickness, and their flesh, as if not racked enough by disease, is maimed and torn by their so called religious rites. (Miller 1849: 24)

Although somewhat dramatically, this vision of the diseased body of the 'distant heathen' condensed within it precisely the same relationships between the interior space of anatomy and the exterior context of superstition evoked in the anecdotal reports of Livingstone and Fitzgerald. Only anecdote had now become a formalized object of missionary medical knowledge, a device to inform the gaze of the student doctor by inculcating a sound appreciation of the fundamental premise underlying missionary medicine: 'The sickness of the body is a continued type of sin' (Marley 1860: 45). Concretizing this generic formulation of the relation between sin, disease and the heathen body, Holden wrote in 1867 that 'consumption' in Africans

> is not so much hereditary as bought on by undue exposure. One great source from which it springs is their night orgies, in which singing, dancing and adultery are often carried on to great excess ... This is kept up until a late hour, until the body becomes exhausted; the pores are thrown open, and a chill ensues, which entails disease and death. (Holden 1963/1867: 371)

It followed from this connection between the diseased body and sin that 'the medical attempt "to do cures" remains cognate to the missionary attempt "to cast out devils", even to the end of the world' (Marley 1860: 49). But how was such benevolent exorcism to be translated from the rhetoric of sermonizing into practice?

For the practitioner of missionary medicine up until the 1920s (when theatrical healing began to be dissolved by the less spectacular methods of hospital medicine), this demanded that he be as accomplished an actor as he was a doctor. For not only should his actions in treating the sick heal their sins, but so too should they be witnessed by as many others as possible. Speaking to the reticulation of words through the very community this method constructed, Burns Thomson (1854) advised that practitioners recruit each and every patient into the role of publicist, and in this way build an ever-expanding network of the converted around the body of the healed.

> When the man sick of palsy was healed, he was charged to tell no man. But he went out and began to publish it much, and to blaze abroad the matter … The missionary will be known, talked of and beloved, in circles in which he has never personally made his appearance. Multiply the services of the medical missionary and groups of grateful hearts are multiplied throughout the community … Every person in the neighbourhood of the medical missionary knows his liability to disease, to the very evil which the benevolent power in his vicinity has come to mitigate or remove; and there is awakened in all hearts a feeling of comfort at the thought that, in the event of sickness or pain, that power will manifest itself in their behalf. (Burns Thomson 1854: 22)

Dependent upon the medical instruments being displayed and the work of healing witnessed, the likelihood of this method's success was enhanced where the doctor could maximize the spectacle of an operation, the setting of broken bones, or even the routine administration of medicine. Alluding to this, G. E. F. M. wrote in 1898 that 'wherever the Medical Missionary pitches his tent, spreads out his surgical instruments, and opens his medicine chest, he may well exclaim, "the weapons of our warfare are mightily through God, to the pulling down of strongholds"' (G. E. F. M. 1898: 5). It is therefore appropriate to make at this point a visit to one such theatre of healing, and join the audience as they observed the doctor at work.

Within the theatre of healing

> The fame of the cures effected spread far beyond those that had experienced these benefits; and of the vast numbers of strangers who throng the capital, few return to their homes without paying a visit to the dispensary, to witness the benefits conferred upon others or to seek relief for themselves. (Lowe 1886: 67)

Foucault began *Discipline and Punish* (1977) by reproducing a description of the public execution of Damiens the Regicide which took place in March 1757. As argued in Chapters 2 and 4, Foucault chose this example to exemplify how sovereign power operated by being visible to those on whom it had its effects, the presence of the king signalled by dramatic public displays and outward shows of ostentation.

Strange as it may seem, it was with these same mechanisms of sovereign visibility and outward display that the nineteenth-century theatres of missionary healing were built. Only within them it was not the executioner who represented God or the king, but the doctor; not the body of the condemned that swayed above the onlookers on a gibbet, but the body of the infirm African which lay sprawled on the examination table; and not the tools of torture and pain that glinted and bubbled in the sun, but the instruments of healing – the scalpel, the stethoscope and the catheter. This was evident in all its splendour as Dr J. P. Fitzgerald set to work on a distended bladder in 1856.

> Late this evening three Kaffirs belonging to Siwani's Tribe ... came to me one of them suffering excruciating agony from retention of urine which has been coming on for the last five days. The bladder was very much distended and he could not pass a single drop of water. I placed him standing against the wall in my consulting room, took out my Instruments and after a little delicate manipulation I succeeded in intorducing [*sic*] a small Catheter into the Bladder, and drew off an immense quantity of Urine; when the Urine began to flow through the Instrument, the Kaffirs were struck with wonder. The two wild painted children of Nature who were standing at my back looking over my shoulders exclaimed 'Nothing can beat the English, or the English can do anything' ... His two friends said, they would leave him with me, and as it was late hurried away filled with delight and astonishment. This will travel all over Kaffir land and the removal of leaves, branches and Trees, Sticks and Stones, Lizards and Toads as practised by my Professional Brethren in their uncivilized state, will in future make but a faint impression either on this patient, his two friends, or my two interpreters who saw with their eyes my whole proceedings, the flow of urine, and the relief afforded. I dare say in a very short time this will reach the trans-Kei constellation and help to extinguish his [the witch doctor's] light. These are practical illustrations for the Natives, which all the prophets and Witch Doctors in South Africa cannot gainsay ... There was a man suffering agony which all the Witch Doctors in the world could not relieve, they saw me place the patient against the wall, take out my instruments, select one, pass it into his Bladder, they saw the Urine flow, and the man instantaneously relieved, they saw with their eyes and believed, just as old Macomo told me the other night 'I believe in your work, because I see with my Eyes'. (Fitzgerald 1856, in Cory Library: Folder 1, 65–6)

A quintessential instance of sovereign power at work, this spectacle in Fitzgerald's theatre of healing spoke to the simultaneous play of discipline as it circulated through the deep gaze of pathological anatomy. For even as the drama unfolded with Fitzgerald at its centre and the 'wild painted children of Nature' looking on, so there crystallized before the very eyes of the watching the African body with organs.

> This day I had three Kaffirs from the Chief Sandilli's place beyond the Kei River ... One of them was very bad suffering from disease of the lungs and spitting of blood. I examined him with the stethoscope and over the part affected I had to apply the Cupping Glasses they were surprised at the flow of blood. (Fitzgerald 1856, in Cory Library: Folder 1, 16)

The spectacle of sovereignty addressed the onlookers in whose beliefs and deeds were reproduced the forces of darkness that had to be made to bow to 'civilization'. But running alongside, almost incidental to the drama that attracted the Africans' attention, coursed the whispering currents of disciplinary power: through the doctor, through the catheter and stethoscope, and through the body of the patient whose blood filled the cupping glass.

Reflecting the instability of this power regime, further confirmation of the dual powers invested in these rituals oscillated between accounts that privileged their sovereign component and others that isolated the play of the disciplinary gaze. For instance, the sketch of Dr de Prosch at work near the Zambezi singled out the onlookers' awe at his actions, to leave the patient an almost invisible prop: 'Doctor de Prosch is surrounded by sick folk waiting their turn, and watching with gaping mouths and craned necks the application of the magic art. He is just bandaging with some lineament ... the limbs of a leper' (Collard 1900: 218). Elsewhere, the focus swerved from the drama of doctoring to isolate for scrutiny the reactions of the patient and the sympathetic ripples through the community of converts created by the cure.

> It is surprising how soon an isolated case of sickness will become an epidemic, as soon as it has become known that the 'Moruti' has dispensed medicine. At one place a man came to me saying he was suffering from certain pains in the stomach. I treated him for indigestion. On the morrow I was amazed to find some dozen or more people coming to my wagon. They all wanted medicine, and strange to say, for the same complaint as that I had treated the previous day. (Williams 1887: 115)

Just as the act of cupping blood and the treatment of indigestion interpolated ordinary Africans as active participants in this diagram of missionary medical power, so too were more calamitous disasters

rendered productive. Relating the increased number of Africans attending catechumen classes to drought and rinderpest in Bechuanaland,
Dyke (1898: 216) wrote: 'this is a black picture, but it has its reverse ...
The trials and losses which have come upon the Basutos have not been
without fruit. The spiritual harvest has been rich and abundant.' However, in some situations the theatre of healing operated to produce less
than the unambiguously positive results claimed for it by most mission
doctors. Thus, a 1906 account of surgery to the anaesthetized body of
an African patient revealed the procedure as producing a distinct sense
of unease on the part of the audience, owing to the doctor's apparent
power over both the death and the life of the patient.

> A curious moment is at the end of an operation. We operate at 7 in the
> morning before consultation hours. A convalescent stands outside our reed
> enclosure to prevent people coming too near. Then when it is all over, there
> is a whole crowd of people sitting at a distance watching us carry the patient,
> still asleep, in our arms. We lay him down on his mat and leave him while
> I see the new patients, change dressings, and my wife cleans and dries the
> instruments. The natives look on distrustfully; there is still some blood on
> my blouse. What if I suddenly decided to kill them too, and bring them
> back to life like the one they have just seen? (A. C. J. 1934/1906: 34)

Despite such exceptions, the repeated confirmation in practice of
techniques that blended the spectacle of sovereignty with the silent
force of the deep gaze found their formalization in teaching texts of
the 1920s that instructed readers in the art of making spectacular the
mundane (see Martin and Weir 1923; Moorshead 1926): 'The way of the
doctor ... [is] a mighty highway to the human soul ... Impossible as it
seems to influence suspicious and hostile peoples by any other method,
medical, and especially surgical work,' provides a way which leads to
the very citadel of their being' (Moorshead 1926: 49).

Even as these texts that drew upon the diagram of sovereign power
to shape the medical missionary endeavour were being written, so a
new strand was beginning to unwind into the discourse of missionary
medicine: this was the hospital. For while permanent dwellings of a
rudimentary nature had often served alongside the wagons and other
temporary staging points at which mission doctors conducted their
theatres of healing, it was only in the 1920s that there began to emerge
any accounts of the relationship between Africans and the fixed space
of the hospital.

Mission hospitals and the manufacture of African misery The theatre of
healing had deployed the tactics of clinical medicine upon infirm African

bodies as a vehicle of visibility to broadcast outwards and towards the watching the sovereign power of God and 'civilization'. Installation of the hospital reversed this relationship of visibility, and the dominant power investing in the work of the medical missionary switched from that of conspicuous sovereign to silent surveyor of African suffering and superstitions that 'rudely and barbarously destroy the last remnants of decency and modesty … and envelop the intelligence in a perfect maze of lies, deceit and folly' (McCord 1926: 197).

> Loathsome lepers … sleeping sickness victims, hideous and demented … babes, bellies pendulous and eyes lack-lustre … This ugly aspect of Africa's need is highly coloured. No one needs to paint it to emphasise its hideousness. The real truth is that one dare not reveal to an unprepared Western public all the horrors of it. (Tilsley 1924: 44)

Where the healing spectacle had allowed more than a glimpse of the barbarism that made African bodies prey to illness, it was the 'ward round' and the 'outpatient department' that could now serve as moral microscopes which magnified not the figure of the mission doctor, but the misery consequent on immersion of the African patients they treated in the beliefs of witchcraft.

> Next comes a woman grandly dressed in skins, horns and bones. A lady friend, during a difference of opinion, has bitten her at the base of her thumb … This lady is a witch-doctor, and during the dressing of the hand is asked why she has not treated it herself … She replies that witch-doctors cannot cure themselves, only other people. (Grist 1924: 9)

Exemplifying this reversal was Aitken's *Who is My Neighbour?* (1944). A book that 'does not contain any dramatic accounts of wonderful operations and amazing cures' (Preface), this replaced the drama of the doctor at work with a vision of 'the lame, the blind and the possessed' as seen in the ward round:

> I have just finished the evening round of the wards and here are some of the patients whom I saw. In a corner of the male ward is Andries … The poor fellow has a fractured spine, and is completely paralysed from the waist downwards … Not far away from him is Hlamalini, the boy whose leg was bitten by a crocodile. His amputation stump is healing now and he is making a good recovery … Out on the verandah are two men suffering from consumption … In the female maternity and surgical ward we have several mothers with newly born babies, and three or four expectant mothers … In a ward by herself we have a woman who is suffering from mental disorder. She firmly believes she has been bewitched by some of her relatives. (Aitken 1944: 33–5)

A device for seeing far beyond the individual bodies into which it located disease, the ward round also functioned as an observatory that radiated the gaze of mission medicine into the space between African beliefs, behaviours and bodies to cement these as their objects of intervention. 'Because he believes that his racking cough is due to a pursuing spirit, the African creeps into his dark, stuffy hut to escape, and lies there at night with his family round him; so tuberculosis becomes the scourge of the Bantu race' (H. P. Thompson 1932: 11). Repeated like a litany in other texts of the 1950s and 1960s (Barker 1959; Doell 1955, 1960; Ingle 1963; Kjome 1963; McCord 1951; Schimlek 1950), the patients seen in the ward round and the ills of each were first recited – 'Sinoia, who had a bladder stone … Koko, an old woman … was suffering from high blood pressure' (Doell 1955: 28) – and in response followed a story or more probing analysis of the social conditions and cultural beliefs that lay behind the suffering of each individual. As Paterson commented after two accounts of children who had each had a leg amputated as a consequence of their parents' 'backwardness, ignorance and super-stition', these 'are not extraordinary stories at all', the point in telling them being to

> indicate ignorance and superstition rather then evil intent or wilful neglect. The average native parents are not neglectful of their children, and, though strict, are usually very fond of them and treat them very well according to their lights. The fact remains, however, that their lights are exceedingly dim when it comes to illness and accident … It is impossible to estimate the number of Native lives that must be lost every year as the result of sheer ignorance and superstition, to say nothing of the ghastly amount of suffering that must be going on at this very moment all over the country, suffering which could be relieved if only reasonable medical care and attention were available. (Paterson 1950: 94)

The purpose of the medical missionary endeavour being to lead Africans 'from darkness into the light of the Gospel' (Grist 1924: 9), accounts of mission hospital practice illuminated not only the suffering that called for the African's salvation, but also the missionaries' success in countering it. As if the hospital's clinically sanitized domain were the very light of the Gospel, Turvey's (1951) description of the 'Mkambati Leper Settlement' juxtaposed the space of misery in which it was set with the benign and regimented order achieved within: 'The colony busies itself daily with the tremendous task of healing those who come with bodies mutilated, disfigured and pain-racked, with minds filled with fear, ignorance and superstition' (Turvey 1951: 8). Against this grim parade of corporeal corruption:

> In neat rooms, surrounded by flower beds, live the patients who are able to partly look after themselves: they stream up early each morning to their special bath enclosure for their daily bath and unction of Oil Chaulmoogra;[2] then they file over to the surgery block to drink their daily dose of yeast and fruit juice, or for special dressings and treatment which often includes painful injections, and, for most of the patients, large doses of the sulphide drugs ... It is nothing for them to swallow up to 30 tablets a day. (Turvey 1951: 9)

The mission hospital thus constituted a sharp line of separation between two great systems of power, which Gale (1943) delineated in a health propaganda pamphlet aimed at convincing Africans that 'they ought to use the new doctors and nurses and hospitals, and not go to the witch-doctors any more' (Gale 1943: 3). Beyond the space of hospital medicine lay a world of animism in which it was 'the spirits which caused sickness ... They did things on purpose and they were very clever. They were much stronger than men, but they were the same as men in being able to be angry, to hate, to try to get the better of others, and so on' (p. 4). By contrast, the space of the hospital was a clinical world governed by 'the laws of nature', where sickness was caused by things which did not think and did not see. 'Some, but not all, of these are living things. They are called "germs". "Germs" grow (like plants) and get bigger in numbers, but (again like plants) they have no thoughts, no under-standing. They do not know what they are doing' (p. 5).

When African bodies crossed this threshold separating superstition and magic from salvation and science, its impact could be clinically observed in the very physiology of the patient:

> One boy came in for an operation; he did well and was at the point of going out ... when I was called to see him. The nurse told me that he was running a high temperature and was in a very excited condition. I went very carefully over him ... and I could find nothing to account for his mental condition or the high temperature ... Next morning I enquired about him. The nurse said he was normal and quiet. 'Only' she said, 'he wants to be a Christian.' Medically I should not have thought much more about it had not a similar thing happened to another patient. (Drewe 1925: 41)

For many mission doctors (e.g. Grist 1924; Humphreys 1958; Turvey 1951; Schimlek 1950), the greatest symbol of the hospital's power over the heathen was the witch-doctor patient.

> It was with fear and trembling that a witchdoctor patient came for treatment. All seemed well until the hands of the white sister touched her. 'Please need it happen again?' she appealed to one of her race, because she

had not slept for great restlessness after the first contact, and was afraid she might lose the powers of witchcraft. (Turvey 1951: 6)

In Doell (1960), and presented as the climax of a moral fable illustrating how 'good can come out of evil', hospital treatment of a witch-doctor patient resulted in the draining of his 'magic' along with the blood of his body. The story related how a witch-doctor, 'the Great Horse', had been pilfering needles, sutures, scissors and scalpels from the hospital to remove cysts from the heads of his patients. Unfortunately for him, one such operation was upon a 'cirsoid aneurysm'. Plastering the patient's head with cow dung to staunch the blood, 'the Great Horse' then stole his car, but while fleeing a tyre burst and the car crashed not far from the hospital. Both he and his patient were soon in the same hospital for treatment, and the scene was set for the final denouement as told from the mission doctor's viewpoint.

> I went to his bed and woke him ['the Great Horse']. 'Friend', I said, 'a man has just arrived whom you nearly killed yesterday morning by cutting into his head. He has lost so much blood that he needs some blood from someone else. I will test your blood to see if you have enough and if it suits him; if it does you will have to give me some for him' ... 'I will not give the blood', said the Great Horse, 'it is special blood and must not be used for other people' ... With that I inserted the needle into his vein and drew off the required amount of blood. He protested all the time, but to no avail ... Among the people the story spread that Ihashinkhulu's magic had been drained; the doctor had 'taken off all his blood', and his power over evil spirits with it. White magic was stronger than Black magic ... Not many months later the Great Horse contacted the mission and started his preparation for baptism. His son and daughter followed him into the fold. Several years later he sent his son to university to become – a medical student. (Doell 1960: 72–3)

From revelation to confession: the speaking subjects of missionary medicine

A system of moral sanitation that deployed disease and its cure to make visible the superstitions of witchcraft and replace these with a Christian belief in God, the gaze of missionary medicine pervaded the soul of the African that alongside the body was its object and effect. The problem was how to 'free' this soul from the grip of superstition so that Africans could be taught and transformed into agents of 'civilization'. In Tilsley's words:

> The disease of Africa's dismal past and of her dark present is diagnosable in one word. That word is CARELESSNESS. Careless in life, the Ethiopian is

equally careless of death, amazingly, unbelievably careless. He has got to be made afraid by outsiders. He needs inoculating with a virulent fear. Fear of disease, for instance, fear of death, fear of sin, fear of ignorance, fear of carelessness, and, above all, comprehendingly all, a holy fear of righteous God. (Tilsley 1924: 46)

Because it aimed so explicitly at producing new subjectivities, the African's voice rang loudly through the theatres of healing, hospital halls, clinic waiting rooms, and the pages of the journals, teaching texts, books and propaganda pamphlets that composed the discourse of missionary medicine. Indeed, since 'spiritual data are not of a kind to permit of tabulation' (Moorshead 1922: 18), verbal accounts from the mouths of African patients were the most important form of 'evidence' for success that medical missionaries could marshal. It is therefore appropriate to conclude this investigation of the medical missionary method by giving the final say to the Africans that were contingent on this regime of moral sanitation. For the words put into their mouths were presented both as proof of African recruitment into the power of the medical missionary endeavour, and parables that confirmed its power as a device of colonial and Christian expansion.

Corresponding to the two phases of this regime (the first exemplified by the spectacular theatre of healing, the second by the ordered observation of the hospital), there was a discernible shift in what was said by the African subjects produced in each of them. In the theatres of healing, their ostentation was mirrored in the revelationary character of the words spoken by the Africans it interpolated, as the surprising cures they witnessed disclosed to them the benign truth of Christianity. In the mission hospital – where 'every patient was a treasure, an investment in the golden future; we examined each with exemplary thoroughness and treated those who came like dukes' (Barker 1959: 47) – the words of its African patients were more confessional in nature, the speaking subject being also the object of what was said.

To begin with the theatre of healing, its emphasis on the spectacular echoed in the emotionality of what the converted had to say as they verbally prostrated themselves at the doctor's feet. In some instances, their words no less than deified the medical missionary to construct the Africans that uttered them as awe-struck supplicants to the power of God's Medicine. Take the 'native prince', who on being healed of wounds inflicted by a witch doctor said to his European 'preserver': 'It is vain to tell my people you came from this or that place, they will have you came down from above' (G. E. F. M. 1898: 28). Or again, 'Chief Kabuti', who at being saved from death exclaimed: '"You are my saviour! You have brought me back from the grave! You have resurrected me!" Such were the words of Chief Kabuti, as he stood near the dispensary door' (Church Missionary Society 1902). In other instances the confirmation of conversion was conveyed through the metaphor of death, the medical missionary God's killer of African profanity and evil. Hence 'A Black Woman's Description of a Missionary's Work' published in 1896 had her say of medical missionaries:

> You are ... hunters who are returning from your expedition. You have had good success. We are the elephants and hippopotami, we blacks, and you are come from shooting us down. Many have been killed outright for the glory of the Lord Jesus. But there are some who have only been wounded by the Word. Then you have looked at the ground, and you have followed their bloody traces in order to overtake and despatch them ... We are glad that you are like the warrior who returns from the battle living and victorious. (Anon. 1896: 209)

Other examples of what African patients said in the theatres of healing were more mundane but, perhaps because of this, they better illuminate the underlying diagram of a medical power that in the corporeal proof of the healed body entered into even the remotest of huts and removed of communities. Thus, following treatment to her legs and feet at the hands of a mission doctor, an African woman left: 'carrying a new message, a new hope. She said "We have not understood the people at God's station. They are for our good. See me. I was carried, now I walk"' (Lynch 1900: 297).

Before examining the African identities formed through the statements of patients in the space of the mission hospital, it is important to pause and consider these words, for their contrived quality makes it unlikely they were ever actually spoken by Africans. Neither, however, is there any evidence in texts of the time to indicate that they were considered outright fictions. But questions as to whether they really were said by Africans, or whether those who read them at the time of authorship believed in their authenticity, are less significant to this analysis than the fact of their centrality to missionary medical discourse. Indeed, that they may have been pure fictions on the part of their authors only underlines the nature of this power as one that required not only the African body as an object, but also a consciousness that could be made visible in words and monitored through speech.

The identity of the African emanating from the revelations induced by the theatres of healing was typified by its emotionality and outward focus on the figures of God and the doctor. By contrast, and doubtless a manifestation of how 'the native people were becoming more and more hospital conscious' (Paterson 1950: 91), the words spoken in the space of the mission hospital were of a more confessional character, suggesting how the gaze had been internalized to recruit each patient as a self-objectifying cell in the diagram of discipline.

Schimlek (1950) could thus describe the following conversation, in which a cured patient reflected upon the error of his ways in having first sought treatment at the hands of a witch doctor:

> As soon as he saw the missionary who had translated all his complaints to the doctors he said: 'Father, you know I wasted 17 oxen on our medicine-men, only to become worse. Now I have been here for a few days and can move all my limbs except my little finger. But the doctor says that will come right too, and I believe what he says, because he is a great doctor. All I had to pay so far were a few shillings. The white man is indeed the doctor of all doctors.' (Schimlek 1950: 80–1)

By the late 1950s, and converging with Aitken's earlier call to avoid 'the temptation when writing or speaking of medical work among Africans … to emphasize what I may call "horror stories"' (Aitken, 1944: 18), the words reportedly spoken by African patients increasingly reflected the routine of work done in ante-natal clinics, child welfare clinics and hospital outpatient departments. For instance, in Barker (1959) the reader could eavesdrop on an exchange between the doctor and a patient's husband who refused to let his wife remain in the hospital.

> With an outward show of reasonableness Thomas Gumede arrived on the fifteenth day. 'About my wife, doctor.'
> 'Yes?'
> 'We have an important feast at home which I wish her to attend.'
> 'When is that?' He mentioned a date a few days ahead. 'She's not ready to go home yet, you know,' I told him.
> He countered: 'It is most important according to our custom that she should be there.' …
> I lost my temper first. 'For heaven's sake don't be a fool, man,' I raved, 'this is your child that I'm trying to save and you come here bleating about some abominable custom which you ought to have left behind with your skins when you put on trousers.'
> Gumede looked pained. All the advantages were with him. 'I understand the doctor's view perfectly, but I'm afraid my wife must be at home for the feast.' (Barker 1959: 145–6)

By the mid-1970s the last of South Africa's mission hospitals and dispensaries had been brought under a state umbrella and became components of a secular clinic and hospital network (Gelfand 1984). With this secularization the remarkably stable discourse of missionary medicine, and the loquacious African as its object and effect, vanished as abruptly as they had emerged some 120 years earlier.

A watershed of power

The mid-nineteenth-century emergence of moral sanitation marked a key moment in the transformation of the anatomy of power. From a conventional perspective on power as a weapon to be seized and wielded by one group over another, its significance as a watershed between sovereignty and discipline is likely to be ignored in favour of emphasizing how this discourse misrepresented the 'truth' of African illness and the place of traditional medical beliefs. Such readings are flawed in two respects. First, no matter how exaggerated missionary descriptions of African evil and misery may have been, they none the less spoke to a power that for the first time allowed the body and beliefs of the African to emerge from below the threshold of description and become the target of discipline as opposed to the brute force of sovereignty alone. Second, arguments that traditional African illness beliefs are not the evils that the missionaries claimed them to be only became possible from the mid-1970s onwards. For, as shown in Chapter 10, it was only then that a further mutation in the anatomy of power allowed for a medicine that instead of suppressing traditional healers sought to recognize their role in the social fabric as a constructive one, and recruit them into the socio-medical enterprise.

This study now turns to a very different organ in the anatomy of power. This was the machinery of mining medicine, which as a vast industrial Panopticon spread an observing network of disciplinary surveillance throughout Africa to create its workforce of migrant labourers as a strictly regimented army of individual bodies. In sharp contrast to the regime of moral sanitation with which it coexisted, this was a medicine not of loquacious bodies, revelations and confessions, but of numbers and the mechanical medical examination of individual bodies, both dead and alive; a medicine not of a quest to 'civilize' but of a drive to make each individual a docile object of industrial exploitation. Underlining these differences between mining and missionary medicine, and also between missionary medicine and the more general discourse of public health (see Chapter 8), the 'civilized' bodies of missionary medicine were for these secular methodologies not part of the solution to African illness, but instead part of its cause. For as many secular doctors noted in their submissions to the 1914 Tuberculosis Commission:

In and around the townships and elsewhere where European influence is felt, large huts are built with little windows which is a good thing but the more civilized native affects European clothing and I think is more easily affected by cold: he ruins his teeth and digestion by eating biscuits and sweets and by drinking tea. The missions are largely responsible for this, I think. A raw native may be covered with dust, but the mission boy is too often covered by clothes saturated with decomposing sweat. (Union of South Africa 1914: 297)

Notes

1. Confirming the status of surgery as the medical missionary's technique of choice, Holland (1923: 1) wrote: 'What department of Medical Mission work is most effective? I would ... without the slightest hesitation reply "surgery". For there can be no doubt that among savage and uncivilized races surgery makes a far deeper impression than medicine. It is also more effective from a spectacular point of view.' Similarly, a 1919 Editorial in *Medical Missions at Home and Abroad* chose to illustrate 'God's providence in modern medical missions' by showing how ether, chloroform and antiseptics had 'at once widened immensely the field in which safe operative surgery was possible. The whole body indeed became the surgeon's field' (Editorial 1919: 270).

2. 'Chaulmoogra Oil is their chief treatment. A line of men stands, each rubbing it into his neighbour's back, while they sing a native song. Then many have a dose of it injected, or others take it as a medicine; the nastier it is, the more good they expect from it' (H. P. Thompson 1932: 45).

CHAPTER 6

The Industrial Panopticon: Mining and the Medical Construction of Migrant African Labour

Foucault's *Discipline and Punish* (1977) linked the eighteenth-century rise of capitalism with the spread of discipline that enabled supervision of a massively expanded workforce: 'It would not have been possible to solve the problem of the accumulation of men without the growth of an apparatus of production capable of both sustaining and using them; conversely, the techniques that made the cumulative multiplicity of men useful accelerated the accumulation of capital' (Foucault 1977: 221). This dovetailing of accumulative technologies characterizes many labour-intensive industries across Africa. It is, however, most obvious in the medical micro-powers which accompanied the expansion of South Africa's gold-mining industry between 1900 and 1950. For the industry's crystallization around the calculable bodies fabricated by mining medicine epitomized the disciplinary diagram inscribed in the Panopticon's abstract formula of a very real technology, that of the body and of individuals. Such is the omnipresence of this Panoptical schema that since the late 1970s when critical histories of the industry's labour practices began appearing (e.g. Crush 1992a, b; Crush et al. 1991; Marks and Andersson 1988; Moodie 1976; Packard 1989; Van Onselen 1980), these studies have themselves participated in its reproduction, studiously ignoring the Foucauldean perspective on power in favour of repressionist analyses that fabricate precisely the authentic African subjects they claim to liberate.

This chapter presents the Foucauldean alternative to these conventional perspectives, by analysing how mining medicine fabricated African mine workers as visible objects possessed of distinct attributes that provoked particular strategies for their management in health and disease. Indeed, rather than concealing and repressing the authentic African body, it was precisely through this industrious medicine that the African body as a target of repression existed at all. The operations of sovereign power and discipline are never mutually exclusive, and interpenetrated each other in this context of mining medicine to sustain a quintessential regime of discipline and punishment.

The heat chamber as punishment and Panopticon

In 1935 Dreosti described 'the experimental chambers' and 'heat tolerance test' developed to assess African mine workers' capacity to withstand the heat and humidity that prevailed underground, and which induced in some instances a 'hyper-pyrexial' type of 'heat-stroke'.

> The native, usually of good physique, while working, and without any premonitory signs or symptoms, suddenly develops a condition of acute mental excitement or wild delirium. He shouts and rushes about blindly, struggling violently if any attempt is made to restrain him. He becomes a danger both to himself and to those who are trying to control him. The European miner in charge will report that the native was working quite normally and 'suddenly went mad, requiring four or more men to control him in order to strap him on to the stretcher for transport' ... This condition of mental excitement is soon followed by muscular tremors going on to generalised muscular twitchings and often convulsions of an epileptiform type; coma supervenes and finally death may occur in the comatose condition. (Dreosti 1937: 32)

Aimed at modifying the African body to prevent such reactions, the 'experimental chambers' were lined with perforated pipes that released humidifying steam, and by unperforated pipes that circulated steam to generate heat. Running through each chamber were two trays for rock, 'the shovelling ... of which is similar to the type of work on which most natives are employed underground where hot working conditions exist' (Dreosti 1935: 44). Observation windows made visible the interior of the chambers to an external observer. During the 'heat tolerance test' Africans were ordered to strip naked and each given a shovel. Monitored by a 'boss boy' to mimic underground conditions and ensure constant work, they were lined up along each tray, whereupon 'each native shovels the rock to his neighbour until all the rock is accumulated at one end of the tray, and so on' (Dreosti 1935: 46). Situated outside the 'experimental chamber', a mine medical officer supervised the proceedings, to make general notes on the behaviour of the Africans, and treat any special cases. After the first and second half-hours of work, the subjects were seated and their temperatures recorded a second and third time. They then remained in a 'cooling chamber' for a further hour, at the end of which their temperatures were taken a fourth time.

According to their 'heat tolerance' as revealed by this test, Africans would be allocated to different 'acclimatization' groups, where they worked in a controlled environment until re-testing indicated they had developed sufficient 'heat tolerance' to work underground.

Clearly, much more occurred during this procedure than the creation of medical knowledge about the body's heat response (e.g. Jokl 1935). In addition to fabricating a new physiology, it can be read in at least two ways. First, it was a ritual of debasement that demonstrated the mining industry's power over its African recruits. This reading reflects the idea of sovereign power, and it is this reading which underlies conventional critiques of mining medicine. Commenting on the 'heat tolerance test', a 1976 study concluded that the enforced nakedness and other privations seemed 'unnecessary, except as a way of initiating the miners into a subculture which is deprived of any values about human dignity' (Moodie 1976: 6).

But the 'heat tolerance test' was also an instrument of discipline, a clinical Panopticon that produced the individuals and bodily attributes it observed through the techniques deployed to monitor the workings of African bodies. The very design of the 'heat chamber' ensured that those examined could not see their examiner; the repeated temperature measurements made each body its own control, and through photographs, tables and charts the attributes of the resultant individuals were turned into information upon which calculations, comparisons and selections could be made. The 'heat tolerance test' thus combined in a single technique the operation of discipline and the force of sovereignty simultaneously to create and punish the individual.

Turning to the domains of anatomical pathology and epidemiology, the mine medical examination, and the design of the compound, this underlying diagram of the Panopticon repeated itself throughout this regime of mining medicine to maintain the perpetually visible and constantly calculable body of the African miner as its object and effect.

Inventing an economy of human bodies: anatomical pathology and epidemiology

Rose (1988: 184) noted that a prerequisite for managing an economy is to conceptualize a set of entities and relationships as an economy amenable to management. Analogously, the birth of the migrant labour population as an economy of human bodies required the deployment of methods able to transform the collective and individual bodies of Africans into a systematized domain of knowledge about how disease, deviance and normality circulated within it.

Thus, when Brodie and Rogers (1894) anatomically dissected the bodies of African miners,[1] they introduced the possibility of a medically disciplined African labour force by making visible the previously irrelevant inner structures and organization of the African body. For in so doing they confirmed the localization of disease to the inner confines of the body, since disease was constituted in anatomical pathology and the medical task thus became the identification and treatment of that discrete lesion. Their work, however, pre-dated by some twenty years the widespread application of anatomical dissection, during which time the less penetrating but equally productive technique of epidemiology was applied to invent the collective contours and boundaries of the migrant labour population.

Prior to the formation of the Witwatersrand Native Labour Association (WNLA) in 1900, the recruitment of miners from across Africa was haphazard, left to 'independent individuals' (Irvine and Macauley 1905: 344), who more often than not 'sent all but the most obviously sick and lame, including many recruits only marginally fit for mine labour' (Packard 1989: 69; Transvaal Archives Depot, SNA 162/275/02). Similarly, there was no monitoring of disease and deaths among African miners, a 1904 Chamber of Mines inquiry reporting that before September 1902 'it was impossible to tell what the death rate was. No one knew how many died – no records were kept' (Transvaal Archives Depot, FLD 15/147/57). Unanalysed by this coercive system of sovereign exploitation, African miners were as much a risk to the industry as a benefit, its efficiency undermined by high levels of disease that provoked increasing African antipathy to recruitment. While this problem was undoubtedly recognized by the mining houses themselves, it was only under pressure from the state that in 1903 (Cartwright 1971: 17) there commenced application of the indirect, aggregating technique of epidemiology.

The first statistical profile of disease and death by territory of origin among Africans on Transvaal gold mines appeared in the evidence of the 1904 Transvaal Labour Commission (The Transvaal 1904: 75–80). This transformed the previously perplexing mass of bodies into an ordered statistical community by which the Commission drew a qualitative picture of the 'character of the natives' and districts from which mine workers were recruited.[2] In the same year, the Chamber of Mines began making the recording of death and disease a constant feature of all mine hospitals, recommending a uniform set of procedures, listing the information to be obtained, and defining the format for monthly reporting (Transvaal Chamber of Mines 1903).

This epidemiological mapping turned the otherwise negative fact of death and disease into an opportunity for the surveillance of not only illness, but also the disease-resisting capacity of 'normal' Africans in the regions from which miners were drawn. Repeatedly applied, it could render visible changes in how disease was distributed among Africans employed on the mines, isolating for closer investigation particularly problematic mines and sectors of the migrant labour population. Why were death rates among Mozambique recruits from north of latitude 22° south excessive, while among miners from south of this line they were acceptable? However, while it created the possibility of asking such questions, epidemiology could not show what underlay the disease patterns created by these statistical techniques.

Pathological anatomy presented itself as the technique by which to provide the answers, and by 1910 was increasingly applied. As an introduction to their comparative investigation of 'Bantu natives from Portuguese East Africa', Maynard and Turner (1914) evaluated the labour potential of nine 'tribes', each illustrated by drawings of 'native faces … chosen as typical of the race they represent' (Maynard and Turner 1914: 129). The 'Shangaan', 'an uncircumcised race of superior type to their neighbours' (p. 125) and the 'Agawa', 'the predominant race, both mentally and physically' (p. 127), distinguished themselves from the 'Parapatos', 'a tall but otherwise not physically a fine race' (p. 129). Acknowledging that 'it is not so easy to determine the tribe of a native when seen in the mortuary after death' (p. 125), their investigation none the less demonstrated the interaction between 'tribal' classification; anatomical variables such as 'skull thickness', the weight of organs (spleen, cerebrum, heart), height and full body weight; and exposure to mining: 'The native with the heavier brain and shorter stature conforms more closely to the European ratio of cerebrum weight to height, and he may therefore represent a higher type of development than the mean of his race, and thus be less stable, also less resistant to abnormal conditions' (p. 140).

Other papers, like Maynard's (1913) enquiry into pneumonia among 'tropical natives', were more circumspect about the aggregation of Africans by 'tribe', preferring to do so by geographical district instead, since 'in recent years so much intermarriage has taken place that, except on very broad lines, tribal distinctions are not maintained' (Maynard 1913: 2). However, whether aggregation was by 'tribe' or district, these studies confirmed this as a medical regime that constructed Africans first and foremost as members of groups, 'and it was these groups, rather than individuals, who were said to possess distinctive psychologies and bodies' (Vaughan 1991: 11). Further, it was from the physiological and anatomical make-up of these composite bodies that differences in death rates emanated, a 1913 editorial observing that 'no one factor can explain them, and there must be a more or less complicated interplay of various factors of race and environment' (Editorial 1913: 254). By mapping its geographical distribution, the migrant labour population was partitioned into aggregates of differing disease susceptibility, and an anatomical topography to guide the practices of recruiting super-imposed upon the geographical face of the continent.

By the mid-1920s a more differentiating and individualizing gaze had developed. Conceptually articulated in the 'virgin soil theory' of tuberculosis (Cummins 1929), this viewed tuberculosis susceptibility as determined not by evolutionary forces, but rather by the body's exposure to the conditions of industrial life. As such exposure was prolonged, so immunity should increase, and it was possible for an individual to move from immunity to susceptibility in the space of years. It was this assumption that shaped the work of the Tuberculosis Research Committee (hereafter TBRC) between 1925 and 1932. Using the most sophisticated methodologies available, it was regarded at the time of its release as the most exhaustive enquiry into tuberculosis among Africans yet produced. As an instrument of discipline, its surveys, tuberculin tests, radiographic examinations and pathological investigations impelled the gaze of mining medicine into the most distant corners of the migrant labour empire, and the deepest recesses of the African body.

Pathological anatomy (Fischer 1929, 1932) and radiographic pathology were prominent among the Committee's methods, and photographs of lungs labelled with the age, tribe and mine number of the deceased illustrated its report. The lungs were 'removed intact along with the trachea and larynx. The lungs were then inflated through the trachea with a bicycle pump and Kaiserling's No. 1 fixing fluid run through them … The main mass of the heart [was] cut away and the photograph was then taken' (TBRC 1932: 123). Through repeated application these techniques first fabricated and then confirmed the interior of the individual body as an object of social consciousness, to be classified according to what its structure revealed about its functioning in life. It was, moreover, in this medicine's capacity to erase all signs of the productive relationship between method and object that its ability to create individual and racial anatomical differences resided. Hence the Committee could write that conclusions as to racial differences in anatomy and physiology (e.g. in lymph nodes and movement of the chest walls) 'were gradually forced on us during the course of investigation' (TBRC 1932: 178). This gaze was reluctant, even resistant to perceiving such difference, and it was not the method that constructed its object, but rather the object that imposed itself upon the medical gaze:

> This want of resistance to tuberculosis is ... a biological character of the African Native which can only disappear with the lapse of time and during many successive generations of industrial contact. This biological lack of resistance exists quite apart from any risk incurred in the mining industry or any other industries. (TBRC 1932: 254)

The African body fabricated as a disease container, technologies were required to monitor the transmission of disease between bodies, and the practice of anatomical pathology was soon matched by an elaborate system of surveillance that radiated into the spaces between bodies to create these as a space traversed by power. Through the device of perceiving bacterial exchange between the sick and the well as the means of disease transmission, tuberculin tests, random sputum examinations and household surveys comprised an extended medical gaze that spread surveillance from inside the body to its exterior, and into the spaces of social contact between the sick and the well. This 'Dispensary Gaze' established 'the reality of the social by identifying diseases of social space, of contacts and relationships' (Armstrong 1983: 11), and in 1927 Lyle Cummins could note that the repatriation of tuberculous Africans to the native territories 'is calculated to disseminate infection and depreciate health' (Chamber of Mines Archives 2308/1544).

Consequently, and as clearly set out in the Tuberculosis Committee's report, the 'Dispensary Gaze' brought the history of each miner's contacts and his family into sharp resolution within the industrial Panopticon. 'The third line of investigation was the tracing of Natives repatriated from the Rand with tuberculosis. Those who could be seen were examined and also as many contacts in their families as possible' (TBRC 1932: 234). Thus the intimacy with which previously anonymous individuals could now be known, such as:

> Disc 5499, Tom Ngqukumbana, aged 43 of St. John's district, a Pondo. Married, three wives and three children, all healthy. Repatriated on 29th July, 1926. Examined on 24th September, 1928. This man appeared well-to-do, and when seen he was selling his crop of mealies. He is able to walk about and carries on his own farming operations. He had no cough and no sputum, and his general condition was very good. (TBRC 1932: 238)

The 'Dispensary Gaze' fabricated not only the social networks of individual miners but also the cultural practices that the path of disease illuminated. Among the more central factors determining the spread of infection from person to person was contact with European civilization, which eroded traditional values and practices (e.g. farming and dietary habits) that for mine doctors would have lessened the risks of infection were they to have remained intact. As a report on the tuberculosis survey of the Ciskeian and Transkeian territories noted:

> Tuberculosis is stated to be on the increase among the natives, and the reason for this increase is that the natives are discarding the red blanket. If this is taken symbolically, it is probably true, for the natives are discarding many of their old customs which acted as a safeguard. (Chamber of Mines Archives 2308/1544)

As pathological anatomy fabricated the biology of the individual miner as insufficiently evolved to withstand the assault of the mining industry and disease, so too was the body of the social, which through the survey was invented as having yet to attain a level that could sustain the individual 'when a life of monotonous leisure is suddenly exchanged for one of strenuous and unfamiliar exertion' (TBRC 1932: 264).

In thirty years the migrant labour population was transformed from an inchoate corporeal mass into a closely supervised army of individuals, the device of infectious disease a constant monitor of African movement through social and geographical space. These procedures were not, however, designed to identify diseased and otherwise deviant individuals at the point of recruitment. To do so required a human sorting house, a technology able to inspect the interior and exterior of the living body, and, by comparing individuals within a group, establish a norm to isolate those who failed to measure up to it.

Debasement and discipline: the mine medical examination

Among the practices by which mining medicine constructed its objects, the initial and periodical medical examinations were central. Until the 1940s the primary purpose of screening miners for illness and infirmity was linked into the repressive strategies of confinement that banished diseased Africans to the 'native territories'. For instance, the Miners' Phthisis Act of 1916 stated that wherever Africans entered urban and industrial areas there be instituted medical examination procedures 'sufficiently stringent to detect any native suffering from active tuberculosis so as to prevent him leaving his district for the Rand' (Union of South Africa 1916: 142). Within each mine, the initial medical examination determined which bodies were acceptable, 'detentions' to be retained for further scrutiny and 'fattening up', and 'rejects', who were 'sent home' (Maynard 1913: 3). The 1916 introduction of periodic weighing wove the examination into a miner's career as a constantly repeated ritual,[3] and from 1925 all miners were examined at the end of their contracts (TBRC 1932: 110). In short, the mine medical examination was the cornerstone that fixed individual miners in organizational space.

This analysis, however, accords the examination a power only as great as that of the authorities who conduct the procedure. This is a 'clinical power [that] can be likened to sovereignty, the doctor equated with the king in the control exercised over bodies' (Armstrong 1987: 69).[4] Such interpretations of the examination's sovereign function may be of value in challenging the more debasing elements of its earliest incarnations. But what of the modern examination, or even that of the mid-1950s, where in some recruiting agencies veterinary tactics gave way to more humane and discrete procedures? Did their arrival mean the body was no longer in power's grip, that somehow it was free? To answer these questions requires descending to the immediate point where the techniques of examination play upon the examined, into that capillary space of power where discipline fabricates its object, the individual.

In 1906 Dr George Turner, a WNLA medical officer, investigated pulmonary tuberculosis and 'kindred diseases ... in the kraals south of latitude 22°' (Turner 1907: Foreword). Using a camera, weighing scale and measuring tape, he produced a set of anthropometric and somato-metric standards for selecting individual African miners. Reflecting the early fabrication of composite bodies, his report minutely detailed individual bodies as 'specimens' of 'tribal' units. A relay of disciplinary power, the report configured the subjectivities of its readers (mine medical men and recruiters charged with selecting and classifying migrant labourers), whose scrutiny of the photographically regimented bodies would enhance their ability to calculate, compare and discriminate. 'The following illustrations ... permit one to judge of the physique of the East Coast native as compared with other classes of recruit. Picked specimens of each type of boy have been taken' (Turner 1907: 78).

Production of these images and anthropometric measurements required considerable manipulation of the Africans' bodies. After being weighed, heights noted and chest measurements at forced inspiration and expiration taken, they were made to strip naked and adopt a uniform posture against a portable white screen. This regulation rendered the collected photographs isomorphic to the perfect comparability of the numerically tabulated anthropometric indices. Mathematically combined into an equation, these supplied a fixed measurement standard for recruiters accurately to compare 'kaffirs of different tribes' and 'individual boys and gangs of boys' (Turner 1907: 77). This trained the medical gaze towards greater 'objectivity', for 'I would warn the observer not to be deceived by the black colour of the skin, which usually leads people to over-estimate the measurements, and to infer the subject of observation is a much finer specimen of humanity than he really is' (Turner, in TBRC 1932: 302). Textual comments and other photographs underlined the violence of this gaze, which debased and primitivized the human objects that were its effects. As well as constructing elusive tribal differences,[5] this cemented a gulf between 'civilized' European and 'barbarous' African. Eight pictures inspected the open mouths of men with teeth filed to sharp points, the accompanying text and a 1911 article (Turner 1911) presenting this as evidence of cannibalistic tendencies (pointed are better than straight teeth for tearing human flesh). Eighteen images of cicatrized torsos offered corporeal confirmation of their subjects' 'paganism', and depictions of albinism, hermaphroditism, dwarfism and 'other deformities' suggested the teratological potential of these atavistic races (Turner 1907: 70).

Turner's report epitomized early mine doctors' perception of the African bodies that were the effect of their corporeal investigations. The Panoptical layout of its photographs (four per page arranged in a grid to permit comparison of the bodies) also reflected how the recruiting examination itself occurred in the concrete space of interaction between doctor and recruit. From the early 1900s to the 1970s, the examination commenced with recruits being 'paraded' and inspected in 'batches'. In so doing the observer could establish a norm for each group and isolate those individuals who failed to measure up to it. Because stationary bodies might conceal a lack of agility or physical deformity, the 'parade' also included a regimen of physical exercises. A 1923 examination schedule (Chamber of Mines Archives 2325/713: 5) thus listed 'bodily defects' that 'are definite causes for rejection' (e.g. 'weak chest'; 'flabby muscles and loose skin'; 'weight under 105 pounds, unless under five feet in height'), and in 1928 a further set of guidelines choreographed the ideal examination procedure:

> Line up all the natives entirely stripped (they must not be allowed merely to drop their trousers and retain them about their ankles). Stand them in line about 20 feet away from the medical examiner. Make each boy walk towards the examiner, observing his gait and whether he is lame etc. When about five feet from the examiner cause him to rise on tip-toe, then squat, then rise again, then extend both arms above his head, extend the arms at right angles to the body laterally, then forward, then flex the elbow joints. When in this position cause him to clench and open his hands, and then rotate each arm parallel to the long axis of the body. Turn him around and look at his spine … Ask the native a simple question in an ordinary voice to ascertain whether he is deaf. Look at his ears, his gums and teeth. Cover each eye

separately, and ask him to count the fingers of your hand to test for blindness. Look at the skin, noting the presence of any large scars or varicose veins, or herniae, or flabbiness of muscles or skin. Now examine heart and lungs. (Native Recruiting Corporation Ltd 1928: 7–8)

Aimed at inducing systematic bodily contortions to externalize any signs of infirmity, the procedure was also a form of 'dressage', where the will of the examiners must subdue that of the Africans examined.

When examining the chest, and with the effect of confirming the African body as a container of disease, some doctors used 'a screen to prevent the boys breathing in one's face while one is examining them' (Stoney 1923: 4). The screen was a sheet of zinc, the back of a paraffin tin, or a chart-board, and 'one got a native attendant to hold it in front of the patient one was examining'. For some doctors it gave those examined more confidence to breathe freely, and assisted stethoscopy by keeping breathing sounds from the stethoscope; for others it hampered examination, as 'some of them [Africans] ... have a sort of idea it was used for some express purpose other than what the medical man used it for' (Stoney 1923: 4). It was surely to such suspicion that Fanon referred when he described a 'visit to the doctor': 'The doctor rather quickly gave up hope of obtaining information from the colonized patient and fell back on the clinical examination, thinking that the body would be more eloquent. But the body proved to be equally rigid. The muscles were contracted. There was no relaxing' (Fanon 1978: 234).

This same rigidity of resistance where the body contorted against the doctor's gaze appeared in materials documenting the 1951 examination ritual at WNLA's Johannesburg compound hospital (Chamber of Mines Archives 1898/3642). Following deverminization: 'the recruits parade naked and in daylight carrying their medical history cards completely filled in. They are then grouped according to how they were recruited ... and again according to good physique, poor physique and poor condition' (Skaife 1925: 2). This device of multiple groupings ensured that a visual norm was established to select individuals, and that the parade functioned to monitor the standards used by recruiting agencies in various districts. Thereafter, 'the Natives are drafted in batches to the examination rooms' (TBRC 1932: 84) where they underwent a procedure that quite literally brought their breathing patterns into conformity with the 'European chest' against which the techniques of auscultation and stethoscopy were designed. Because 'raw natives are exceedingly stupid and do not try to expand the chest when observations are being taken' (TBRC 1932: 309), or, in a more charitable view, 'very nervous and apprehensive', training in 'how to breathe deeply' (p. 84) was essential. The recruits' resistant breathing patterns reconfigured to permit accurate evaluation of their lungs, the naked recruits were then lined up in rows before the medical examiners, and their lungs examined: 'the native standing with his hands clasped behind his back. He is then made to turn around, and, with his arms folded in front, the posterior aspect of the lungs is examined' (Skaife 1925: 2–3). 'A [chalk] mark on the chest' (TBRC 1932: 84) coded bodies requiring further investigation, following which were X-rays and inspection of 'the limbs, eyes and glands, [and examination of the genitalia for] ... signs of venereal disease' (p. 84). With fingerprinting and pass allocation the regularizing gaze of the medical examination inscribed the individualized body of each miner in the archival apparatus of the state.

Beyond the bodily resistance provoked by these veterinary examinations, some records show them inciting more direct opposition. In 1909, the Government Native Labour Bureau temporarily suspended the examination of mine workers in a nude condition. Following complaints by 'chiefs' in recruiting districts, it was feared that naked examination may exert 'a prejudicial effect on recruiting due to some of the natives disliking this mode of examination' (Transvaal Archives Depot, GNLB 5/2910). In 1957, also due to its disruptive effects, the examination procedure at WNLA's central compound depot dispensed with enforced nudity and collective examination. Instead, miners were examined in individual cubicles. Walled on three sides but open to the front, this Panoptical arrangement allowed doctors to view each recruit but not the recruits to see one another. Individuals entered clad in trousers, which they removed only when the doctor examined them. Before examination they viewed a filmed depiction of it, designed to lessen their anxiety. Although by 1976 (Moodie 1976) not all mining houses had made similar changes to the initial examination, the trend was clearly away from its construction as a humiliating ceremony of sovereign power towards the more subjectifying lines devised for white miners.[6]

Correctly, it has been the excessive brutality of this most unnatural selection of the fittest that has incited resistance by the Africans examined and by social scientists. It is, however, the notion of sovereign power on which such resistance rests that both creates and restricts its value in understanding the interplay of power and the body in the mining industry. The prominence of punishment in the early examination procedures undoubtedly achieved some success in defining the roles of dominator and dominated. It is also certain that resistance to such tactics forced their abandonment, to leave a clinically sanitized domain in which the doctor, distant behind a battery of electronic body-investigation devices, was scarcely visible, as during the 1945 procedure of mass miniature radiography:

> Two rotating anode tubes face two upright stands, while two patients stand side by side. A smooth mechanism moves the camera-cum-screen from one patient to the other. Two high speed lifts are provided, having nine height adjustments, so that patients from 5ft. to 6ft. 3in. can be accommodated. The patients are lined up 70 at a time, tallest on the right, shortest on the left ... As the two patients step on to their respective height adjusted platforms, their numbers are placed against permanent magnets within the top left of the screen areas ... Next, the tube opposite the first patient is excited; next, by pressing a button, three operations take place. First, the spool in the camera is wound to position; second, the high tension is switched from the first to second tube position, and third, the camera-cum-screen is moved to the second position and then the second tube is excited. Both men then step down and are replaced by two more men. (Collender 1945: 37)

However impersonal, whenever the medical examination occurs it renders those inspected for ever subject to the knowledge that they have been observed and cannot know what about them has been seen, heard and recorded, or how such information may be used. It is this silent induction by the medical examination of its objects into ceaseless surveillance that remains hidden by those who resist only the repressive components. By provoking increasingly inconspicuous procedures for investigating the body, sovereign resistance widens the gap between the knowledge gained of the individual and what the individual knows to have been gained.

A therapeutic operator: compound design and disease control

Channelling patterns of production, reproduction and social interaction, buildings fill bodies with power: 'Stones can make people docile and knowable. The old simple schema of confinement and enclosure – thick walls, a heavy gate that prevents entering or leaving – began to be replaced by the calculation of openings, of filled and empty spaces, passages and transparencies' (Foucault 1977: 172). This is particularly apparent among buildings intended as 'total institutions', such as the asylum and the mine compound. By design, these are keyed to the medically fabricated nature of their inhabitants and the mechanisms by which diseases and disruption spread between them.

In mining medicine's pre-bacterial era of contagionist theory (c. 1880 to 1920), high-level carbon dioxide levels promoted the spread of disease between bodies. Consequently, the chief architectural weapon against disease was the manipulation of cubic air space and the forced ventilation of huts. Under the 1905 'Coloured Labour Ordinance' (The Transvaal 1905), this truth produced the 'Rand Mines Type of Hut' in which sleeping arrangements for occupants were 'shelves and nothing between the shelves' (Orenstein 1922: 3), while large ventilators producing cold draughts of air prevented the build-up of dangerous levels of carbon dioxide (Pearson and Mouchet 1923: 31). The huts were distributed around the interior walls of a large open square. Entrance to the compound was by a single gate next to the mine manager's office. The manager could thus survey from his office the entire square, monitor workers' movements into and out of their rooms, and control their movements into and out of the compound (see Crush 1992a; Pearson and Mouchet 1923).

In the early 1920s pre-bacterial theories of contagion gave way to the knowledge that 'infectious diseases are either transmitted by immediate contact or by indirect contact' (Orenstein 1922: 3). With this knowledge the previously latent disease prevention potential of compound arrangements that maximized the balance between surveillance possibilities and physical techniques of separation could now be realized.

> The great anti-hygienic factor in compounds is, of course, the aggregation of a large number of people under one roof ... Something much better must be provided to counteract the effect of this bringing together of thousands of people from various parts of the country and from various tribes and races, of different susceptibilities to disease. (Orenstein 1922: 2)

Criticizing recommendations of the Gorgas Report (Gorgas 1914) that family housing replace the barrack system which divorced labourers from their families, Orenstein argued for a mechanism that could separate individuals and maintain a high number of occupants per compound hut.

> It is not necessary to separate people by so many yards of air space – the same can be achieved by introducing some mechanical obstruction to the projection of bacteria from the nose, throat, or mouth ... [This] can be achieved by ... simply interposing some isolating mechanical device during the hours of sleep when they may, and do, come in close proximity. (Orenstein 1922: 3)

This 'device' was a simple pair of boards. Placed on either side of the bed, they created 'a sort of cubicle principle' (Orenstein 1922: 6), just large enough to contain a single supine body. A better example would be hard to find of the disciplinary principle of partitioning by which space is 'divided into as many sections as there are bodies' so that 'each individual has his own place, and each place its individual' (Foucault 1977: 143), and by the 1930s (A. Gordon 1935) most mines had complied with Orenstein's prescription to partition sleeping arrangements.

Complementing this individualizing system of isolation within the dormitories, compounds were also partitioned along ethnic lines. This precluded the dangerous intermingling of Africans of differing disease susceptibility, and minimized the traffic of infection across tribally defined borders of personal cleanliness.

> The Shangaan has a mania for washing himself and keeps his body beautifully clean and oiled, the Zulu and Swazi are clean personally, the Xosa is indifferent and usually dirty, while the Pondo is one of the dirtiest of mankind and often does not wash himself for six or nine months. (Chamber of Mines Archives C2309/F1806)

Not only beds and barracks, but each and every surface was calculated to minimize contact between individual bodies, like the latrines: 'of a special design ... and so constructed that it is almost impossible for a native to squat on the seat. The flush is automatic, [and] ... 5 gallons per seat is delivered at required intervals, usually twenty minutes when the natives are not at work underground' (Gordon 1935: 9).

Beyond the dormitories, both underground and in the open spaces of the compound, separation gave way to surveillance. Here the concerns of mine doctors fused with those of mine managers to maximize the transparency that compound arrangements afforded in relation to the behaviour of their inmates. Published in 1923, Pearson and Mouchet's *Practical Hygiene of Native Compounds in Tropical Africa* lent strong emphasis to surveillance in its discussion of compound arrangements: 'The general features which we should seek to embody in any arrangement are those which conduce to easy supervision and maximum accessibility to all installations combined with as great a degree of compactness as possible, in view of the necessity for avoiding too great proximity between natives' (Pearson and Mouchet 1923: 23).

The importance of surveillance to disease control emanated from construction by the 'Dispensary Gaze' of the social as a space of danger through which disease-causing bacteria were constantly passing from one individual to another. Spitting was perhaps the most conspicuous habit to be isolated as a mechanism of disease transmission, and in 1925 tuberculosis prevention campaigns were 'centred against the carrier and distributor of the infection: for his sputum is the cause of all the trouble' (Chamber of Mines Archives 2309/1777). To police such behaviour required that all mine workers be subject to constant observation and the knowledge that whoever 'expectorated' would be seen and punished.

Hence a system of 'sputum espionage' wherein 'Whenever a native, or indeed anyone, is seen to expectorate anything more than saliva, a smear should be made and sent to the Institute with the name of the expectorator attached to it; the Institute would report to the Mine Medical Officer the result of the examination' (Chamber of Mines Archives 2309/1777).

While the ranging characteristics of the 'Dispensary Gaze' meant it could be deployed independently of any particular spatial configuration, its efficiency was enhanced where such arrangements facilitated supervision and hierarchical observation. Noting this, Pearson and Mouchet (1923) paid special attention to the compound arrangement deployed at the City Deep mine on the Rand.

> The dwelling-huts are erected in long lines which radiate fanwise from a centre at which the compound offices are situated. The plan is devised to give maximum ease of supervision by the compound manager, who can survey the whole, or almost the whole, of his compound area whilst sitting at his office window. (Pearson and Mouchet 1923: 26)

In 1923 this 'fan compound' was the only example of its kind, and as Crush (1992a: 6) has also noted it would be difficult to find a more precise architectural realization of Bentham's Panoptical design for the maximization of surveillance. In addition to affording visibility, the 'fan compound' overcame the limitation on building expansion imposed by the closed square format, since extra huts could be added along each spoke of the wheel 'without sacrificing the possibility of instant surveillance from the compound manager's office' (Crush 1992a: 6). Coinciding with the expansionist phase of the mining industry, the Panoptical compound design became, from the late 1940s through to the 1970s, 'the industry standard' (p. 6).

The disciplinary descent of mining medicine

In each domain of mining medicine this chapter has examined, clear changes occurred in the discourse by which African mine workers were constructed and controlled from 1900 to 1950. By briefly extending the time-frame into the 1990s, it is evident that techniques of anatomy no longer fabricate racially distinct bodies, but instead discern individual differences in the internal structure and organization of bodies. The concept of 'susceptibility' has been displaced by the ideas of deprivation, poverty and exploitation in explaining the incidence of tuberculosis (e.g. Packard 1989), and in place of the earlier 'Dispensary Gaze' by which culture was fabricated as a determinant of disease exposure, there are now open-ended interviews and attitude surveys (Steinberg 1993). Such techniques work not through the eye and observation, but rather through the ear and hearing, to constitute their respondents not as mute and passive objects, but as the subjectified authors of their own attributes and identities, whose most intimate secrets concerning sexuality and personal sanitation are entered into the space of surveillance and the design of disease prevention programmes.

The examination remains a key component in the machinery by which the bodies of individual miners are graded, allocated and monitored. Along with the increasingly sophisticated manner in which it is conducted, so has there crystallized an increasingly subtle discourse around the possibility that miners may consciously or unconsciously manipulate or resist the examination, in the shape of psychometric and psychiatric scales and interviews designed to test for somatization, malingering or deliberate symptom minimization.

Complementing these medical procedures for the fabrication of a more autonomous individual are changes that have occurred in the design and layout of the mine and mine compound. Since the mid-1970s, and in the face of an upsurge of worker protest on the mines, mine compounds started to be known instead as 'mine villages'. In these, the stark square or radial arrangements of the compound, which broadcast to those observed the fact of their constant surveillance, were replaced by interior environments that create a sense of openness, with park-like surrounds and less bleak living quarters (Crush 1992b: 833). But in them is a system of surveillance 'without windows, towers, walls or guards' (Poster 1990: 93), these having been replaced by the computer, the barcode and the swipe card, through which it is possible constantly to monitor the movement and location of every worker, both above and below ground (Crush, 1992b).[7] All these developments point clearly to a decline in the importance of sovereign power as a means of achieving control over the individual and social bodies of miners. But, at the same time, every development represents a conscious attempt to increase the intensity, intimacy and invisibility of the monitoring gaze by which disciplinary power articulates itself within the individual and pervades the social.

Notes

This chapter is adapted from an earlier version appearing in *Social Science and Medicine*, Vol. 42, no. 2 as 'The Industrial Panopticon: Mining and the medical construction of migrant African labour in South Africa, 1900–1950', pp. 185–97. It is reproduced with kind permission from Elsevier Science Ltd, The Boulevard, Langford Lane, Kidlington OX5 1GB, UK.

1. Brodie and Rogers' 1894 paper on 'acute specific rhinitis' was one of the first instances involving the application to Africans of pathological anatomy. Attempting to explain the relatively sudden onset of death (when compared to Europeans with the same disease) in the African miners they examined, they concluded: 'the brain of the uncivilized Kaffirs – and they were all raw Kaffirs – is less responsive to the effect of disease than that of the highly organised brain of the white man' (Brodie and Rogers 1894: 181).

2. This Commission operated as an extended Panopticon, the evidence collected from observers in different regions of the sub-continent allowing the state and the mining industry simultaneously to survey and compare the 'usual work ... food ... pay ... physique, aptitudes, (and) special ailments' (The Transvaal 1904: 2) of Africans from different regions of South and Central Africa. In addition to a majority of sober evaluations from its witnesses, the evidence included descriptions of 'cannibals' and 'pygmies' (see The Transvaal 1904: 380).

3. In 1936, Dreosti described how:

All natives are weighed once monthly and their weights recorded. Any native who shows a loss in weight of 5 lbs. or more, since his last weighing, or 6 lbs. or over on three consecutive weighings, is brought up before the medical officer for examination. The weighing is done by specially trained Europeans whose duty it is also to look out for any apparent ill-health in the natives being weighed and to bring such natives before the medical officer irrespective of weight. (Dreosti 1936: 8)

4. This was also the level at which it was most commonly contested by individual miners. For instance, in 1920 a miner named Nontswaku was the centre of a dispute between WNLA medical officers and the medical officer on the mine to which he was allocated.

I was told (at the WNLA compound) there was nothing wrong with my chest and that I was to return to work at the mine. I returned to the mine but the Mine Medical Officer contends I have something wrong with my chest and I am not allowed to go to work ... I have made a mistake in not complaining to the Inspector before this. (Transvaal Archives Depot, GNLB 211/29151)

5. In the introduction to his report on the survey, Turner alluded to the necessity of an active gaze in discriminating tribe from tribe: 'It has been a difficult matter to keep within any very strict lines of description, the native tribes and their customs seem to merge into one another so much that for the sake of comparison one has often to diverge considerably in describing them' (Turner 1907: 5).

6. A 1939 report on anthropometric indexes and average values by which to establish the condition of miners, noted that European miners are weighed 'in trousers and socks only, but braces or belt (unloaded) may be retained' (Bedaux Company for Africa 1939: 7).

7. For instance, by the early 1980s on the HJ Joel mine in the Orange Free State, Anglo American's 'Human Resources Information System' was installed

to monitor constantly the movement and location of every worker, both above and below ground:

> At Joel, the mine complex (itself enclosed by security barriers and guards) is partitioned into a series of self-contained spatial zones – including the residential 'village', kitchen and dining rooms, indoor and outdoor bars, shops and recreation areas. These zones are bounded by impenetrable physical barriers (such as walls and fences). Each zone has a fixed entry and exit point at which there is a gate or turnstile and check-in points where workers have to swipe their bar-coded ID cards before proceeding. Each transaction is automatically logged in the data banks of the mine computer in the central security tower. The movement of every worker around the mine can thus be continuously monitored and their geographical location fixed in an instant. (Crush 1992b: 835–6)

CHAPTER 7

Discipline and Danger: Psychological Science and the African Personality

Resistance to power has an important place in Foucault's diagram of discipline. However, unlike its role in conventional analyses (where it blocks power and protects people from its damaging effects), resistance in relation to discipline is a mechanism of power's extension and elaboration: 'As soon as there is a power relation, there is a possibility of resistance. We can never be ensnared by power: We can always modify its grip in determinate conditions and according to a precise strategy' (Foucault, in Kritzman 1988: 123).

Resistance provokes discipline, and its consequences are intensified techniques of individualization, a lowering of the descriptive threshold that occurs in a positive relationship to the degree of resistance. As resistance intensifies around technologies that ignore individuality or fail to recognize subjectivity, so the very agents of resistance increasingly confirm their interiorization of the gaze until they become the subjectified objects of their own self-analysis. This was perhaps what Foucault meant where he observed that 'resistance ... does not predate the power it opposes. It is coextensive with it and absolutely its contemporary' (Foucault, in Kritzman 1988: 122).

Using this Foucauldean formulation of resistance, Chapter 7 explores the emergence and dissolution of the 'African personality' as it was produced by the psychological sciences in South Africa.[1] A case-study in the productive effects of conflict, it highlights the creativity of colonial discipline as this fabricated an African psychology to set in place a new space of domination and subordination.

Lunatics and nervous systems

A first glimpse of the African psyche as a possible object of knowledge occurred in 1875 as the effect of a psychiatric gaze to insane Africans in the Town Hill Hospital at Pietermaritzburg in Natal, South Africa.

> 53. Majonda, a tall powerful male native aged about 25 years was admitted
> on 20th October, 1875 suffering from Dementia. This inmate was a prisoner
> in the Central Gaol Pietermaritzburg, where he began, a short time ago, to
> show certain peculiarities indicating insanity. When told to do anything he
> would laugh in a silly and vacant manner, and when spoken to would answer
> by entering on a rambling and purposeless conversation. At the same time
> he began to be dirty in his habits, besmearing the walls of his cell with
> porridge etc. He has become quarrelsome in his manner without cause and
> is under the delusion that his head is filled with water. (cited in Minde 1956:
> 288)

To search any earlier for signs of the African psyche is to toil under a
delusion, for until the 1870s when special provisions were made for the
identification, treatment and confinement of lunatics, the conditions
necessary for its emergence had yet to exist. Prior to this point the
insane had no separate existence from the criminals with whom they
were confined (see Burrows 1958: 344; Foster 1990). The emergence of
madness as a relay of discipline that connected an African mind to
behaviour thus dates to this point and the passing of lunacy laws that
constituted the insane as a particular class of people composed of
various sub-categories such as: 'persons dangerously insane, either with
suicidal tendencies or criminal inclination'; 'persons of unsound mind
but not dangerously so'; and 'an idiot or person of unsound mind
incapable of managing himself or his own affairs' (see Burrows 1958:
344–6). Coinciding with these laws, the first asylums dedicated to the
confinement, observation and treatment of lunatics were built (see
Burrows 1958: 341–7; Foster 1990: 29–32), and it was with this new
practice of isolating the insane to intensive inspection that the first
distinctive strand in the genealogy of the 'African personality' became
possible.

Built to confine the mad, the early asylums also functioned as observatories into the nature of the 'normal' African nervous system.
Delineating insanity as a disease localizable to lesions of the physical
body and the brain, they produced the psyche as no more than bundles
of nerve fibres and neurons. In 1895, for example, Greenlees at the
Grahamstown Lunatic Asylum could observe that the preponderance
of mania and rarity of melancholia among African patients indicated
that in 'normal' Africans 'the higher and latest developed strata' of the
brain had yet to evolve, and therefore that 'the native brain has its
analogue in the European child's cerebrum' (Greenlees 1895: 72). This
he demonstrated through 'a series of observations on the naked-eye
appearances and the microscopical characters [*sic*] of the native brain',
which combined with statistical information on mental diseases among

Africans revealed their place on the scale of evolution (Greenlees 1895: 75).

Confirming the primary spatialization of insanity to the neuronal networks of the African brain, insane Africans were confined in surroundings commensurate with the 'sensitivity' of their 'nervous systems'. As the 1879 Commission of Inquiry into the Cape's Robben Island Asylum reported:

> the modern plan of constructing asylums instead of having these large buildings, is to erect a series of cottages – to have a large space of ground, which is dotted over with separate cottages, so that all can get the benefit of quiet. With regard to the Kafir, the closer you can assimilate his condition to that of his normal state the better. I think it would be a mistake to confine Kafirs to a house and tie them to one spot. They would be better if they had room to roam about a little. For that reason I think the asylum on Robben Island is particularly suited for natives. (Cape of Good Hope 1880a: 3)

Elaborating on this theme, the head of the asylum argued that owing to the greater 'sensitivity' of their 'nervous systems', Europeans were 'more amenable to such influences as scenery' (Cape of Good Hope 1880a: 8) than Africans, and that a 'double classification' (i.e. segregation) by race and type of insanity should be implemented. Violent and incurable African and European patients (such as those suffering from dementia) could be housed together, since with such conditions racial differences in nervous system sophistication were obliterated, and 'all classes become assimilated' (Cape of Good Hope 1880b: 1–4).

This first interpolation of an African psycho-physical space into the anatomy of power was restricted to the interior of the confining asylum. However, in producing the African nervous system as a discrete entity in a particular relationship to the environment, the conditions were created for a subsequent radiation of the psychological gaze into the most intimate and the most public of colonial spaces.

Impulsive insanity and the perilous black

In 1893 a Johannesburg newspaper warned its readers: 'Beware of your houseboy, for under the innocent front may be lurking and lying latent the passions of a panther, or worse!' (cited in Van Onselen 1982: 49). This response to the attempted rape by a black servant of his white 'madam' catalysed a series of 'black peril' scares that traversed the Witwatersrand between then and 1912. Over these years 'the curse of the black peril' recurred sporadically in response to similar instances of black on white violence, peaking when in 1912 the *Rand Daily Mail* organized a petition and submitted some 52,000 signatures to parliament demanding that it curb the 'black peril'. The social historian Van Onselen (1982: 50–3) has shown how most incidents clustered among economically less stable working- and middle-class households, to argue that as a collective phenomenon the 'curse of the black peril' was driven by 'periods of stress and acute tension within the political economy of the Witwatersrand as a whole' (Van Onselen 1982: 51).

An anachronistic fiction of the history of the past, this economist explanation for the 'black peril' conceals the underlying power shift that made it possible in the first place for violence to serve as a tactic of visibility by which the inner workings of the African mind could be exposed to the eyes of everyone. For even by this point the power of discipline to fabricate the African psyche as its target was producing increasingly intimate domains of domination and resistance. In 1910, a Johannesburg doctor communicated the following facts of which he felt obliged to inform the Secretary for Native Affairs 'in the interests of the public welfare':

> On the 26th Jan. 1909 I find a certain native named Isaac was sent to the Pretoria Asylum certified insane. It appears that he was liberated from there some months afterwards. A few weeks ago this same native was arrested for assault, or threatening to stab his mistress. He was sent up to the Fort by magistrate V. d Berg for medical observation. I am of the opinion that he is a dangerous person, because he has moments of perfect sanity, and afterwards he is apt to lose all control of himself. He says if he is balked or thwarted he feels like murdering the party doing it. In short he suffers from what I call 'impulsive insanity'. Now, it appears to me highly necessary that when a native has been in the asylum and authorities consider it necessary to liberate him, that the fact of his having been in the asylum should in some way be stamped on his pass. You or I or anybody else might innocently engage such a native and expose our families to the utmost danger, whereas if he is known to have been in an asylum he will through force of circumstances ultimately be compelled to return to and remain at his kraal. The community would be well rid of such a character. (Transvaal Archives Depot, AG 202/10 LD 1786)

Emanating from the space of danger produced by the close intermingling of natives and Europeans, 'Isaac' was a marker of how ruptures in the boundaries of crude repression were inducing a shift in the psychological gaze towards problematization not of the nervous system itself, but rather of the relationships between the internal space of the African mind and the external space of the environment. As Conroy (1907: 36) noted, 'the baby when born is treated by such barbarian

1. Herbert's 1638 Hottentot man and woman (Hirschberg 1967).

2. Monstrous men – woodcuts from Hartman Schedel's
Liber chronicarum (Schedel 1493).

3. Linschoten's cannibals of 1596 (Hirschberg 1967).

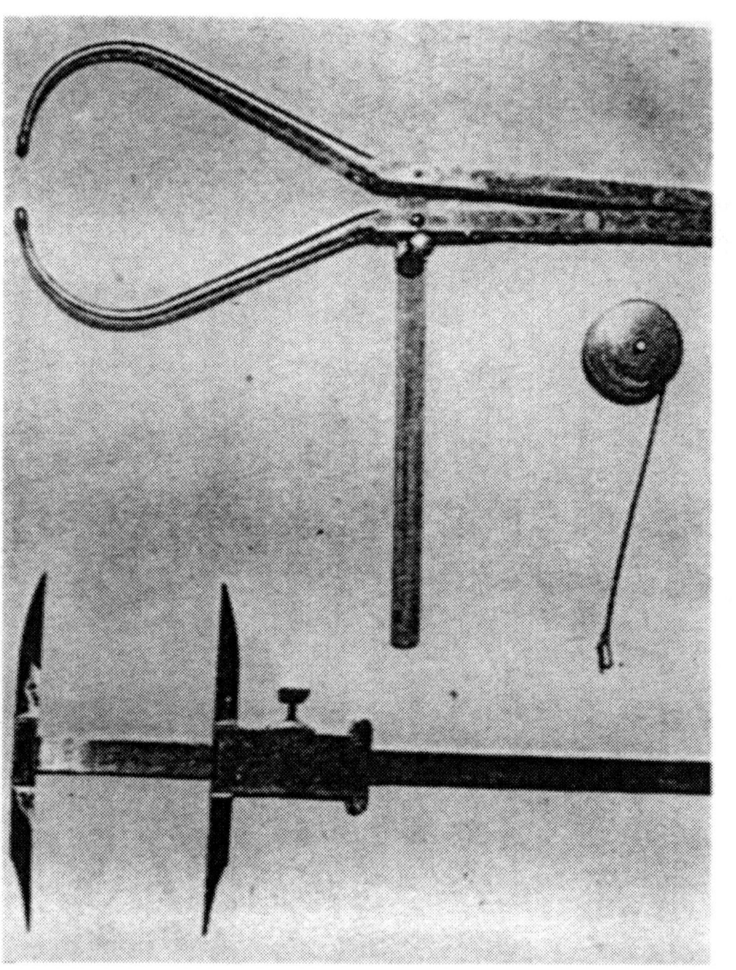

4. Instruments for measuring the skull (Bruwer et al. 1958).

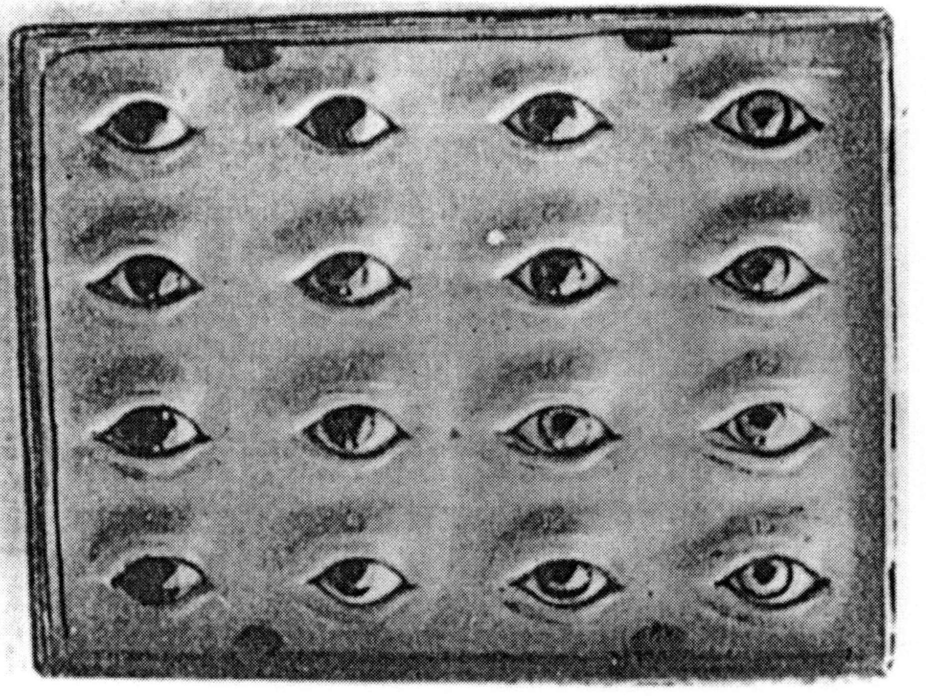

5. Scale for comparing the colour of the eye (Bruwer et al. 1958).

6. Scale for comparing the colour of the skin
(Bruwer et al. 1958).

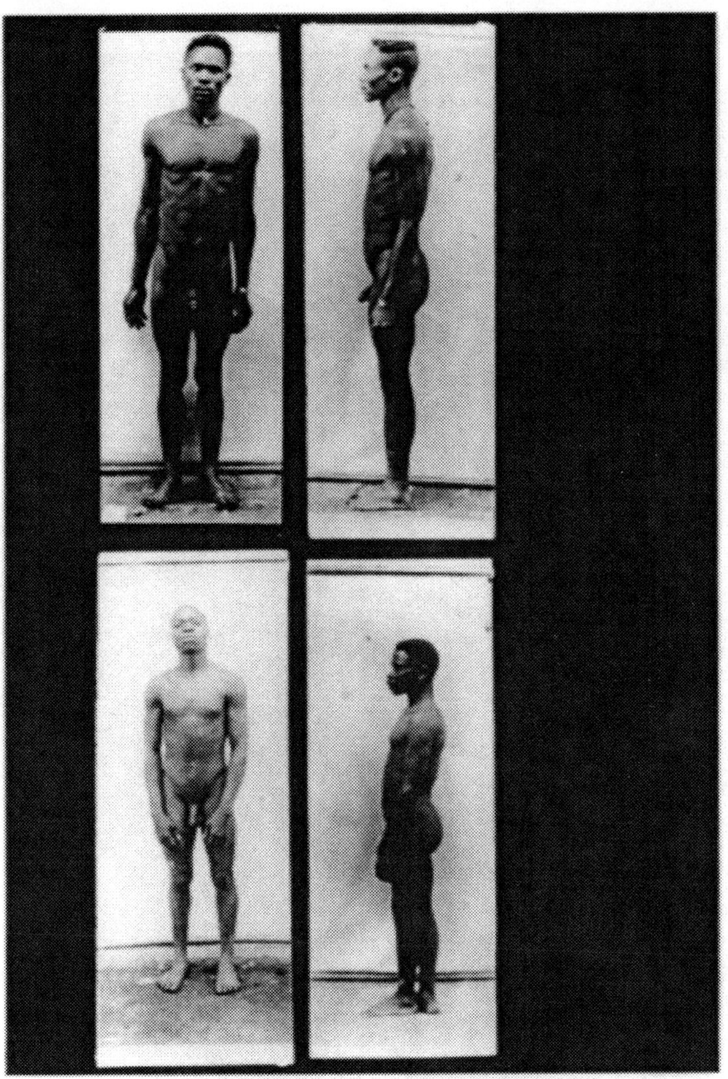

7. Types of Mozambique native (Turner 1907).

8. Heat tolerance test (Dreosti 1935).

9. Heat tolerance test (Dreosti 1935).

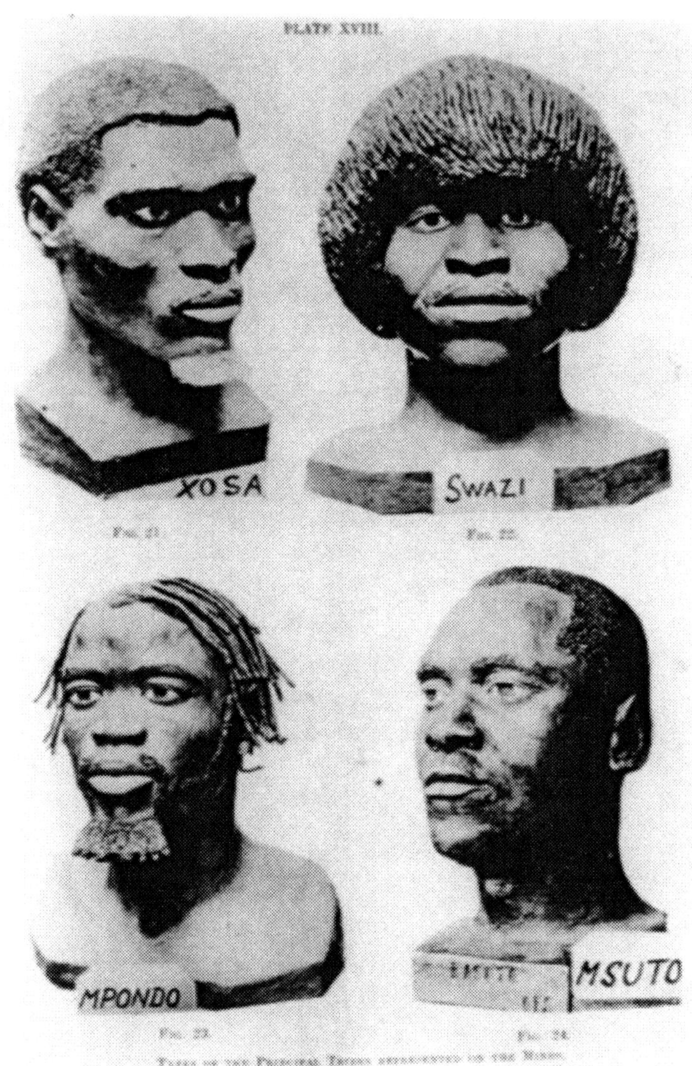

10. Types of the principal tribes represented on the mines (TBRC 1932).

11. Top: A fan compound in Johannesburg (circa 1950);
Bottom: A 'mine village' (circa 1985) (Chamber of Mines Archives).

12. Mass miniature radiography (Cartwright 1971).

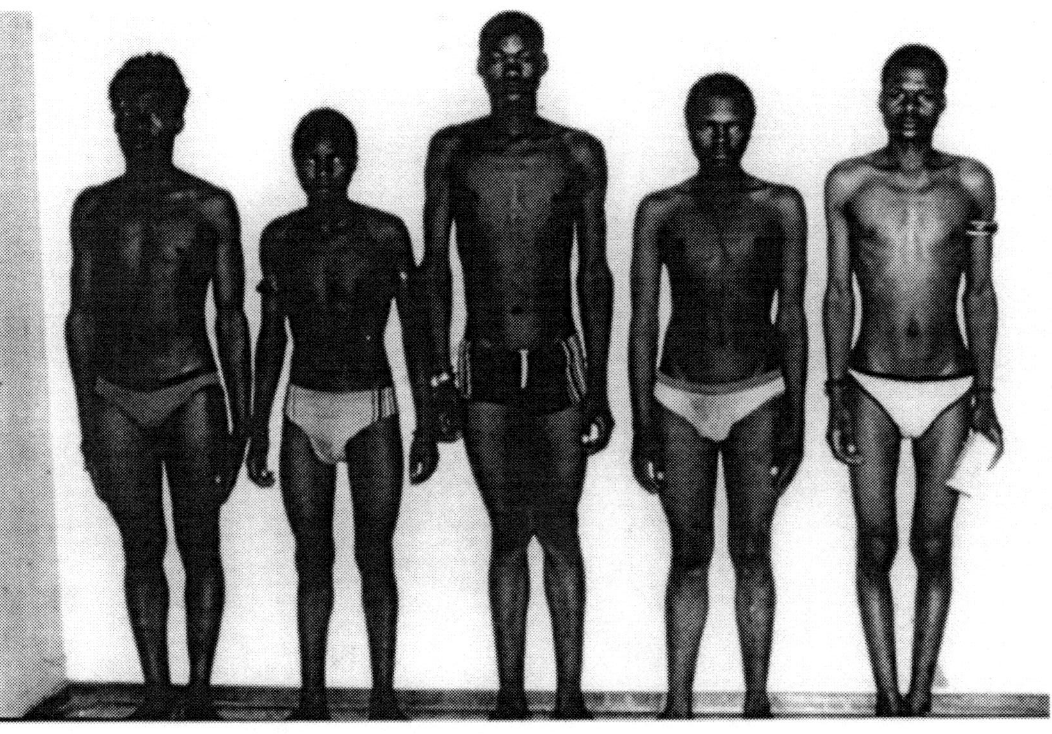

13. The 1980s mine medical examination (Chamber of Mines Archives).

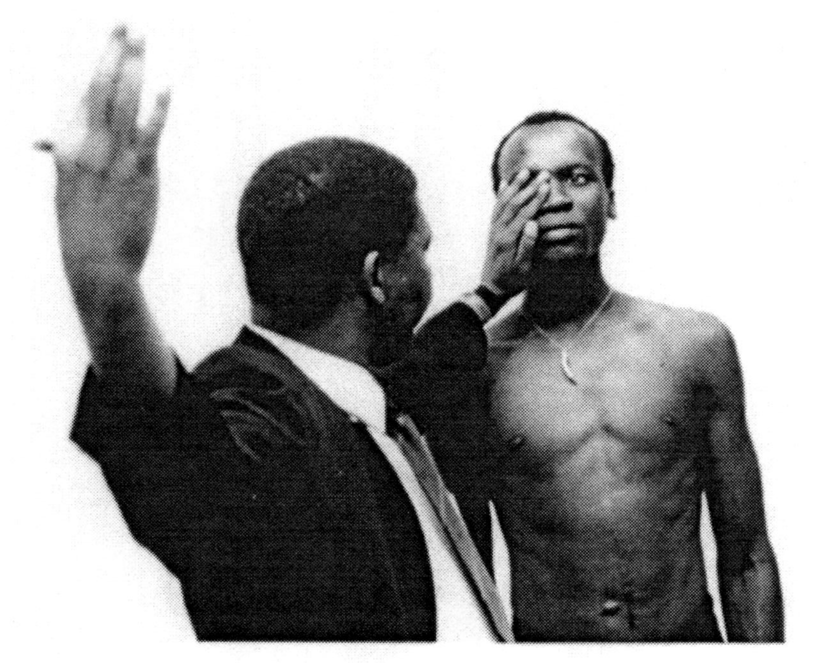

14. The 1980s mine medical examination (Chamber of Mines Archives).

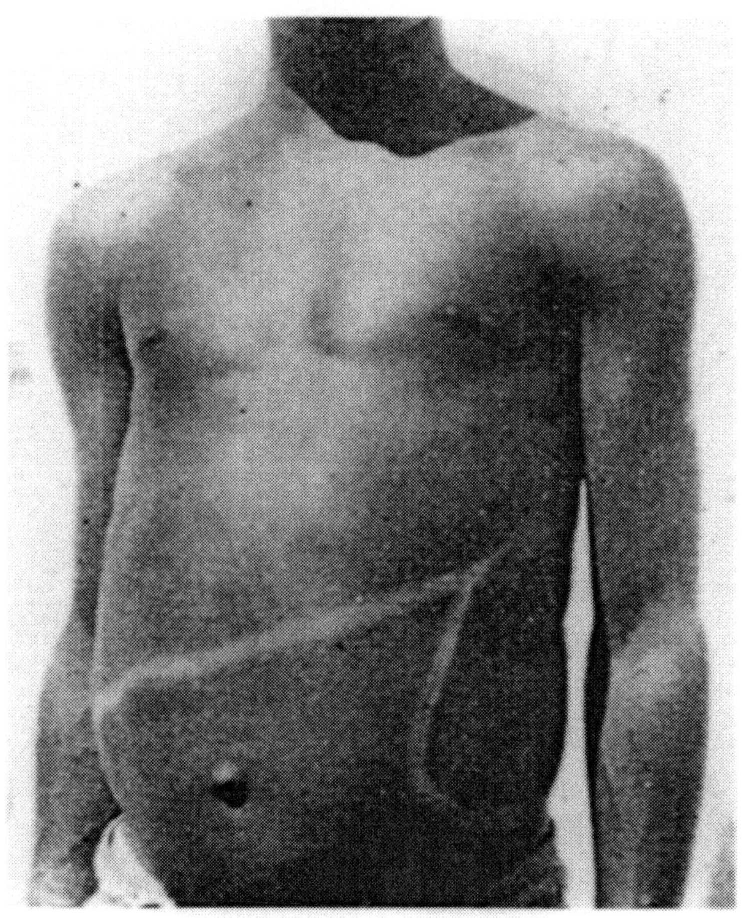

15. Bilharzial cirrhosis of the liver and splenomegaly (marked in chalk)
(Gelfand 1943).

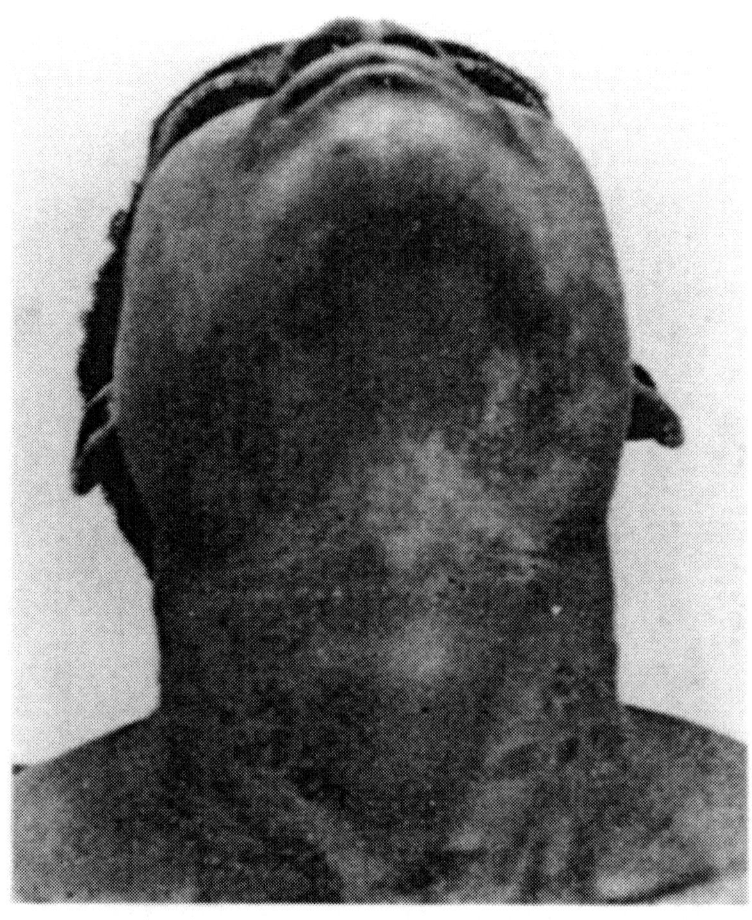

16. Pellagra with 'collarrette' resembling lizard skin in the lower
region of the neck (Gelfand 1943).

methods as are likely to sew the seeds of chronic disease'. Inscribing the same line of environmental determinism, a 1912 editorial could thus argue for 'the curse of the black peril' to be dealt with through 'a scientific treatment of this social evil on exactly the same lines as if it were a human disease' (Editorial 1912: 201). Fabricating a psychological analogue of the 'dressed native' that at the same time entered public-health space (see Chapter 8), it defined 'the black peril' as a consequence of removing Africans from their tribal environment and then failing to substitute this in the cities with an equivalent set of contextual restraints on African sexuality:

> We have taken enormous hordes of young adult savages or semi-savages, eminently virile in more senses than one, from their own environment, and have placed them in an environment absolutely teeming with every possible stimulus to the sexual impulse at the same time that they are, necessarily, kept celibates ... We have not even tried to put them in the social mosquito-proof house of a reproduction of a native community, but, on the contrary, have freely exposed them to all the stings of a class of human mosquitoes whose interest is to inoculate them with every kind of human vice, and, as regards some forty thousand of them at least, have permitted their employment in duties of all other most calculated to raise the sexual impulse. (Editorial 1912: 203)

In fabricating an interdependence between African sexuality and socio-cultural context, the African in the city was rendered 'normally abnormal', and therefore the target of interventions directed to ameliorating such 'abnormality' through a combined system of segregation and social sanitation.

Obsolete machinery and the poor white problem   The 'curse of the black peril' and irruption of a psychological gaze to the impulsive African established African behaviour as a possible object of rational management at the level of the population. In 1918 the anthropologist J. S. Marwick published a paper on 'The Natives in the Larger Towns'. One among many similar papers of the time (e.g. Boehmke 1928; W. Flint 1919; Loram 1922; Radcliffe-Brown 1923; Rheinhallt-Jones 1926), this argued for drawing Africans into a system of 'positive law' that would regulate their conduct in urban settings: 'In the early history of the towns the presence of Natives was not a matter that called for regulation by positive law, as their numbers were not great, and their duties and obligations were not easily evaded in a small community' (Marwick 1918: 593). This 'early history' now buried beneath the demographic changes accompanying industrialization, the problem had become one of discipline:

> The regulation of the routine of human existence in our larger towns, so that Europeans and Natives may live on such terms that mutually satisfactory relations shall subsist between the two races. This foreshadows the necessity of a finely adjusted organisation in which good legislation, good administration and good citizenship shall each bear a part. (Marwick 1918: 590)

For Loram (1922), the securement of 'mutually satisfactory' relations between Africans and Europeans required deployment of the psychological sciences: 'The machinery for dealing with the Native question has become obsolete and ineffectual ... Just as the war needed the chemist, the physicist, and the engineer, so the Native question needs the human-nature scientists, the political scientist, the economist, the psychologist and sociologist' (Loram 1922: 100). These arguments for social scientific solutions to the 'native problem' invented as a surface of intervention the interface where black bodies infiltrated the strictly delimited domain of white bodies, and so threatened to destroy the lines of sovereignty that had previously kept them apart.

At the heart of the 'poor white problem' and the Carnegie Commission's Inquiry (Carnegie Commission 1932) into it was the conviction that through social and sexual intercourse with blacks indigent whites would lose their European identity and destroy the perception by blacks of European superiority. 'Going kaffir' (Carnegie Commission 1932: xix) was a colloquialism that expressed this fear, and connoted the worst scenario, poor whites breeding and living with and in the same way as Africans. In its findings, the Carnegie Commission was unequivocal as to the deleterious effects that extended contact with 'inferior coloured races' would have on Europeans, and in concluding that its 'primary causes ... have not been physical' (W. A. Murray 1932: 127) localized its origin and solution to the domain of economics and the psychological sciences.

Construing the native component to the 'poor white' problem as of the colonists' own making, since 'under European rule the native population has greatly increased in numbers' (Carnegie Commission 1932: xix), the Commission propelled the psychological sciences deep into the interstices between white and black bodies to invest these spaces with the dividing power of discipline. Spread through the minutest points of contact between African and European (the kitchen, the nursery, the road gang, the factory and the mine shaft), these were established as an analysable network of body boundaries and breached spaces between black and white minds. This objectified the African as a source of corruption and the European as a victim, whose Protestant ethic was undermined by psychological proximity to the coarse and careless African.

Uncivilized native habits often affect the white family and break down the work of the Church, the school and the home. The native has no re-finement, taste, or sense of propriety, according to European standards, but is coarse and immodest; without realizing it the whites are influenced detrimentally by contact with him. (Albertyn 1932: 40)

Cementing this increased visibility of African mentality was the invention of 'intelligence' as a quantitative surveillance device that partitioned the population into a hierarchy of groups and individuals against the norm of the 'intelligence quotient'. Accordingly, and as had Fick (1927, 1929), Wilcocks (1932: 169) showed that while the environment operated to lower the intelligence quotients of poor whites, 'the majority of poor white children ... [and] poor white adults possess normal, and, in part, even more ordinary innate intelligence'. By comparison, the 'average intelligence' of Africans was equivalent to that of 'mentally defective whites', the Africans' 'learning ability' insufficient for them 'to compete on equal terms with the average European, except on tasks of an extremely simple nature' (Jansen van Rensburg 1938: 43). Contemporaneous with this wave of intelligence-testing arose plans for eugenic measures to protect the purity of white racial stock through the encouragement of breeding only within races and only between the 'fit' whose 'germ plasm' was 'good'. Such direct eugenic measures were, however, never implemented, and references to eugenics in the *South African Journal of Science* abruptly ceased in 1932 (see Appel 1989: 612).

The psychiatric gaze as it played upon lunatics to invent the African nervous system as a discrete psycho-physical space; the 'black peril'; the 'poor white question'; mass intelligence-testing and the putative eugenic reflex. Each of these problems signified difference under siege, a triangular assault upon the biological 'truth' of European racial sovereignty which incited a new language of government that not only managed racial distinctions but would actively cultivate a culture of difference.

A 'better native': indirect rule and the cultivation of culture

By the 1930s African customs and culture were constituted as a distinct body of knowledge in the writings of anthropologists, ethnographers, psychologists and psychiatrists. This issued from the formalization of the psychological sciences in general and of sub-specialities devoted to studying the African in particular. In 1921, Radcliffe-Brown was appointed chair of the Union of South Africa's first department of anthropology (at the University of Cape Town), and in October 1921 the first edition of *Bantu Studies and General South African Anthropology* was published. In 1925, G. P. Lestrade was appointed to head the new ethnological section of the Union's Native Affairs Department, and within a few years courses in 'Bantu studies' and anthropology were offered by most universities (see Dubow 1987: 80).

Unifying these sciences was the common object that was the effect of their investigations: the African mind, behaviour, and their relation to a surrounding social and cultural space. As such they were components of a single power apparatus, a Panoptical system for the production of individual minds and surveillance of a social space traversed by power. Along with other African colonies (see Bhaba 1986; Vaughan 1991), these developments enabled previously irrelevant aspects of African life to be interpolated in the gaze of coordinated scientific research and become components in the regulatory mechanisms of 'indirect rule'. The notion of 'indirect rule' described the tactics adopted by Europeans to resolve the crisis posed by the perception that 'civilization' was eroding the malleability and docility of Africans, thereby endangering social control and threatening the economic base of cheap labour. To contain this threat the discourse of indirect rule translated African dissatisfaction into the vocabulary of ethnology, anthropology and psychology. Signs of 'native restlessness' thus became symptoms of 'deculturation' or 'acculturation', iatrogenic consequences of the colonial cure for African barbarism. By bolstering African adherence to 'custom', obedience to traditional leaders, and cultural or tribal identity, such threats could be averted (cf. Vaughan 1991: 109).

Eiselen, a lecturer in 'Bantu studies' at Stellenbosch University, could thus argue in 1929 that: 'The duty of the native [is] ... not to become a black European, but to become a better native, with ideals and a culture of his own' (Eiselen 1929: 12). Two years later, this emphasis on cultural purity was modified to form the 'adaptationist position', for which the 'ideal' African would be manufactured by fusing elements from both African and European traditions:

> There is a middle way between tying him [the native] down or trying to make of him a black European, between repressionist and assimilationist schools ... It is possible to adopt an adaptationist attitude which would take out of the Bantu past what was good, and even what was merely neutral, and together with what is good in European culture for the Bantu, build up a Bantu future. (Lestrade 1931, in Dubow 1987: 85–6)

Urbanization and surveillance of the African unconscious Within the political and economic context of adaptationism, cultural and racial difference took on a new utility. Instead of a negative incitement to suppression, difference was now a productive element in a novel machinery of discipline that operated through its cooption to render too little difference just as problematic as too much.

It was within this context that the mind of the African attained further depth through the deployment of psychoanalytic techniques. By drawing a line through culture, the unconscious and behaviour, the domain of instinct, desire and emotion was now fabricated as a distinct entity (the 'African personality') within which strategies of disciplinary surveillance could articulate. Two 1937 studies marked the emergence of this psychoanalytic gaze: B. J. F. Laubscher's *Sex, Custom and Psychopathology: A Study of South African Pagan Natives*, and W. Sach's *Black Hamlet: The Mind of an African Negro as Revealed by Psychoanalysis.*[2]

A senior psychiatrist in South Africa's Union Mental Service, Laubscher combined ethnology with psychoanalysis to impel the psychological gaze into the most intimate corners of 'Tembu tribal life', and behind the resistant front of African antipathy to European surveillance. Like the back lighting that reveals to the Panoptical observer the grid of cells in which inmates are objectified, this device identified the personalities of individual Africans as mere nodes in a matrix of indigenous culture: 'It will be seen that the cultural pattern to which the native belongs, determines the nature of his mental content'(Laubscher 1937: xi).

Established in this way as 'phylogenetically on a par with the Oedipus phase in ontogenetic development' (Laubscher 1937: 58), Africans isolated from their tribal settings were psychologically ill-equipped to cope with the sudden surges of instinct and libido that emanated from the deep psychic well of the now distinctly defined African unconscious: 'The native is not by nature bloodthirsty, but his aggressive instinctive or pugnacious propensities are excitable, easily roused and explosive ... His aggressive libido flows outwards, becomes readily externalized, and sudden, impulsive assaults, often fatal, are common' (pp. 306–7). Now a visible complex, the African unconscious became a site for the installation of a psycho-social calculus directed to managing the African body through the African mind.

Finding that 'sadistic sexual acts on European women' (p. 257) occurred infrequently among rural Africans as compared to Africans in the towns, Laubscher concluded that their prevention in urban settings could be achieved by manipulating tribal rites relating to African masculinity. So, because neglect of the circumcision rite created 'a marked instability ... in behaviour and attitude to practical things' (p. 134), it should not only be permitted but actively encouraged among urban Africans (p. 134). In contrast to this stabilizing rite was the 'racial characteristic of sharing and mutual assistance' (p. 135). In rural areas this was an admirable attribute. In the towns, however, it 'facilitates his comprehension of communistic ideals ... and makes the native prone to the influence of agitators' (pp. 196–7). Such altruism was therefore to be met with an educational antidote that could engender a desire for private property that was consistent with 'capitalistic administration' (p. 197).

Where Laubscher's ethnological approach began with the construction of traditional African culture through its direct observation, Sachs (1937) concentrated the psychoanalytic gaze to raise a single individual – 'John' – into the eye of disciplinary power. Sachs too fabricated the interzone of European civilization and African tradition as a psychological no man's land which, lying between the clearly demarcated domains of the kraal and the city, produced African psyches that were flawed and split: 'John, moreover, had an additional tragedy which shadows the life of almost every African. The circumstances of his life, the clash of his two worlds, constantly caused inner division. Every African leads a double life in the full sense of the psychological concept' (W. Sachs 1937: 174–5).

While Laubscher and Sachs interpolated the African soul into divergent political projects – Laubscher's an inferiorizing and repressive one, Sachs' a paternalistic one – their disagreement solidified the space between African tradition and European civilization as a region of psychological disintegration bounded on the one side by the 'noble savage', and on the other by the psychologically cloven 'detribalized' African of the city.

Further recognition of detribalization's dangerous effects came with R. E. Phillips' *The Bantu in the City. A Study of Cultural Adjustment on the Witwatersrand* (1948). One of the first questionnaire-based surveys of the African psyche, this elicited responses from '232 Africans in 49 different occupations' to dissect the interface between rural tradition and urban 'civilization'. By extending psychological surveillance into the eye of the urban African, this became an ocular relay in a normalizing network of gazes that isolated for inspection those situations which stimulated 'increases in anxiety and inner tension' (R. E. Phillips 1948: 74), thereby to enable monitoring of 'the emotional orientation of the African and the dominant role which the personality of the acculturator plays in the matter of cultural transference in Africa' (p. 187). Alongside the negative effects of the violent police methods used in suppressing African resistance, the corrupting effects of urbanization were located to all those situations where 'decent, coloured natives', observed 'the white man under conditions which are not favourable to the development of respect on the part of the observer':

African youths seem to be everywhere; they see everything ... To illustrate: the writer found a lad of about fifteen years of age ... engaged as a helper to an elderly woman who kept a magazine stall on Eloff Street, Johannesburg, for the sale of overseas *pulps* – 'True Confessions,' 'Modern Romances,' 'Love Magazine' etc. When visited, the lad was engrossed in his reading of a profusely illustrated pamphlet with actual photographs of nude White women, entitled 'The Beauty of the Female Form.' (R. E. Phillips 1948: 105)

The imposition of apartheid and installation of moral surveillance The 1948 imposition of statutory apartheid in South Africa involved a draconian extension of existing state controls over the geography of African mobility. By 1952 'Africans required official permission to travel and not to travel, to work and not to work ... Permits were required to look for jobs, to take jobs, and then to change jobs' (Posel 1991: 116). The 1953 introduction of 'Bantu Education' complemented these repressive controls with disciplinary tactics to cement further separate development through the manipulation of mind and language. The result was an intensification of organized and informal African resistance. In turn, this provoked a resurgence in the development of psychological surveillance devices to monitor the African personality and trace the behavioural outcomes of its mutation under the pressures of urbanization and apartheid repression.

In 1953 Biesheuvel published his 'Moral Attitudes Inventory', a questionnaire that interrogated 'the manner in which Africans become aware of the conduct that is required of them in their relations with Western society' (Biesheuvel 1953: 13). By 1957 the 'Moral Attitudes Inventory' had been applied to more than 1,000 Africans from 'all walks of life' and 'from all parts of the country and many native reserves and locations' (Biesheuvel 1957: 310).

An understanding of what Africans know concerning European manners, morals, ethics, and legal codes, of the attitudes which they are adopting towards the standards of conduct to which we expect them to conform, is ... exceedingly important for the citizen generally and for those who as educators, administrators, social workers or law-makers have the well-being and future development of Africans in their hands. (Biesheuvel 1957: 309–10)

An observatory that transformed resistance into a calculable capacity, the inventory inducted Africans into imaginary conversations with five 'speakers' by having them rate the 'wisdom' of each speaker's opinions. These opinions were reflections upon everyday situations involving questions of belief, manners, ethical conduct or legal duty. For instance, 'William' said: '"One must be courteous for it is the custom of our own people"', while 'Jack' thought: "'Why should the African be courteous to the white man, who is never courteous to him?"'(Biesheuvel 1957: 310). Through their responses, ordinary Africans objectified themselves within the categories of this colonial discourse on culture and behaviour to feed the machinery of surveillance with information about the stability of the social order.

The attempted control of African attitudes and relations towards white authority in the late 1950s was thus enabled through manufacture by the psychological sciences of the African mind as the origin and container of attitudes and values. Through instruments such as Biesheuvel's (1957) 'Moral Attitudes Inventory', R. Sherwood's (1958) 'hypothetical personality models' of the ideal 'Bantu clerk', and Reader's (1963) 'marginal man', these values were scrutinized and used to plot the lines of opposition and acquiescence running between the sovereign centres of white domination and black resistance. The effect of this was to problematize further the question of African personality. For where studies such as Biesheuvel's had shown most Africans manifested loyalty towards the government and acceptance of South African society's moral and legal codes (Biesheuvel 1955, 1957, 1959), other researchers had found less acceptance, and even outright hostility to the state (e.g. Bloom 1960).

The disparity between fabrications of the African as apartheid's loyal subject and its resistant opponent provoked claims that questionnaire-based measurements of personality were flawed, that they measured not the African personality itself, but instead revealed 'mere lip-service to the culture of the dominant group, prompted by fear of disapproval or by an attempt to please the examiner by giving him what one believes he wants' (Biesheuvel 1959: 145). A solution to this problem crystallized in the shape of the projective test. Using pictures rather than words to provoke the unconscious into revealing its tendencies, this could bypass the African's readiness to 'please the examiner' by penetrating to the black skin concealed by the white mask of what was now recognized as pseudo-acquiescence to colonial domination.

Projective testing and the creation of the African as a dangerous individual Following Lee's (1950) early experiments on the projective testing of Africans, Sherwood had by 1957 developed an 'area-first' approach to thematic apperception testing. This dissected the personality into discrete yet interacting sub-components such as the relationships between 'father–son, father–daughter, mother–son', and other constructs such as 'person alone, aggression, love triangle' (E. T. Sherwood 1957: 166). In this way, individuals subjected to the procedure were fabricated as microcosms of their surrounding authority figures, intimate relationships and cultural norms that had been internalized or were being eroded by detribalization.

A method that penetrated the innermost core of the African personality it manufactured, this Africanized Thematic Apperception Test allowed a new substrate of unconscious energies to crystallize beneath the ethico-moral topography of contact between black and white that the earlier regime of attitudinal surveillance had illuminated. Manifest from 1960 to 1975 in a spate of studies devoted to refining the methodology of African projective testing (e.g. Baran 1971; Erasmus 1975; Minnaar 1975; Pretorius 1977), this ballooning of the African personality invented urban African townships as analysable constellations of individual minds criss-crossed by the projections, perceptions, impulses and needs that originated from the personalities of their inhabitants.

The threshold of psychological description lowered beneath the line of consciousness, urban Africans were interrogated not through the overt meanings of what they said, but rather the 'unconscious' dynamics that now underlay the spoken word. '[A] *TAT* picture [is] ... a question addressed to the subject – addressed both to his conscious and his unconscious mind' (E. T. Sherwood 1957: 167). Epitomizing the paradoxical power of discipline to increase itself through resistance was De Ridder's 1961 publication of the *Personality of the Urban African*. Against a background text that microscopically detailed the apperceptive interstices of 2,500 Johannesburg Africans, De Ridder noted how 'recent developments have focused attention upon a particular type of individual' (De Ridder 1961: 118). These 'developments' were the 'antipass' campaigns of Langa and Sharpeville, where in 1960 black resistance and apartheid oppression led to the shooting of sixty-seven Africans. The 'particular type of individual' was a resistance leader – 'usually referred to by the Europeans in Africa as an agitator or an African nationalist' (De Ridder 1961: 118) – and it was this threat that provoked De Ridder to lend a full chapter to analysing the personality of this dangerous individual. Leaving no doubt that treason itself was an epiphenomenon when viewed against the personality, De Ridder concluded that:

> The subject is definitely not adjusted to the prevailing social conditions. He shows very strong feelings of insecurity and anxiety feelings and is frustrated in the satisfaction of his needs, desires and ambitions. His resulting embitterment and his feelings of being discriminated against find outlet in criticism of the prevailing social set-up in general and of Europeans in particular. (De Ridder 1961: 127)

Unsurprisingly in this context of struggle between black and white for a hold over sovereign power, the last projective test designed to assess the African personality was explicitly targeted to identifying the African as an imminent danger to Europeans. Published in 1975, the 'TAT Zulu' ('TAT-Z') was presented to respondents as 'a test to measure the power of your imagination' (Erasmus 1975: frontispiece). Concealing in this concern with imagination the productive power of psychological surveillance, the 'TAT-Z' was preoccupied with relationships of domination and subordination, control and rebellion. The 'aggression card', for instance, invented as its objects of surveillance the 'extent of underlying aggression towards Whites ... [and the] degree of aggression ... among the Blacks themselves' (Erasmus 1984: 17). A scientific rendition of the earlier 'curse of the black peril', the scoring manual's hierarchy of response types supplied a code to seriate Africans on a ladder of threat towards the European.

The people are fighting, but the White man in uniform will control them successfully	20
Perceives aggression towards the White but he himself is *clearly* negative towards this aggression and *rejects* it	16
The people are fighting; although the White man in uniform will not be able to control them, they do not harm him	14
It is a festival and the White man in uniform is merely a spectator	12
They are fighting, want to attack White man [*sic*] or are aggressive towards him without the respondent's taking up an attitude in favour of the figure	3
They are going to attack the White man but not necessarily kill him	2
They are going to kill the White man	0

(Erasmus 1984: 51)

Monitored by European psychologists as a pre-given entity that would ultimately yield its 'truth', the early 1970s confirmed the African personality as also the effect of a more general power mutation. For it was then that the psychological gaze became autonomous of its scientific conduits and internalized by Africans themselves.

Black consciousness and the alienated African

Viewed by conventional historians as among the high points of African resistance to colonial oppression, the 1970s emergence of Black Consciousness was also the moment where disciplinary fabrication of the African personality found its greatest confirmation.

> At the heart of this kind of thinking is the realization by the Blacks that the most potent weapon in the hands of the oppressor is the mind of the oppressed … Hence thinking along lines of Black Consciousness makes the Black man see himself as a being, entire in himself, and not as an extension of a broom or additional leverage to some machine. (Biko 1988/1972: 83)

For with Black Consciousness the African personality could exist even without the formal technologies of the psychological sciences. Instead, Black Consciousness being 'essentially an inward-looking process', the African personality was now the end-product of a confessional discourse in which the speaking subject was also the object of what was said. A recursive mechanism that refracted the psychological gaze through a revisionist history of the past, Black Consciousness invented Africans as the outcome of their own subjugation:

> It becomes more necessary to see the truth as it is if you realize that the only vehicle for change are these people who have lost their personality. The first step therefore is to make the black man come to himself; to pump back life into his empty shell; to infuse him with pride and dignity; to remind him of his complicity in the crime of allowing himself to be misused and therefore letting evil reign supreme in the country of his birth. (Biko 1988/ 1970a: 43)

Exemplifying the disciplinary process by which a positive power that creates is concealed in the identification of a repressive power being lifted, Black Consciousness enabled the recognition that 'blacks are suffering from inferiority complex – a result of 300 years of deliberate oppression' (Biko 1988/1970b: 35). Expressed as a strategic relation, knowledge is the other side of the power coin, and it was now possible through the device of 'alienation' to shape a new African personality that was the mirror image of the old.

In 1973 Manganyi's *Being-Black-in-the-World* compared the body image of healthy black subjects with that of black paraplegics. The effect of this investigation was to pathologize all Africans, for far from the 'dangerous individuals' of white psychological surveillance, the healthy subjects manifested the same diffusion of body-boundaries associated with the non-coping life strategies of hospitalized paraplegics (Manganyi 1973). Installation of the ordinary African as a psychological paraplegic demanded that the aetiology of this dysfunctionality be defined, and Manganyi's work fabricated the African body as an effect of racist socialization:

> [I]n the African experience there was over time developed a sociological schema of the black body prescribed by white standards. The prescribed attributes of this sociological schema have ... been entirely negative. It should be considered natural under these circumstances for an individual black person to conceive of his body image as something entirely undesirable, something which paradoxically must be kept at a distance outside of one's self so to speak. (Manganyi 1973: 51)

Borrowing from Fanon (1967), Manganyi later defined this second order problem as 'a racial epidermal schema' (1977: 15), and by 1981 the imperial forces that sustained this 'white mask' had been lifted further into visibility through historical investigations into how 'Euro-American psychologists have had a definite function and role in the history of (neo)colonial oppression' (Bulhan 1981: 25).

Feeding on its own resistance to invisibility and confirming the inevitable extension of surveillance into every dark space of the social and the psychological, the disciplinary micro-powers of the psychological sciences had moved full circle by the 1980s. So, just as the African personality had coalesced under the earlier regime to invent the African as a dangerous individual, it was now the personality of the white man that was the source of danger, corruption and alienation.

A liberatory psychology and the diffusion of danger

In 1985 the first edition of a psychological journal called *Psychology in Society* was published. This collected the previously scattered writings of 'critical psychologists' to consolidate a new psycho-social space, 'firmly rooted in the context of a changing South Africa and in the service of liberation' (Editorial 1986: 1). Against the preoccupation of earlier regimes with interrogating a pre-given African personality, the new focus was a human subject as the product of a dialectical relationship between the individual and the social:

> Critical psychology is based on the rejection of the polar extremes of psychologism (the reduction of cultural phenomena to psychological categories) and sociologism (social determinism). To the extent that sociology exclusively embraces the study of supra-individual forces while dismissing spsychic [*sic*] structure and agency it becomes sterile and devoid of meaning. But, on the other hand, to the extent that psychology tries to explain social phenomena by appealing simply to individual subjectivity it succumbs to the ideology of subjectivism which obscures the penetration of the individual by the social order. (Ivey 1986: 23)

Under this new theoretical configuration the 'African personality' was dissolved (Couve 1986), for within it the very notions of personality and the individual were themselves constituted as ideological fictions of industrial capitalism (Dawes 1986: 33–4).

Consistent with its mission to 'carve out the foundation of a practice which contributes to the real, not imagined, social arrangements in which full human lives may be lived' (Foster 1986: 65), this new psychology traversed a space of historical depth and interdisciplinary breadth: from the beginnings of colonial occupation at the Cape (Lambley 1980), into the possible future of a democratic state (Seedat 1993); and from the exploitative interests underpinning capitalist industry (Muller and Cloete 1987), to the sinister darkness of torture and detention chambers (Foster and Skinner 1990).

The danger that had provoked the initial installation and continuous renegotiation of the African personality was thus relocated from the individual and diffused into an all-pervasive threat which infiltrated each and every person, profession, practice, relationship and environment. By the 1990s, danger, which initially had resided only in the dark space of mind, had with this most recent power mutation come to be seen as lurking everywhere, each and every individual an agent of moral surveillance, scrutinizing others with infinite care so as to locate them in an unwritten taxonomy of psycho-political correctness or deviance. The diffusion of danger is therefore complete and totalizing, and the psychological sciences, for all their characterization by some of the sentries of sovereignty as irrelevant and ineffectual in an African context, are, as a mode of discipline, omnipresent and inescapable.

Notes

This chapter is adapted from an earlier version appearing in *Social Science and Medicine*, Vol. 42, no. 2 as 'The Industrial Panopticon: Mining and the medical construction of migrant African labour in South Africa, 1900–1950', pp. 185–97. It is reproduced with kind permission from Elsevier Science Ltd, The Boulevard, Langford Lane, Kidlington OX5 1GB, UK.

1. For a social and intellectual history of the 'African mind' and 'ethno-psychiatry' in Kenya, Madagascar, Rhodesia (now Zimbabwe), and other African countries, see McCulloch (1995).

2. A 1996 reprinting of this text (W. Sachs 1996) includes two introductory essays (by Saul Dubow and Jacqueline Rose) that offer a social history of Sachs and the origins of a South African psychoanalytic tradition.

CHAPTER 8

Filth, Food and Freedom: Public Health and its Changing African Objects

Preoccupied with gaps between bodies and the interface separating bodies and the non-corporeal world, public-health technologies ex-emplify the productive power of disciplinary space, which is the contextual condition of possibility for the identity of the objects within it. Following Armstrong's (1993) use of Mary Douglas's *Purity and Danger* (1966), one way of exploring this space is to view its characteristics as produced by the hygienic rituals codified within public-health practices.

At one level, hygienic rules are a means of identifying and keeping separate that which must be kept apart. To illustrate this, Douglas (1966) analysed the dietary rules in Leviticus and Deuteronomy which give a listing of animals, distinguishing between those which may and may not be eaten. She argued that the only way of understanding the allocation of animals to either of these two classes was the principle of completeness or 'holiness' which demanded that different categories of things were not confused.

> In the firmament two-legged fowls fly with wings. In the water scaly fish swim with fins. On the earth four-legged animals hop, jump or walk. Any class of creatures which is not equipped for the right kind of locomotion in its element is contrary to holiness. (Douglas 1966: 55)

For example, because the eel and the shellfish live in the water but do not have fins and scales, they were part of an anomalous group and therefore unclean: '"Everything in the waters that has not fins and scales is an abomination to you"' (Leviticus xi, in Douglas 1966: 42). Analogously, 'dirt' or 'filth' – which feature so prominently in the discourse of public health – are essentially matter out of place, and rules of hygiene themselves function like religious interdicts to keep separate that which must be kept apart.

What Armstrong (1993) adds to this analysis is an examination of a further effect Fof pollution rituals for, in addition to ensuring the purity of the spaces they are designed to keep separate, these rituals highlight the boundary itself:

> The boundary between 'protected' spaces is a line across which pollution threatens to pass. But in closer focus it can appear to be more than a linear dimension: rather it becomes a space or region marked out by its own conceptual axes and containing its own anomalous objects excluded by the contextual classification system. This boundary line is a residuum of social order, a twilight place of outcasts, danger and pollution … Seemingly within the line itself, in a space without volume, lurks threat and danger which cannot be ordered, only contained. This unruly region separates and defines the fundamental spaces of social life, yet somehow seems to lie outside of the social. (Armstrong 1993: 393–4)

This chapter follows Armstrong into this unruly space of productive power by analysing the public-health practices that from the second half of the nineteenth century have had as their object and effect the relation of the African body to public-health space.

Sanitary science and the emergence of a body boundary zone

During the mid-1900s a respatialization of illness occurred that for the first time made it possible to conceive of the volume of the African body as a distinct space alongside the physical space of the environment. Previously (see Chapter 4), disease illuminated not bodies but the characteristics of places, for the causes of sickness had been seen to reside in the interplay of the air, the soil, water and the sun (e.g. Kay 1834; Lichtenstein 1812). While this geo-climatic spatialization of disease sustained the technique of quarantine aimed at keeping diseased and non-diseased localities apart by preventing the movement of bodies between them, those bodies themselves (their characteristics, attributes, identities and so on) remained irrelevant and therefore unanalysed.

Around 1850 this public-health focus on places was reversed by a concern which replaced the geo-climatic space of old with a socio-physical one. This was 'sanitary science', and problematized not movements of disease into the body from the atmosphere, but rather the reciprocal exchange of energy and matter between human bodies and external space. This new gaze established as its effect and as the primary object of public-health surveillance the boundary zone which separated anatomical from environmental space:

> Man lives in a medium on the surface of the Earth – absolutely necessary for the support of life and that medium is pure atmosphere. Essentially

necessary for the preservation of his health or for the recovery of his health when lost. Fish live in a medium and that medium is water. Water, either fresh or salt, if one poison the water in proportion to the amount of poison will the Fish sicken and die. In like manner if one poison the atmosphere, man will either sicken and die – in proportion to the amount of poison contained in the atmosphere, because the blood unless it can be subjected to the influence of pure atmosphere in its passage through the Lungs becomes hurtfull [*sic*] to the body, oppressive to the Brain, unfit for the reproduction of healthy tissue, the freedom from disease and the support and nourishment of the Body in General. (Fitzgerald 1859, in Cory Library: Folder 3, 200–1)

In this new regime it was the body itself that was the most prominent source of danger to atmospheric purity, for: 'A body in a state of disease is like a volcano in action and is constantly eliminating from the Lungs, skin and various organs of the Body Noxious matter and Effluvia hurtful to it and no longer to be endured' (Fitzgerald 1859, in Cory Library: Folder 3, 201). Purity of the body and purity of the atmosphere were therefore each contingent on the purity of the other, and it was through the deployment of rules directed at controlling the exchange of matter between these two categories of completeness that the African body entered the regime of sanitary science.

The 'Christianized Kaffir' as a public-health problem By the 1870s the boundary zone delineating anatomical from environmental space was itself located in a more encompassing pair of categories. On the one hand, the 'natural' and therefore pure category of 'tribal' life, and on the other hand the equally pure category of the European city and 'civilization'. In between was an indeterminate region that gave rise to the 'Christianized Kaffir' who, belonging to neither the tribe nor the town, was an anomalous object and so particularly hazardous to health. This danger issued from the incomplete 'civilization' conferred by 'Christianization', which altered clothing habits to interrupt the proper exchange of matter and energy between the body and the environment:

Among the ... Kaffirs, cases resembling phthisis are often met with; but I believe that most of these are cases of pneumonia becoming chronic through neglect. This is more especially the case among Christianised Kaffirs, because the wild Kaffir wears only a blanket, and when he gets wet, as soon as he returns to his hut he throws off his blanket, and does not sit or sleep with his wet blanket round him but lies naked on a mat before the fire. But the Christianised Kaffir, who wears European clothes, does not trouble to change them when he gets wet, as it is too much trouble, but keeps them on and sleeps in them, and is thus, through help of civilization, more subject to bronchitis and pneumonia, the latter often through neglect terminating in abscess of the lung. (Egan 1877: 112)

Against this momentary focus on the two-way exchange of energy across the skin of the African, the gaze of sanitary science was, until around 1910, preoccupied with the unidirectional policing of matter moving from the African body into the 'atmosphere' absorbed by European bodies. Particularly hazardous were substances belonging to neither the body nor the environment (e.g. faeces, urine, saliva). It was therefore the bowel and the mouth through which these were expressed that emerged as the dominant objects in this nascent regime of sanitary science.

In 1888, for instance, it could be said that 'the Public Health at Kimberley and other Towns' (Fitzgerald 1888: 4) would be much improved by a sewage disposal system that kept separate categories of human waste which did not belong together.

> [C]an it be conducive to Public Health to have a number of human beings congregated close together in Towns and Cities with a number of Cesspools and one Tub Closets containing fluids and solids in their midst, constantly undergoing fermentation, and giving forth foul emanations poisoning the atmosphere they breathe? Why should we mix solids and fluids together, thus making a poisonous and disease-generating mixture polluting the air? From the natural organization of our bodies, it was never intended we should do so. On the contrary, it is clearly pointed out to us that we should get rid of them as speedily as possible without mixture. (Fitzgerald 1888: 4)

Alongside faeces and urine, the 'microbe' was among the most threatening of objects inhabiting the newly discerned body-boundary zone, 'for there is now scarcely a medical subject ... which is not supposed to have its microbe or pathogenic organism' (Messum 1895: 268). The 'microbe' was less a discovery than a surveillance device, for in demanding that its passage through space be mapped it outlined those bodily regions across which disease-causing organisms might pass into the world of people, places and things. To wherever it turned, the sanitary gaze filled the environment with such organisms as they swarmed from the earth (Public Health Notes 1894: 75), from the blankets and bodies of the African (Fuller 1897: 43), from the 'tools, implements and c.' used by rural Africans (Impey 1896: 32), and from the mouth of the 'church native':

> Properly conducted and careful enquiries ... will nearly always show a focus of infection. This in nine cases out of ten is the servant-maid; she is generally a church native, and almost invariably wears stockings. She, it can be

proved, has wantonly kissed the baby; it gets syphilis. The unsuspecting master also inflicts upon his offspring a chaste and paternal kiss and, as a partial consequence, he gets a hard sore on his glans or prepuce. Thus the disease gradually osculates the whole community. (M.O.M. 1894: 154)

By the turn of the twentieth century the body-boundary zone had thus expanded into a three-dimensional space that established the contours of the African body as an anonymous anatomical container and isolated as immanent sources of danger its points of greatest permeability to the external world. The occurrence of bubonic plague between 1900 and 1904 further insinuated this socio-physical space into the gaps between bodies by illuminating a series of dark corners in the cities which sanitary inspection revealed as especially dangerous owing to the dense intermingling within them of different bodies: 'Whole streets were inhabited by natives, and in some houses close to the leading thoroughfares the cellars were occupied by large numbers of men – Europeans, Malays, and raw Kafirs – all sandwiched together, living in a state of the utmost neglect, disease and vice' (Graham 1902, in Swanson 1977: 400)

If the occurrence of disease could be identified with such admixtures of different bodies, then its prevention demanded that those same bodies be separated out, and through their aggregation the minute interstices of contact between different bodies precipitated the formation of a massive new surface for public-health intervention.

Plague and the new hygiene of 'Location' A means of control through segregation, confinement and surveillance, the idea of 'Location' crystallized an otherwise indistinct relationship between the disorder of urban space and the production of disease. In revealing to the sanitary eye the failure of Africans to manage adequately the passage of matter across their body-boundaries, the plague offered powerful confirmation for the strategy of 'Location' as a means by which to combat such disorder. Its initial effect was to install the African body as part of the environment, as a threat to the European which could not be ordered, only contained. Giving evidence on the plague in Natal, Durban's Medical Officer of Health could observe: 'Of course, with an Indian or Kaffir population constant supervision is essential, for their ideas of sanitation are not sufficient, in my opinion, to allow them to live in any area where Europeans reside' (Munson, in Hill 1904: 9).

Between 1900 and 1904 the productive power of the plague as a disciplinary device was realized in the installation of geographically defined locations outside Cape Town (1901), Port Elizabeth (1903),

Johannesburg (1904), and a host of smaller towns, in each instance as a direct result of the plague appearing within them to shine a sanitizing light into 'every yard, hole and corner' where previously 'everyone ... [was] allowed to go except a policeman' (South African Native Affairs Commission 1905: 652).

However, the strategy of 'Location' transgressed the hygienic rules which demanded that bodies be kept separate to prevent their pollution via the dangerous accumulation around them of exhaled air, sweat and other substances that belonged neither to the body nor the environment. Even at the point of its installation, 'Location' was therefore a site for the resurgence of disciplinary surveillance to the interface between the interior of the African body and the environment. Arguing that local authorities were evading their responsibilities by using the African as a 'sanitary whipping boy', a 1904 editorial called not for the abolishment but rather the refinement of 'Location' as an hygienic strategy:

> When such people are transferred from their own environment to one exacting a totally different habit of thought and practice the clear duty of the white man who has learnt his lesson is to pass that lesson on to them ... Our paramount duty is to face the burden of a better and more expensive hygienic supervision than is necessary with the man of white skin. (Editorial 1904: 71)

'Location' thus became a strategy which combined the repressive tactics of separation and enclosure with the subtle segmentations associated with discipline, at once to enable the sanitary segregation and surveillance of Africans, and produce them as 'docile' and 'regimented' bodies.

> That Natives and Asiatics, other than those employed in domestic service, should reside apart in a specially allotted district of the town is ... highly desirable. These people have moral ideas and social habits widely divergent from those of educated Europeans, and this fact alone fully justifies such racial segregation. To the hygienist, however, the most convincing argument is the facility which is afforded for sanitary control, more especially in respect of communicable diseases. (Watkins-Pitchford 1908: 73)

By interpolating hygienic surveillance into its closed domain, the native location became an observatory for the minute surveillance of the sanitary behaviour of Africans. The effect of this was to revivify the earlier focus on the 'Christianized Kaffir' as an anomalous object produced in the unruly region between African tradition and European civilization.

The dressed native as object and problem   Where previously the sanitary gaze to the African body-boundary had been preoccupied with monitoring matter passed out of it, this was now complemented by an equivalent focus on policing the substances that moved into the African body from the environment. Food, for instance, became the subject of close scrutiny and a device by which sanitary science elaborated the African mouth with teeth, which as the first point of contact for many substances entering it was a particularly dangerous part of the body-boundary zone. Thus, both Mitchell (1908) and Bruce Bays (1908) offered comparisons of the African's diet under 'natural conditions' and in the location: 'Consisting mainly of mealies, pumpkin, sweet potatoes, and sour milk ... with meat occasionally and as a luxury', the tribal African's diet was 'healthy and nutritious' (Mitchell 1908: 258). In contrast, the African in the location: 'may feed at home on the offal of beasts of the slaughter-houses, on coffee, perhaps condensed milk and again on white bread ... [T]he result is that the teeth tend early to decay, and to become organs no longer required' (Bruce Bays 1908: 267).

The minute surveillance of the African body-boundary enabled by 'Location' thus marked completion of the great cycle of interchange involving contamination and purification of the substances exchanged between the environment and the anatomical space of the body. For the African body now existed as the point where the arc of matter moving outwards was met by an equivalent arc of inward movement. Confirming this, a 1914 Tuberculosis Commission report (Union of South Africa 1914) matched each of its investigations into matter which departed the African body with an equivalent focus on that which entered it. Talking of the native's 'apparently ineradicable ... dislike to ventilation in his dwelling' the report observed:

> windows, and ventilation openings he persistently blocks up. If possible he will always have a fire in his sleeping place. The hotter and stuffier the air the better he likes it. Added to this he invariably sleeps with his head wrapped up in a blanket. If the blanket were clean there would be no great harm in this, on the contrary it would act to some degree as a filter both to himself of the air he inhales, and to others of the breath he exhales. (Union of South Africa 1914: 103)

Complementing this attention to the nose and mouth as points where dangerous substances moved into the African body, these were now also visible as orifices that expressed dangerous matter into the environment:

> all natives are in fact most careless and filthy in regard to their nasal and buccal secretions. He will foul his fingers with it and after 'cleaning' them

on his own bare leg, on the floor or the neighbouring wall of the hut, or anything else convenient, he may dip into the common eating utensil. (Union of South Africa 1914: 102)

Contemporaneous with the crystallization of the 'dressed native', McVicar had in 1908 argued for a system of medical inspection and health instruction in 'native schools' as a means by which hygienic habits could be inculcated in the African: 'It is they who are likely to spread infectious or contagious disease. It is their unhygienic habits and their ignorance that require to be remedied' (McVicar 1908: 314). Such suggestions directed to recruiting individual Africans into managing their own body-boundaries were, however, signs of a public-health regime to come, for it would be another thirty years before they began to find any sustained application in relation to the African. Instead, and cementing the invention by sanitary science of the dangers to health as residing in the lines between the anonymous anatomical body and the environment, the regime of sanitary science gave rise to a centralized control technology aimed at policing the movement of impurities across the body-boundary through tactics of 'prevention and suppression'.

Policing impurity: the Public Health Act of 1919 Until its formalization in South Africa's first Public Health Act of 1919, the requirement for a centralized health administration was evident more by its absence than in its presence. For example, editorials criticized the fact of 'similar health calamities [being] ... dealt with in different ways' (Editorial 1911), because 'Municipalities are not always intelligent bodies ... some doing nothing at all for a long time, and then, under the influence of panic and negrophobism, rushing into paths wherein angels fear to tread' (Editorial 1914: 121).

In 1918–19 the influenza pandemic once again highlighted neglect of the boundary zone between the body and the environment, an Influenza Commission report advocating 'the necessity of devoting immediate attention to the improvement of housing and sanitary conditions in slum areas and locations' (Union of South Africa 1919: 54). In the same year the Public Health Act No. 36 of 1919 established the Department of Public Health as a central coordinating body charged with standardizing the methods of observation and mechanisms for the 'prevention and suppression' of infectious diseases deployed by each local authority.

The end result of repeated inscription in administrative consciousness of the anonymous border between the mass of bodies in the population and the external environment, the Act gave the force of law to tactics for its monitoring and control. Its nine chapters and 161 sections contained no mention of the person as an idiosyncratic individual with thoughts, beliefs or emotions. Rather, its network of hygienic regulations coincided exactly with the body-boundary zone between corporeal and non-corporeal space. Factories, for instance, should be designed to make provision for the prevention of sweating; the regulations governing housing laid down a complex of laws concerning ventilation, lighting, space, the storage of food and disposal of sewage, while the Act's 'Food and Drug Adulteration Laws' set out standards governing the nature, quality and composition of foodstuffs.

In 1923, these procedures found their first systematic codification in Reid's *Sanitation and Public Health*. This instructed readers in how to detect such sanitary dangers as the ill-ventilated room, which 'on entering rapidly from the outside the sense impression gives a good idea as to whether ... its air is fresh or stuffy, oppressive or smelly' (Reid 1927: 50); how to identify for various infectious diseases 'the channels of invasion, or ports of entry into the body'(Reid 1927: 264); and how to fumigate rooms and disinfect 'articles like furs, feathers, bound books and leather goods which would be damaged by steam or liquid disinfectants' (Reid 1927: 241).

Syphilis prevention and personal health In radiating regulatory tactics into the body-boundary zone, the great achievement of sanitary science was to manufacture this as a visible interface amenable to manipulation in the fight against disease. However, this was also its greatest failing, since while laws governing such things as the design of buildings and the quality of foodstuffs could be enforced with relative ease, the external regulation of more intimate bodily activities – such as bowel movements, bathing and sexual intercourse – could not.

Emblematic of this failure was the mid-1920s' recognition of difficulties surrounding the 'prevention and suppression' of syphilis in Africans. Since 1909 'special anti-syphilitic measures' (Colonial Secretary 1910: 1) had sought to prevent its spread by making the issue of passes allowing natives to be present in European areas conditional on their being examined and treated for syphilis. In 'urban areas to which the Urban Areas Pass Regulations apply' (Colonial Secretary 1910: 2), these made it compulsory for all male natives suspected of having the disease to submit to a medical examination for the purpose of its detection. By 1928, however, the Department of Public Health began to comment on the 'special difficulties' attaching to this repressive strategy, which because it did not extend compulsory examination to native females had little effect on preventing the spread of syphilis through prostitution:

Under the pass system obtaining in some of the Provinces, a measure of control can be exercised in regard to males, but action on these lines in regard to females is extremely difficult. Native females are frequently commercialized purveyors of the disease, and in the large labour centres of the Northern and Eastern Transvaal frequently operate in gangs. It was hoped that with the coming into operation of the Natives (Urban Areas) Act, No. 21 of 1923, it would be possible through the agency of matrons of Native hostels and otherwise, to exercise a measure of control and supervision over Native females and to exclude from urban areas undesirable and redundant Natives of both sexes, but up to the present this hope has not been realized. (Union of South Africa 1928: 47)

By 1930 these procedures were not only seen as ineffective, but as inducing effects opposite to their aims of syphilis control. On the one hand, they produced the suspicion that an increased prevalence of venereal diseases was due to 'free and convenient treatment facilities ... [encouraging] exposure to infection and consequent spread' (Union of South Africa 1930: 47). For even as it failed, the creative power of the sanitary gaze was still able to illuminate the African's 'moral' make-up as a potentially important link in the chain of prevention:

A large percentage of such patients is almost entirely 'a-moral' and many are without any feelings of shame or common decency. They will often freely admit to repeated exposure to infection, or even perhaps to incest; re-infections after a period of prolonged, troublesome, and expensive treatment are not uncommon. (Union of South Africa 1930: 47)

On the other hand, attempts to expand the system of enforced medical examination to include 'all natives in domestic service' (male and female) were found to 'arouse intense antagonism and resistance amongst the native population' (Union of South Africa 1930: 47), driving the disease underground where it was inaccessible to the centralized lines of sanitary surveillance. Accordingly, and in place of these prohibitive practices, it could now be suggested that 'tactful methods and friendly persuasion – coupled with suitable methods for voluntary treatment – will in most cases yield the best results' (Union of South Africa 1930: 47).

As the failure of sanitary science became increasingly evident in relation to not only syphilis, but also malaria, tuberculosis and other diseases, so public health mutated into an increasingly synaptic configuration of disciplinary power. Against the concern with 'prevention and suppression', this nascent regime of 'personal health' (Reid 1927: 346) crystallized around the new idea of 'health' as something to be achieved through training the habits of individuals towards greater cleanliness, better diet and closer attention to the well-being of themselves and their families:

> While the liability to contract infectious diseases depends greatly on the environment of the individual, the cause of constitutional diseases depends more on personal habits and ways of living and as to how far the rules of health and laws of nature are obeyed ... Public Acts and Laws are chiefly designed to promote the health of communities through improving environmental conditions, by removing anything insanitary liable [*sic*] to be injurious to the general health. Personal hygiene is mainly directed to the promotion of the health of the individual. It aims at increasing the vital forces of the body so as to prevent constitutional disease. (Reid 1927: 346)

The new vision of personal health found rapid expression in state commitments to 'the dissemination of knowledge of the simple principles of healthy living ... amongst all races and classes of the population' (Union of South Africa 1929: 1), and by 1930 the socio-physical space of sanitary science was rapidly being replaced by the psycho-social space of a new public health. Soon to be known as 'social medicine', its attempts to recruit Africans themselves into the surveillance of anatomical spaces and body-boundaries would 'recognise countless individualities ... each composed of different constitutions, habits and idiosyncrasies' (Armstrong 1993: 401).

Social medicine and a psycho-social space

Summarizing this shift in public-health power, Cluver's 1934 *Public Health in South Africa* stressed the primacy of tactics that could persuade individuals to monitor their own body-boundaries:

> Our first aim will be attained when we have induced the individual to eat food in correct quantity and quality, to live in atmospheres with sufficiently high cooling power whose action is not neutralised by incorrect clothing, to respond to muscular exertion by suitable psychological stimuli, and generally to live in accordance with the findings of the science of physiology. (Cluver 1934: Introduction)

To induct individuals into such a regime demanded that the psycho-social factors inhibiting the adoption of healthy habits be identified, and social medicine was thus the origin of a lowering in the descriptive threshold of power sufficient to manufacture the previously irrelevant customs and beliefs of Africans as its analysable objects and effects. This expansion of public-health space beyond the body's anatomical contours into the intangible topography of beliefs transformed the

African into a more pliable entity than had been sustained by the regime of sanitary science. For, as Gale noted in 1938, the fundamental health problem was now '*the problem of how to win over an illiterate people, still loyal in thought and in practice to medical ideas and customs intimately associated with deep-rooted ancestral superstitions, to a confidence in and utilisation of the sciences and art of western twentieth century medicine*' (Gale 1938: 8–9, emphasis in original).

Intertwined with this emerging focus to the beliefs it installed behind the African's overt hygienic behaviours was the cognitive device of viewing hygiene as coextensive with economic factors and patterns of African domestic economy: 'No amount of medical attention or instruction in hygiene will avail unless the Natives possess the facilities for observing any rules and regulations that may be promulgated ... The observance of instruction in medical hygiene is intimately wrapped up in the economic factor' (Kark 1934a: 18).

To establish this link between hygienic behaviour and the 'economic factor' demanded not only that better statistics be maintained to 'investigate thoroughly the incidence of disease in the native', but also mechanisms of surveillance able to construct the interrelationships between such factors as 'accommodation', 'ventilation', 'diet', 'sanitary conditions' and 'superstitions and other racial traditions' (Kark 1934b: 67). Illness was thus relocated from the elementary space of the body-boundary zone discerned by sanitary science into this complex space of multi-factorial causation, and the nascent gaze of social medicine required a new technology for mapping and monitoring its distribution. This crystallized in the roving device of the survey, which now became an increasingly prominent technique of surveillance alongside the older methods of observation from the geographically fixed points of clinics and notification offices.

Surveying a psycho-social space: problematization of the normal   A system for fabricating immunity through the modification of individual constitutions, social medicine demanded a technology of seeing that could dissolve the binary division of the population into the ill and the healthy and so induct everyone into its network of visibility. Hence a key manifestation was its 'problematization of the normal' (Armstrong 1995: 5). In relation to the African, this commenced between 1935 and 1945 with a swarming of the survey and its diffusion of a normalizing gaze into African schools, townships and rural areas, to bring everyone into the eye of this new public medicine through the medicalization of everyday life.

Established in 1934, the Society for the Study of Medical Conditions among the Bantu (Kark 1935) had as one of its first projects 'a scheme for investigating mathematically several thousand native school children' (Editorial 1935: 3). Suggesting the novelty that attached to this new way of seeing was Achterberg's characterization of native schools and classrooms around Johannesburg as

> an enormous virgin field of medical research lying fallow practically at the very doorstep of the medical school ... In native schools within the municipal area of Johannesburg ... there are enrolled at present 7,000 pupils ... Within a distance of 30 miles from Johannesburg, there are an additional 3,000 pupils ... The possibilities for research work are boundless. Accurate means for judging age and reliable age-norms are needed. There is the fundamental investigation ... of vision, hearing, nose and throat, teeth, nutrition, and the incidence of hookworm and syphilis. (Achterberg 1935: 10)

In the same year Orford reported on a 'somatometrical study of bodily habitus in the Bantu female' that delineated 'the normal types of bodily form' (Orford 1935: 41), and in 1936 Broomberg investigated the blood pressure of '250 apparently normal Zulu adults' to reveal the variability of this normality by showing higher average readings for town-dwelling as compared to rural natives (Broomberg 1936: 32). Fox and Back's (1938) survey mapped the relation between agricultural practices, nutritional status and health in the Transkei, while nutrition surveys (Anning 1938; Le Riche 1938) combined anthropometric measurements with home budget studies to draw a line between bodily dimensions, patterns of domestic expenditure, ideas about the nutritional value of different foodstuffs and occupation. Meyer's (1941) 'physical measurements of Bantu school children' offered 'indications regarding the processes of bodily growth' by which deviations from the norm could be detected, while health surveys of African school children (Becklake 1943; Kark and Le Riche 1944) provided a perceptual grid in which to locate individual children on a continuum of health through the normalizing inspection of 'build' ('linear, intermediate, lateral'), 'posture' ('satisfactory, fatigued, scoliosis'), 'skin' ('elastic, dry, rough, mosaic'), and so on (Becklake 1943: 30).

By impinging upon the bodies and minds of all Africans, the survey erased the earlier distinction between the sick and the well to manufacture everyone as ill.

> Sit in your car ... and watch the people who pass to and fro along the sidewalk. They are folk, white and black, who make up the main bulk of our population ... Do they appear to be healthy? ... The answer is, quite definitely, no ... The people do not achieve that optimum of health which

we really mean when we talk brightly about an A1 nation. (Anning 1938: 7–8)

In short, the survey superimposed a new psycho-social space upon the socio-physical space of sanitary science. This psycho-social space was a series of gaps between bodies that were important not only for the 'microbes' passing to and fro, but also for the meaning that flowed between them, and so could now be caught up in a systematic health education campaign directed to their hygienic modification and regimentation.

'To the back of the black man's mind': educating the individual The survey's problematization of normality established a new objective for the practice of social medicine. Since everyone was now ill this required that everyone be made well, and with the survey's elaboration as a perceptual technique there arose a complementary focus on analysing 'health propaganda' and 'health education' as components of an expressive technology directed towards the manufacture of a healthy nation. 'A Ministry of Health!' exclaimed the South African Department of Public Health in 1937: 'the nation must be made health conscious and health minded rather than sickness conscious and sickness minded' (Union of South Africa 1937: 26).

No longer only the passive object of a centralized Panoptical power, the individualized African of the survey was now becoming its vehicle, an active conduit of discipline which through proper education could be recruited into the machinery of this new medicine as his own overseer, exercising surveillance over, and against, himself. Hence the possibility of a public-health gaze that extended to the very 'back of the black man's mind':

> Does the European doctor or Sanitary Inspector really believe he can get at the back of the black man's mind, or trace the history of an outbreak of disease among the kraals as a native can? I believe that the [best] approach to the black man is by the black man supervised by the white and also that the main attack must be educational and that it must be kraal to kraal … The country people … must be tackled at their homes, by visiting and demonstrations … and the iron hand of the law is best hidden in the velvet glove of persuasion. (Park-Ross 1937: 29)

Confirming the synaptic nature of the disciplinary power productive of this new regime, Anning observed that through health education each individual should be made into his own diagnostician, for 'the root of national and individual health … depends primarily upon diagnosis, and the primary diagnostician is the sufferer' (Anning 1938:

10). What this required was a technique to increase the efficiency of individuals in reading their own state of health, for so long as 'consciousness of social incapacity' instead of 'subjective state of disease' continued to guide the search for treatment, so would people continue to remain sickness- rather than health-minded. 'We must think in terms of the opportunity for everyone to maintain and develop their health, and of assisting them to detect and suppress the first signs of illness' (Anning 1938: 8).

With this transformation, the repressive legislation and 'usual herd methods of examination, when all and sundry are stripped and examined in the mass' (Union of South Africa 1937: 57) that sanitary science had applied to the control of venereal disease, were now 'contrary to usually accepted health principles in so far as they tend to destroy co-operation and sympathy'. Instead, and where compulsory examination in the pass office and native clinic did still occur, it was transformed from a ritual of repression into a relay for the constructive power of discipline. 'The ... medical examination ... is a channel for health education and propaganda ... and much could be done through this contact to awaken his [the African's] intelligent interest and cooperation in hygiene' (Union of South Africa 1937: 57–8).

Complementing the transformation of pass offices and clinics into relays for the dispersal of hygienic discipline was the new figure of the 'native health assistant', an ambulatory agent of health propaganda designed to internalize the vigilant gaze of social medicine within the homes and minds of everyone:

> These men, of good address and of sufficient age to carry weight with their fellows, have a background of intensive instruction in the working of the human body, the meaning of infection, the methods of spread of infectious disease, and the prevention of that spread. They have been equipped to follow up cases of infectious disease, and the contacts of such cases; to gain the interest and the confidence of the sufferers and their families in order to encourage them to attend at the clinics; to deliver lectures on health topics in beer halls, cinemas and schools; to prepare health pamphlets in Zulu; to inspect and report on defects of housing and sanitation. (Anning 1937: 7)

The aim of health education being to recruit each and every individual into the service of monitoring their own body-boundary zones, this could be facilitated by having native health assistants promulgate a device such as Hertslet's (1946) 'score-card' for a 'better home' and 'better family' competition. Taken 'into the Native locations, townships, black belts and reserves' (Hertslet 1946: 22), the 'score-card' first analysed the sanitary environment of the home and garden into thirty elements, each to be scored out of 10 or 20. The second part addressed twenty-five 'parts of the body' (e.g. eyes, gums, kidneys and bladder, sleeping, and 'mental'), each of which was evaluated for each family member according to its condition. For instance: 'Bowels: Open once or twice daily without medicine (3); No discomfort (2); No diarrhoea (2); No bleeding (1); No pain or burning (2)' (Hertslet 1946: 26). Completion of these sanitary and bodily inventories would establish for each individual and each family the reality of hygiene and health as inscribed in the relationships between the body and the environment, which once internalized would 'help their people to walk ... and practice the ways of clean and right living' (Hertslet 1946: 22).

Crystallization of health education as a tactic of health promotion also found its way into the native school. Through native health assistants and teachers specially trained in the subject, social medicine now realized the long recognized potential of the classroom as a site for the creation of individual health, where 'the *learner provides in his own person the subject-matter* with which both the training and the study are concerned' (Dugard 1944: 418). There was education and training in nutrition, domestic science and school gardening aimed at cultivating 'a taste for protective foods which will last him through life' (Dugard 1944: 418), while training in physiology, disease transmission and personal hygiene made each child's emotions the locus of their own sanitary supervision:

> My experience of Native children has been that they simply do not mind having dried food and nasal discharges and flies all over their faces ... In other words, it does not seem to be much good telling a child *why* he should be clean ... Our real aim should be to create in him an active dislike of dirt, so that his reaction to it is emotional rather than intellectual. (McGregor 1944: 419)

Finally, and as the tactic by which discipline could engrave itself at the subconscious level of pride in the body, there was the new focus on 'physical culture': 'Knowledge of the body in action must be studied and through the application of psychological and hygienic principles along with a better appreciation of the dynamics of movement, physique may be fortified, resistance to disease increased, and thus life may be healthier, happier and more productive' (Shearer 1938: 13).

The 'physical education lesson' thus established an alliance between the free yet controlled movement of bodies and the regime of personal hygiene, as through the game of 'the mulberry bush', where to the tune of 'Here We Go Round the Mulberry Bush' were substituted verses depicting such hygienic rituals as washing the face, cleaning teeth, hands, feet, combing the hair and running to school (Huntley n.d.: 78). Such games and exercises were at one and the same time a means of observing the body and disciplining it: 'While they are singing they should fit appropriate actions to the words ... The teacher should see that the actions are correctly performed, and that during the singing of the chorus the children skip or run neatly, with small, vigorous, skipping steps' (Huntley n.d.: 78–9)

The Polela Native Health Unit and the African as a person Deployed independently, the productive capacity of surveys and health education was subject to clear limitations. Alone, the survey was restricted to making visible patterns of health and disease in the population. Without this information, health promotion and health education lacked any clearly defined targets. To maximize their productive power required that the receptive technology of the survey be closely synchronized with the messages identified to the expressive device of health education. Ideally, the two should be fused into a seamless exercise of surveillance–subjectification, the dissemination of health knowledge occurring at the same time as the recording of surveillance information. In 1940, following Gear's (1938) proposals for 'experimental health areas' where continuous surveillance coincided with ongoing intervention, the Polela Native Health Unit was established in Natal to realize just such a fusion of surveillance and subjectification, and with it a concentration of discipline sufficient to produce the African as a person.

The geographical space of the Polelea unit was first rendered calculable by 'mapping', whereby the entire area was partitioned into subdivisions small enough for a single native health assistant to record the place, personal identity, family configuration and various indexes of sanitation, hygiene and health for the occupants of every homestead in his area. Into this objectified nucleus for the maintenance of 'population records ... and epidemiological data' (Union of South Africa 1941: 63) were then intruded an array of surveillance techniques, every one a conscious attempt to make visible the web of human relations and recruit each individual into this synaptic network of disciplinary power.

During 'home to home visits of ALL the homes in specific areas, regardless of the presence or absence of ill health in a particular home' (Union of South Africa 1945: 36), members of each family were encouraged to talk about sanitation, vegetable-growing, eating habits, sleeping patterns and so on (Kark 1942). This information was recorded on special cards that tabulated the relationships between health, education and employment indices for each individual in the family, such as the dimensions of rooms in the homestead; to what uses the rooms were put and what furniture they contained; diet, and qualitative observations concerning the family's 'health consciousness'. The family as a network of interpersonal persuasion was thereby constituted alongside the individual as a key object and conduit of this social medicine, and any illness within it could be related to such intimate observations as the fact that 'poultry share this hut with the family during sleeping hours', and while 'the head of the family is keen to progress ... his present wife is an extremely backward person, lazy and unkempt, and the home, unfortunately, reflects her personality. It is kept in an untidy and filthy condition' (Kark 1944: 46). Available to doctors treating patients at the unit's clinic and in the schools during routine medical inspections, these cards joined the otherwise separate fields of visibility represented by the school, the clinic and the home, to make each patient and his or her social spaces an integrated and open field of medical visibility: 'Instead of being cyphers, each man and woman, each child whether at school or not becomes a living entity with a home and a background, with thoughts and behaviour patterns – and each becomes an important part of our lives' (Union of South Africa 1945: 36).

Extending the power of this gaze to produce the African as a 'whole person', the unit had by 1945 phased out its 'specialised disease clinics' due to their

> 'dividing the indivisible', namely the patient. To such an extent has this become the case that a person is known and classified by the disease from which he suffers. Should there be two or more main pathological entities, e.g., syphilis, dysentery and tuberculosis then the person is put into three separate pigeonholes ... It is our contention that this is harmful and often leads to neglect not only of understanding a person as a person but of even missing some additional pathological factors influencing the individual's health. The Health Unit ... must therefore strip itself of this 'dividing of a person' and must use specialists and special clinics only where the practitioner of social medicine finds it necessary in the interest of the patient. (Union of South Africa 1945: 36–7)

Complementing home visits by which the medical gaze pervaded the psycho-social fabric of the community it constructed, a corresponding series of devices replicated the pattern of surveillance established at London's Pioneer Health Centre, where surveillance of the community had been achieved by bringing the community within the centre's own walls (see Armstrong 1983: 36). In the same way that all schools in Polela were used as observatories of health status and conduits for the creation of health in the home, so the formation of a Polela People's Club, and Saturday 'nutrition clinics' (National Health Services Commission 1944:

8653) infused the buildings and grounds of the unit's headquarters with the power to monitor and mould the health behaviour of the Africans that visited them.

Community health

While recognizing the 'countless individualities' it had recruited into its synaptic web of personal hygiene, social medicine had at the same time been a totalitarian regime. For although the individual was its relay, personal idiosyncrasies and cultural variations were acknowledged more as barriers to cultivating a regimented health consciousness than as conduits to collective well-being. As Kark had noted in 1944 of the Polela Native Health Unit:

> At the beginning we were met with very solid antagonism ... They did not understand these 'black spies' that the Government had sent out into their homes ... The trouble is that you are dealing with something around which there is a considerable number of beliefs. Our first job was to break down those beliefs. (National Health Services Commission 1944: 8650)

Against this totalizing tendency, and contemporaneous with Orwell's (1949) post-war celebration of a liberal-humanist subject, there commenced a reevaluation of African resistance to public health.

An analysis of resistance and the emergence of community In 1947 Kuper wrote on 'the concept of social medicine applied to some Bantu speaking tribes'. Noting that among the Bantu 'new ideas are seldom accepted with alacrity, especially if they involve action by the European government and if they attack fundamental and vital beliefs' (Kuper 1947: 55), this introduced a new way of seeing African resistance to European public health by analysing the 'political implications' of Bantu attitudes to health and medical practices. Reversing the direction taken by earlier assessments of African beliefs from the external perspective of the public-health official, Kuper's analysis adopted a frame of reference internal to the Bantu tribes she investigated.

Accordingly, Kuper could show how traditional medical practices were coeval with the structure of tribal authority, its hierarchical distribution of power, and an array of sexual and 'magico-social principles' (Kuper 1947: 59) which clustered around food and housing to ensure that 'diet, recreation and housing are never haphazard and uncontrolled', but followed 'traditional codes within the framework of tribal experience' (p. 58). The effect of this analysis was to reconfigure the African as an object of public-health practice by replacing the earlier focus on regimentation through rational persuasion with the idea that social medicine should be synthesized with African institutions in general:

> The modern European concept of social medicine is a historical development in a particular sociological setting. In Bantu society, with an entirely different background, we find a different approach to medicine ... To suggest that the African be simply 'argued out of his belief in witchcraft' – is useless, not because of any innate differences of mentality, but because of the different social conditioning. Our treatment of African health must therefore be regarded as part of the approach to African institutions in general. Only on that basis can 'social medicine' as conceived by twentieth century sociologists and medical men be made effective in the new environment of the Bantu. (Kuper 1947: 66)

Concretizing this shift by which the analysis of African resistance induced a current of public-health power within the capillary spaces of community force relationships was Schaap's (1953) paper 'Health Visiting Among the Urban Bantu'. This explored urban Africans' antagonism to health visitor instructions that premature babies be placed in special boxes to ensure they slept alone. Noting in some cases that the midwife's attempts to introduce the box to the mother were rejected by the infant's grandmother, the health education strategy was not to override but rather to coopt this newly recognized authority relationship:

> Much talk and persuasion on the part of the health visitor was required to convince that most important person in an African home, the grandmother. Thereafter, she tended to think the box her own idea and its magical properties the reasons for the child's survival. It is well for any health visitor starting work amongst the Africans to realise the importance of getting the grandmother on her side. (Schaap 1953: 534)

In 1957, and based on a similar analysis of African antipathy to health propaganda which failed to acknowledge the internal structure of African society, Goddard described a new series of venereal disease films which replaced earlier versions that had employed white actors: 'They caused great excitement because of the local setting, Bantu cast and the narrative which was woven around Bantu domestic life, its traditions and customs' (Goddard 1957: 18).

Albeit only hesitantly, these scattered commentaries on resistance signalled the formation of a new public-health space premised on a new dynamic of disciplinary power. For rather than trying to erase them through force of reason, the new space of community health had begun to transform the traditional structures and health beliefs of African society from anomalous objects into lines of force that could themselves be coopted into the production of health.

A community gaze   Exemplifying the object of community as an effect of this nascent 'community health', Kark and Steuart observed in 1957 that 'while effective health education must have precisely defined objectives, an attempt is made to avoid substituting one rigidity (ours) for another (the peoples')' (Kark and Steuart 1957: 133–4). Thus, where health education aimed at 'change in the interests of progressively improving states of health', it should at the same time 'achieve its ends by means that leave inviolate the rights of self-determination of the individual and his community' (Steuart 1962: 65):

> Health education will then be at odds with itself if it tries to perpetuate … 'the vandalism of restoration', if it attempts to re-fashion society on the model seen through the refracting lens of the health worker's culture. Manifestly this applies with increasing force, the greater the difference between the social and cultural make-up of the expert on the one hand, and the community he serves on the other. (Steuart 1962: 65)

The recognition of cultural relativity reconstituted the codes of public-health perception. Social medicine had involved complete calculability of the psycho-social through its precise mapping as a clearly demarcated series of relationships between epidemiological disease distributions, personal habits and economic factors, from which flowed the precisely measurable objectives of promotive health. Now, the very precision that had enabled social medicine to itemize public-health problems was itself seen to be a problem. As social medicine had criticized sanitary science for dividing the indivisible in the shape of the individual, so the community gaze now criticized social medicine for its fragmenting of the community:

> Whatever ends may be served by the necessary specific [*sic*] definition of clearly articulated targets, the range of targets should be based on the implicit recognition that the health and disease of a community cannot be described purely in terms of discrete items but also as a single complex, contributed to by the whole pattern of everyday living. (Steuart 1962: 68)

This 'single complex', which was the cognitive object of community health, could now begin to crystallize as a new strategy of attention localized illness and health to the interrelated points between which power was reflexively exercised by community residents. As Cassell (1962) observed in respect of 'community diagnosis', what 'would otherwise appear as a series of inexplicable interrelated acts' (Cassell 1962: 238) on the part of Africans refusing health-centre treatment for tuberculosis, found their own internal logic when viewed through a knowledge of cultural patterning and the social situation:

> A firm conviction existed that patients presenting symptoms of pulmonary tuberculosis were suffering from a disease that could only be treated by a skilled *inyanga* and about which White physicians could be expected to know little ... Should the Health Centre viewpoint be accepted, therefore, the patient was in danger of being feared and ostracized by the community. (Cassell 1962: 239–40)

'Community diagnosis' was, however, a mere precursor to the more important task of community treatment, which involved stimulating 'those processes of community in a community which might lead to active promotion of health' (Kark and Kark 1962: 9). One example of how such stimulation was to be achieved was the Steuart (1962) system for the cooption of 'primary groups' through the deployment of 'community structure files'. 'An index system of carding every group of whatever kind as it was "discovered" or use made of it in a programme' (Steuart 1962: 83), the primary groups it invented functioned as networks of concern which modulated the strains of everyday life to embed each individual in a self-regulating circuit of care:

> Internal communication among the members is likely to be continuous and intimate and deeply toned by an everyday familiarity. Primary friendship groups could be expected to exert, on the one hand, conformity pressures of a powerful kind because of the deep-seated attractiveness of membership and the fundamental human urges for acceptance and belonging. On the other hand, they may be able to tolerate certain differences among the members without rejecting them, and when pressures to conformity operate in respect of these differences, to be so coloured by personal friendship that conformity will result without undue strain on the individual. (Steuart 1962: 82)

A direct consequence of the South African state's repression of public-health activities in the early 1960s (see Lapping 1961; Letlhaku 1961), 'community' was in the decade that followed noticeable only by its absence, an editorial of 1967 calling for 'the organization of community-orientated, curative, preventive and promotive medicine. If disease lies hidden in our community is it not our task to root it out?' (Editorial 1967a: 662). By 1970, however, and coinciding with the emergence into clinical medicine of a 'cross-cultural outlook' (see Chapter 9), the community gaze began to reassert itself. In 1970 Silbert could thus publish a paper on 'the Cape morbidity survey'; in 1971 this was followed by a second morbidity survey in Uppington (Movsowitz 1971), and in 1975 an editorial announced 'the recognition of community medicine' (Editorial 1975: 32), which Spencer described as a 'specialist branch of medicine, which does not deal primarily with individual patients, but with communities, determines community health status and priority health needs by epidemiological techniques, and prescribes and makes operative the means optimally to maintain health' (Spencer 1975: 35). Epidemiology was the technique of choice for this rediscovered and finally formalized community medicine of the 1970s, and over the next decade there occurred a flurry of studies that linked patterns of health and disease to demographic, socio-economic, educational, familial and socio-cultural variables. This epidemiological renaissance installed what Power and Heese (1978: 409) called 'the new morbidity' ('behavioural disorders, adolescent problems, drug abuse and unwanted pregnancy are some of the areas covered by these terms'), and with its rise community health began to decline in the shadow of a new public-health object called 'lifestyle':

> The lifestyle of a community and of its individual members is a product of the environment and the reactions of the community or individual to it. There is every reason to believe that the patterns of health and disease is [*sic*] determined to a great extent by the prevailing lifestyle. (Editorial 1978: 733)

Where it had previously recognized the factors productive of illness and health as immanent in community force relationships, the invention of 'lifestyle' dispersed the dangers to health into the environmental space surrounding communities. Here, it was less illness itself than the precursors of future illness that would become the target of a new socio-ecological focus to the extra-community space of 'risk' and 'risk factors'.

A new public health: the socio-ecological model

Since the 1980s, what has become known as the 'new public health' (Armstrong 1993) or 'socio-ecological model' (Goldstein 1993: Appendix B) has taken shape and embraced the population in a novel strategy of attention. As Goldstein noted, the emergence of this approach resided in a recognition that 'major sectors of the population are unable to make changes in individual risk factors' (Goldstein 1993: Appendix B) owing to their lifestyles being conditioned by sociological and environmental forces that transcend both the individual and the community.

Where sanitary science was concerned with the intrusion of nature into bodies, and social medicine and community health with the dangers that lurked in interpersonal space, the gaze of the socio-ecological model is concerned with the intrusion of the activities of those bodies into nature: 'The new public medicine has discovered that the by-products of economic and social activity can be dangerous and has committed itself to maintain the purity of the natural environment' (Armstrong 1993: 405). Intensely reflexive, the 'socio-ecological model' invents the individual, the community and the social as at once their own greatest sources of danger and the locus at which intervention should occur. Emblematic of this new focus was the concept of 'health promotion', which Tobias and Reddy defined as:

> [A]ny combination of health education with related organisational, political and economic interventions designed to facilitate behavioural and environ-mental adaptations that will improve or protect the health of communities … Many of these health conditions and broader circumstances that result in a compromised quality of life are not within the control of the individual. There is a need to acknowledge the gap between the rich and the poor and the limitations economic inequities place on an individual in adopting or resisting behaviour that compromises health. (Tobias and Reddy 1993: Appendix A)

The effect of this has been to extend the psycho-social space of interpersonal hygiene into a 'politico-ecological dimension', its contours delineated by the intersection of interdisciplinary and cross-sectoral modes of analysis and intervention. For instance, the risk factors sur-rounding violent injuries are transposed from the individual and the community into the subjectifying effects of repressive ideologies that here sustain implosive patterns of interpersonal violence and there explosive patterns of internecine violence (e.g. Butchart and Brown 1991). Through the surveillance of cigarette and alcohol usage, an insidious network of observation and caution now identifies the threat to innocent minds which resides in the products of the advertising industry and its 'particular ramifications for youth who are easily in-fluenced by social factors as they attempt to develop a sense of identity' (Parry et al. 1994: 44). In relation to pollution, levels of bodily exposure to noxious gases and other wastes from car exhausts, coal-fired stoves and industrial plants are revealed through the monitoring of air and integrated into urban-planning diagrams and interventions aimed at altering the use patterns of fossil fuels (Seager 1993). Deforestation of the land in search of wood for fuel has further elaborated this 'green response' in the shape of new strategies for electrification and national tree-planting campaigns, while the prevention of 'chronic diseases' (e.g. hypertension and obesity) is inscribed in strategies that interlink 'lifestyle' with departments of health, political parties, trade unions, large employers and educational agencies (Steyn 1993: 111), to position individuals, communities and societies in a great matrix of corporate, political, governmental and environmental forces.

Thus, whether the environment be that of the socializing patterns set in place by the dynamics of the economic and political order, or the physical environment as it is formed through the chemical outputs of industry and the built environment as it takes shape under the impact of informal settlement and low-cost housing, the space of identity in which the African body of the new public health emerges is a space of subjectivity and personal freedom, a space preoccupied with understanding and protecting the thinking, acting subjects which it fabricates from their own actions, and in that way maintaining the hygienic separation of human activities and nature.

Body production lines

To conclude this chapter's examination of public-health spaces and the identity of the African body it is useful to abstract the essential characteristics of each public-health regime by thinking about public health as a line drawn between bodies.

First, there was the geo-climatic model and its attendant strategy of quarantine by which a line was drawn between places. Second, there was the regime of sanitary science and its concern to police a line separating bodies from the environment. Third, social medicine and its preoccupation with recruiting those same bodies into maintaining a line between each other and the environment. Fourth, the strategy of community health which embedded groups of bodies in the larger social units produced by the lines it drew around communities. Finally, the socio-ecological model of the new public health and in its intrusion of lines of hygienic surveillance 'everywhere throughout the body politic' (Armstrong 1993: 405).

Correlated with these changes in the lines between bodies was the identity of the African body that each regime made possible. For geo-climatic medicine the line between bodies was a line without permeability, volume or depth. It recognized no separate bodies and no individualities, the rules of quarantine and their sovereign enforcement ensuring that these remained below the threshold of visibility and analysis. Sanitary science expanded this line into one with sufficient width and malleability to flow around and in between bodies, to constitute the African as a distinct but anonymous corporeal space in the crowd, its contours delineated by the points of greatest permeability to the environment on which clustered the external control techniques of sanitary segregation. The advent of social medicine further expanded the dimensions of this line to make its volume more significant than its linearity. Its ballooning into the space of mind that was its effect thus allowed the African body to crystallize as an individuality invested with traditions, superstitions, customs, emotions and so on. With community medicine, the volume of this line expanded further outwards to fabricate the edges of a shared social space, the borders of which were folded in on themselves and coterminous with those of the communities this medicine discovered as encasing the individual and the interpersonal. Finally, with the new public health, any vestige of linearity has disappeared, to be replaced by a multi-dimensional 'presence' that invests and sustains the African body as a reflective subject and conduit of an all-embracing socio-ideological context of economic and political activities.

The power of public health to invent, sustain and transform the social body and the various types of individual and aggregate bodies that have materialized within it does not reside within the ordered spaces and categories of health and wholeness that these lines protect. Rather, the productivity of these technologies emanates from the chasm between these regions of completeness, in the abyss separating the fundamental spaces of social life that over the last 150 years has, from its beginnings in the slender and almost invisible line of quarantine, 'rolled back across the landscape, revealing a vast space of limitless dimensions in which the social and the subjective would crystallize' (Armstrong 1993: 409).

CHAPTER 9

Birth of the Bantu Clinic

In *The Birth of the Clinic* Foucault (1976) set out the practices that in Parisian hospitals at the end of the eighteenth century relocated illness from the two-dimensional surface of the body to a point within the three-dimensional volume of an anatomical body: 'In anatamo-clinical experience, the medical eye must see the illness spread out before it, horizontally and vertically in graded depth, as it penetrates into the body, as it advances into its bulk, as it circumvents or lifts its masses, as it descends into its depths' (Foucault 1976: 176).

This final substantive chapter offers a similar analysis of western clinical medicine and its production of the African. In clinical nomenclature the term 'Bantu' was preferred over 'African' until around the 1970s, and in keeping with the history of the present is also the term used here. Defined geographically, 'Bantu' designated all native peoples of Africa south of the so-called 'Bantu line' drawn across Africa from near Mount Cameroun on the west coast, keeping north of the Congo River and Lake Victoria, until the east coast at a point just north of Mombasa.

Although missionary hospital medicine had engaged with its own very peculiar African body somewhat earlier, it was only in the 1930s that the Bantu body started to become an object of secular clinical concern. As Bernstein observed in 1938: 'It was not until comparatively recently that the Bantu peoples existed for the [medical] student as a problem' (Bernstein 1938: 28). By 1973, the sheer repetition of Bantu clinical practice had so imprinted the reality of the Bantu body as different to the European body that Kloppers, president of the Transkei and Ciskei Research Society for investigating disease in rural Africans, could note: 'When I do a ward round at the White hospital and then walk over to the Bantu hospital, I truly have to change over in my way of thinking; I have to take one computer program out of my mind and substitute another marked "Bantu" to work there' (Kloppers 1973: 287).

Consisting in techniques such as palpation, auscultation, invasive instrumental inspections and surgical investigations, the clinical gaze plumbs the living body to construct its most intimate depths and darkest recesses as visible objects of medical manipulation. Correlated with the intimacy of this gaze was the compactness of the objects that were its effects, and it was in the Bantu clinic that the African body achieved its greatest density.

A 1934 description of 'a day in non-European casualty' afforded a glimpse of how even in its earliest configuration the Bantu clinic produced the African patient as quite literally a lump of flesh:

> You start in on the crowd which has now extended ten deep, and wonder if they've been breeding while you were away ... You go into the female cube and find about six perspiring masses of flesh; listening to a chest you hear the wierdest [*sic*] noises, and you realise the steriliser is the cause of it. You sing out for it to be turned off and return to the chest. (Casualty Officer S.S. 1934: 36)

This was a gaze that further divided the body into a series of disconnected segments defined by the pathology that was seen. Here 'a good T.B. chest in the cubicle – one at a time may examine'; there 'an interesting skin case'; and elsewhere 'cases of syphilitic ulcers, mucous patches and gonorrhoeal ophthalmia ... quickly dealt with by sending to Rietfontein' (Casualty Officer S.S. 1934: 36–8). The African as a fragmented collection of body parts and lesions was more than the reductive fantasy of a callous practitioner anxious to display an heroic capacity for clinical work. For this first regime of the 'Bantu clinic' coincided with a wider practice of pathological anatomy, which in actively creating a distinct 'Bantu anatomy' provided the corporeal context necessary to the unfolding of this African clinical practice.

A Bantu anatomy

In 1937 Dart concluded his *Racial Origins* by setting out a future where the Bantu body would be subject to the same intensity of investigation as had the European body in the '400 years since Vesalius':

> The background of our picture has been limned; various highlights have been tentatively painted in; their gaunt relief will be subdued by the labours of those artists whose detailed work is essential to the masterpieces of the future. Their books are works of the time to come and will unquestionably appear when an army, equal to that which has laboured in Europe over the last 400 years since Vesalius, has been organised to collect information about the Bantu similar to that which has been garnered over these centuries concerning Europeans. (Dart 1937: 102)

Frankenstein-like, the anatomy and physiology of the passive body of the African patient began over the following decades to be assembled by the practices of the clinic. 'Every day, instances of variation in some anatomical feature or other are brought to light in work on the Bantu on the operating table, in the post-mortem and in the dissecting-hall' (Tobias 1947: 17). Organ by organ (e.g. the heart [Malherbe 1934]; the intestine [Van Velden 1943]), bone by bone (e.g. the skull [Galloway 1941]; the pelvis [Wells 1933]), and limb by limb (e.g. the thigh [Boshoff 1935]; the hand [Goldberg 1941]), its attributes were isolated and displayed for scrutiny alongside and in comparison to the European body. Thus, what this medicine demanded and what these anatomizing techniques produced was 'a monograph on the anatomical peculiarities of the Bantu', a 'Bantu anatomy' (Tobias 1947: 18) precisely equivalent to Gray's.

As pathological anatomy opened it up to invent and compare its configuration to that of the European body, certain organs, bones and systems of the African body attracted more intensive scrutiny than others. For instance, Sutherland-Strachan published in 1932 one of the first papers to examine what would become colloquially known as the 'Bantu liver', which was a particularly sensitive site from which to monitor the relation of Africans to the elements, minerals and alcohol its pathological analysis revealed to be present in their diet (Sutherland-Strachan 1932). A means of explaining the 'strange difference' between European and African women in 'the obstetrical sphere' (Broomberg 1935: 11), the pelvis of the Bantu female would also become the epicentre of more intensive study, as reflected in 1956 by the publication of *Bantu Gynaecology*: 'Less than twenty years ago the Bantu were an exotic growth to the gynaecologist. Now this branch of the human race has been received in orthodox gynaecological circles and its womanhood forms for the observer an entity' (Charlewood 1956: 1). The African heart was singled out due to the 'social anthropological interest' (Elliot 1953: 29) attaching to findings that it might differ anatomically from the European heart (Brink 1959; Sandeman 1965; R. Singer 1959), and because it was affected by a pathology so foreign to that seen in Europeans as to be labelled 'cryptogenic heart disease' (Higginson et al. 1960). Other anatomical applications analysed the African body's external surfaces, such as the pigmentation of the skin (Wasserman and Heyl 1968) and of the skin within the mouth (Van Wyk 1970), because 'the various patterns which skin pigmentation may assume are not always appreciated. Incorrect interpretation of a perfectly normal appearance may therefore result' (Van Wyk 1970: 177).

These and other applications of pathological anatomy furnished doctors with an intimate familiarity with the African body's otherwise dark and unknown interior necessary to distinguish correctly the signs of real pathology from those that were mere phantoms of an eye, ear or hand unfamiliar with what was 'normal'. As Wells (1949) noted of the African body where he compared it with the European body:

> [T]he anatomist may expect to find differences widely distributed throughout its structure. These can hardly fail in every case to exert an appreciable influence on function. Immediately they assume a practical bearing on the clinical sciences ... since it is agreed that normal function is best preserved or restored by maintaining or re-establishing normal structure. (Wells 1949: 86–7)

This anatomy was not a stable mechanism of normalization and clinical correction, though. From its crystallization in the 1930s, Bantu anatomy would for the next thirty years continue to consolidate itself. From the mid-1960s, however, it began to run alongside a new component in the Bantu clinic that permitted doctors not only to see the pathology but also to hear what patients said as signals of their physiological and emotional interdependence with a more encompassing socio-cultural domain, which by the late 1970s was formalized in the discipline of 'community health' (see Chapter 8). This produced the body of the individual as coextensive with the communal body, and by 1978 Tobias could thus replace the device of an individual Bantu anatomy with that of an aggregate African anatomy:

> While anatomy and physiology deal with the standard individual, [physical] anthropology is the science of the group. Herein lies its great importance in a medical and dental school in this last quarter of the twentieth century; for it is with the group that community health has to deal ... Just as one has to study the anatomy and physiology of the individual as a groundwork for training in personal medicine ... so too does one need to study ... the anatomy and physiology of groups of men or communities, as a baseline for the later emphasis on community medicine and quest for community health. (Tobias 1978: 1067–9)

Turning from this synoptic genealogy of the Bantu anatomy this chapter now examines the African patient as an object and effect of clinical practice, from the 1930s to the 1990s.

The African patient as a lesion-containing body

The Bantu clinic's earliest incarnation developed around the perceptual technique of triangulation involving symptom, sign and pathology. The symptom was a marker of illness as experienced by the patient. The sign intimated disease as elicited by the physician through history-taking and physical examination, and both symptom and sign pointed to an underlying lesion that was the disease (Armstrong 1995: 393). In effect, the patient was the lesion, and as an overture to physical examination by which the lesion was pinpointed deep within it, the doctor's task consisted in 'provoking the lesion to speech' (Armstrong 1984: 738). Pathology itself being voiceless, this could occur only through the surrogate medium of what the patient had to say about where, how and when the pathology made itself known, to problematize all patients who were not fully competent to speak for their pathology.

It was around this component of the clinical gaze that contemporaneous with the 1930s fabrication of a Bantu anatomy there crystallized a discourse devoted to identifying the characteristics of African patients that might limit their ability to speak on behalf of the lesions within them. Initially these writings were somewhat anecdotal, such as Grobbelaar's 1934 identification of 'the snag' that 'lies in the taking of the history of the case, for ... [the African patient] thinks that he is helping you ... if he answers every question in the affirmative' (Grobbelaar 1934: 14).

> For instance: Question: 'What do you want?'
> 'Nkoos, I weep because I am ill.'
> 'How are you ill?'
> 'My whole body is ill.'
> 'Have you pain?'
> 'Yebo, Nkoos.'
> 'Where is the pain?'
> He points to head, chest, stomach with a sweeping downward gesture.
> 'Is the pain in your head?'
> 'Yebo, Nkoos.'
> 'Is the pain in your stomach?'
> 'Yebo, Nkoos.'
> 'Is the pain in your chest?'
> 'Eheu! YEBO, Nkoos.'
> In other words 'You've got it.' (Grobbelaar 1934: 14)

Confirming the correctness of this procedure when examining Africans, Dowie Dunn (1939) spelt out its principles: 'If there was no obvious evidence of disease, one talked in general terms, stating that with this sickness sometimes one got a headache or bellyache and so on. The native always gave the show away by showing definite interest when particular areas of his body were mentioned' (Dowie Dunn 1939: 51).

In 1943 the first edition of Gelfand's *The Sick African*[1] systematized the scattered recommendations of practitioners such as Grobbelaar and Dunn to formalize the notion that clinical practice with African patients 'involves an entirely different angle of approach to investigation and treatment' (Gelfand 1943: Preface). In its chapters dealing with clinical practice, *The Sick African* confirmed the negative significance of what the African patient had to say. Despite a twenty-six-page chapter on 'The Patient' – 'as a patient, he is well behaved, docile and submissive (Gelfand 1943: 6) – and a twenty-page chapter on 'The Examination', what the patient said was mentioned only to alert doctors to how these words might confound apprehension of the pathology:

> [D]ifficulty in obtaining a good clinical history is presented by the patient himself ... He will not speak readily or communicate freely ... He has little conception of time and seldom knows his age ... Often enough, a few hours later, he will give an entirely different account. So the doctor must often rely upon the conclusions which the clinical findings enable him to draw. (Gelfand 1943: 28)

In 1948, Keen published a further exposition on diagnosing disease in the African body. Titled *The Psychological Approach to Bantu Medicine*, this advocated a number of methods for making the virtual voice of pathology audible through the noisy 'mixture of magic, religion and medicine which forms the background of the Bantu's mental reactions' to clinical care (Keen 1948: 6). For instance, because 'the taking of a long history goes against the grain in the Bantu' (Keen 1948: 8), and to mimic the ways of the witch doctor, the clinician should know even before talking with the patient where in the body the pathology was. To achieve this, a practice of surreptitious surveillance in the doctor's waiting area, achieved by

> sending an orderly among the patients sitting outside my consulting room collecting names and tickets. He would tactfully find out what was wrong and as a result, I always had on my desk a list of names with major complaints. The patient would walk into the room and I would look him over and say 'Take off your shirt, I want to examine your chest' or 'For how long have you been coughing,' and then during the examination I would get my history knowing it would be as accurate as is possible in a Swazi. (Keen 1948: 8)

Further, in physically examining the African the course traced by the doctor's hands towards the lesion should reverse the direction taken by the hands on European bodies so that the patient's confidence would not be lost along with a chance to locate the pathology:

> In examining a patient ... go for the main pathology first. For example, you
> have been taught that in palpating an abdomen, where you suspect the
> possibility of appendicitis you must start your examination in the left iliac
> fossa and work across to the right side. The idea of course is not to stir up
> any pain or guarding. That is fatal when dealing with the raw Bantu, as he
> will at once think that you do not know what you are about. (Keen 1948: 9)

Similar recommendations appeared two years later in Storr's 'Medical
Diseases in the Bantu' (1950), and Brebner's 'Surgery in the Bantu' (1950).
For Storr, 'Mr. Medical-diseases-in-the-Bantu' (Storr 1950: 49) was a
particularly difficult patient in which to establish the truth of the
pathological lesion because Africans lacked the historical consciousness
needed to reproduce the lesion's chronological dimensions: 'Thus it is
very difficult to obtain concrete answers to questions where time is
really concerned. For how long has the pain been present; or when did
he first notice that lump; when did he first start coughing up blood?'
(Storr 1950: 50). Other obfuscating factors included 'the pigmented skin'
which hindered the identification on physical examination of such
conditions 'as early jaundice, anaemia and cyanosis' (p. 50).

Transfer of the lesion from the body into the abstract space of
diagnosis was merely a precursor to treatment. Where this entailed
ongoing therapy it demanded that the same lesion exist as an entity
within the patient's own consciousness so that for its duration he would
monitor it. But the African's 'concrete mindedness' and envelopment in
a world where sickness emanated from bewitchment or ancestor influences meant that even this could not be assumed. The clinical gaze
thus configured itself into a technique for training the patient's
consciousness to produce the same corporeal dimensions of the lesion
as seen by the doctor:

> The Bantu, if he sees the trauma, can understand what's what and he then
> recovers because his tissues also have an immunity to infection. Years of
> repeated wounds give his tissues a certain immunity to infections. But woe
> betide him if that infection is hidden. If it is somewhere in his liver or his
> lung where he can't see it, he gives up the ghost very easily. It is in such a
> case that I think it worth while if you can spend the time, in simple language
> to say to him, 'now look, you have got this inflammation inside your body;
> it has to run its course; we'll try and control it.' (Brebner 1950: 47)

This was a means of recruiting the African into the heart of clinical
discipline as his own insightful physician, and for Keen involved showing
the pathology on the X-ray, the urine being tested, and letting the
patient 'look down my microscope. He will probably not see anything,
but it will give him something to fix his mental reactions' (Keen 1948: 9).

While it was the passive body containing the lesion that filled the medical gaze in this first incarnation of the Bantu clinic, the consciousness of the patient was not wholly absent. It is, however, incorrect to argue that this momentary surfacing of how the African patient conceived of his own body represented the tip of a subjective iceberg being discovered by a medicine edging towards a more humanist approach and the 'whole person'. Instead, these techniques of consciousness were directed to the opposite end of having the patient objectify the disease contained within his body. Problematization around 1960 of the African patient's thoughts and feelings as positive objects of clinical medicine therefore represented a break from this old regime. For the African patient as an emotional being was less a discovery of humanist enlightenment than a medical surveillance device to 'illuminate the dark spaces of the mind and social relationships' (Armstrong 1984: 739) within which it occurred.

An emotional patient The second edition of Gelfand's *The Sick African* (1947) merely extended the range of physical pathologies that doctors should seek within the African. The third edition's inclusion of new sections on 'psychological disorders' (Gelfand 1957: 533), and the 'effect on work and the importance of knowing the African' (p. 791), thus constituted a reconfiguration of clinical power that allowed for a patient that was more than an anatomized body containing a lesion. Now Gelfand could argue that the African patient's psychology was an important component of the clinical encounter: 'It is not merely a pathological problem. It is a problem which involves the appreciation of his outlook and his attitude to disease. One must know not only the diseases of Africa, but also the people with whom we are dealing' (Gelfand 1957: 791).

A 1960 paper by Findlay (1960) analysed 'the emotional pattern of the tribal Zulu as it affects pre-anaesthetic assessment and management'. Confirming the psychology of the African patient as an important effect and target of this new clinical regime, Findlay observed that where the patient was a 'tribal Zulu', it was important the anaesthetist pay special attention to this function owing to the culture-bound tendency of such patients to mask the 'stress' occasioned by fear. While emotional capacity was equally well developed in Europeans and 'Zulus', in the latter

> Fear is deceptively masked by the absence of its outward manifestations. Thus the usual reaction to stress can be described as autonomic rather than vocal. The Zulu shares the belief of other warrior races that courage, as

such, should be regarded as a primary virtue, and any display of fear as contemptuous self-indulgence. The psychosomatic implications of this are the actually exaggerated responses anaesthetists encounter daily in the Zulu as a result of moderate physiological and pharmacological interference. (Findlay 1960: 854)

Accordingly, anaesthetists working with patients from 'warrior races' should avoid being 'misled' by their outwardly placid nature and anticipate the emotional infrastructure this concealed. Careful 'psychological preparation' was therefore essential (Findlay 1960: 855).

These works marked a new analysis of disease and its indicators that involved a reassessment of the African patient. Just as the emotional infrastructure of the Zulu patient recognized by Findlay (1960) meant he should not be mechanically pumped with anaesthetic, so at a cognitive level the patient 'cannot be regarded as an open vessel ... or as a vacant vessel, ready to accommodate whatever the doctor wishes to instil in him' (Abramson 1960: 365). Reciprocally, the lesion which the earlier regime had assiduously isolated from the context of the person, family life and culture, now came to serve as a relay for illuminating precisely these factors, and these in turn as a locus of clinical treatment. Illustrating the practical implications of this novel concern with the psycho-social, Crowhurst-Archer (1960) observed that tuberculosis among Africans occurred within a 'patriarchal society composed of large family groups governed by primitive taboos (Crowhurst-Archer 1960: 243). Accordingly, treatment of the individual as an individual would reduce the body's healing capacity by arousing resentment on the part of others and concomitant 'emotional breakdown' of the patient. The entire social unit in which tuberculosis occurred should thus be made the patient, and: 'To this end the wards of the admission blocks of some hospitals where Africans are treated are only separated by walls 3 feet in height so as to preserve the sense of community life' (Crowhurst-Archer 1960: 243).

An emotional component of illness having been identified within the shifting social spaces between bodies, a clinical method was now required to map these social spaces. Since they could be known only through what the patient said, illness was in effect being converted from what was visible to what was heard. 'The Language of the Patient' (Campbell 1961; Editorial 1961) thus advocated a thorough assessment of the doctor's capacity to understand what the African patient might say:[2]

It is morally wrong for any doctor to practice for gain unless he is able to communicate direct with them [*sic*] in a language which they understand well enough to express accurately, not only the overt symptoms of their physical illnesses, but also the finer nuances of their thoughts and emotions, and the true nature of their hidden hopes and fears. (Editorial 1961: 986)

This 'moral' imperative to study the intimacies of African patients' experiences and thoughts was less an ethical necessity than a discursive device to mobilize psycho-social surveillance, and it was precisely towards establishing 'the true nature of their hidden hopes and fears' that the mechanism of the patient survey was first directed in 1961.

In 'What is Wrong with Me? A study of the Views of African and Indian Patients in a Durban Hospital', Abramson, Mayet and Majola (1961) confirmed the distribution of illness in the previously dark vaults of the subjective and the social by asking patients

> a number of general questions concerning the illness, what the patient thought or had been told about it, and the steps he had taken. The patient was also asked whether he thought his illness was related to his food, work, smoking, drinking, or worries, whether he thought he had a 'Bantu disease' or had been 'tricked', whether he thought he might have inherited it or got it from somebody else who was ill, and whether he thought it might be a punishment, or result from any act or omission on his part. (Abramson et al. 1961: 690)

Invention by the patient survey of the social interstices which shaped the body and emotions extended illness well beyond the lesion in the body. There could thus emerge 'urbanization' as a device by which individual African bodies were made coextensive with an aggregate body defined by the factors specific to African culture and tradition.

Urbanization and a cross-cultural clinical gaze Since the early 1900s the idea of 'detribalization' had been installed by the psychological sciences (see Chapter 7) and public health (see Chapter 8), to explain the heightened proclivity of Africans to behaviours that increased their exposure to disease and their tendency towards 'impulsive' aggression. The clinical notion of 'urbanization' etched a far deeper line that ran not only through culture and behaviour, but into the very physiology and biology of the body, to render these inner systems resonant with their social and cultural context. By 1964, studies which some thirty years earlier had been the exception (e.g. Broomberg 1936: 31–2) had become the rule. Thus Seftel's (1964) study of diabetes in African patients attending a Johannesburg hospital could note that 'urbanization ... appears to be a potent diabetogenic factor ... The condition is rare in rural Africans but common in those living in and around cities' (Seftel 1964: 82). Indexical of these urbanizing diseases were those affecting the stomach and the bowel, which from the 1960s became the pathological markers of African urbanization, magnified within the clinical gaze by the cognitive device of 'psycho-somatic' theory.

As Mirvish noted in 1962: 'there has emerged an increasing knowledge of the nature of symptoms in the study of such conditions as headaches, migraine, and many skin-conditions of nervous origin, and of the effects of the emotions on the gastro-intestinal tract, the stomach, and the bowel' (Mirvish 1962: 210). This fabrication of a new class of illnesses defined less by the lesion than emotional and attitudinal patterns called for an equivalent modification in the gaze of the doctor, who must 'be led to appreciate the close and inevitable link between psyche and the soma, and the way in which the one works on the other' (Elliot 1964: 148). A year later, Crowhurst-Archer consolidated this new interest in the patient as an integrated mind and body by advocating that psychiatry's prominence in the medical curriculum be increased, so as to introduce doctors 'to the problem of individual differences and their statistical treatment, the problem of normality and the problem of inter-personal relationship. It should ... prepare him to see *the person* in the patient' (Crowhurst-Archer 1965: 635).

Complementing this new interest in the 'person in the patient' was a reassessment of the place of clinical health education. For if illness was a pattern of emotions, then the categorization of patients into the sick and the well on the basis of the presence or absence of a lesion was no longer adequate. Instead, everyone was potentially a patient, and illness could be established even before becoming manifest through scrutiny of the social fabric it formed a part of. The *South African Medical Journal* in 1967 explored the implications of this new gaze for the clinical examination itself. Because 'some cultures are in equilibrium but others are undergoing change in the process of industrialization and urbanization which results in cross-cultural conflict' (Editorial 1967b: 41), it was essential that doctors 'who work in multiracial communities' understand and interpolate these cultural factors into their clinical practice:

> It is advocated that when case histories are taken on any particular patient, some questions be asked which relate to the patient's general culture. In every community the doctor is in a favourable position to study his fellow men because he can ask any questions he likes in the name of Medicine. (Editorial 1967b: 41)

By the early 1970s the practical translation of this new 'cross-cultural outlook' on clinical medicine was well under way, and in 1971 gave rise to Mokhobo's temporarily definitive re-drafting of 'medical history-taking among the Bantu tribes of South Africa'. Drawing upon Chamberlain and Ogilvie's (1967) demonstration that for some diseases in different stages of their development symptoms could be more important than signs, Mokhobo distinguished 'predominantly historical diagnoses' (e.g. angina, peptic ulcer, vascular insufficiency), and disorders where 'physical findings may be all important' (e.g. meningitis, malignant disease). Because 'many African patients exhibit a pattern of attitudes born of ... traditional influences' inscribed in 'Bantu medical practice', doctors unaware of the illness meanings created by these attitudes were liable to confuse the relative importance of symptoms and signs. Where thirty years earlier the African patient's utterances were a hindrance to accurate apprehension of the pathology, in this new approach the patient's story was central:

> The Bantu patient ... may exasperate the doctor by explaining every one of his symptoms. [But] this self-analysis and diagnosis is, however, a priceless account to the doctor ... The manner in which the patient tells his story, his timed emphasis, all furnish information which may otherwise be hard to come by. (Mokhobo 1971: 112)

Such information was, however, apparent only to the doctor primed in understanding the cultural meanings attached to specific organs and symptoms, and 'a patient's psychological and cultural outlook must provide the mirror through which the clinical picture is viewed' (Mokhobo 1971: 112). This was provided by a compendium of 'tribal terminology' relating to various classes of disorder, a perceptual grid that enabled doctors to recognize how within indigenous African systems of diagnosis and healing 'Priorities of symptoms and signs have a complex but interesting treatment. A patient with gonorrhoea will give undue prominence to backache and not mention penile discharge, the reason being that the damage may have been inflicted on the kidney, which is an important organ of potency and masculinity' (Mokhobo 1971: 112).

Mokhobo's realignment of the relationship between signs and symptoms and his observation that traditional African healers saw these as nodal (rather than focal) points in a network of feelings and social relationships suggested an entire complex of semantic needs that for doctors under the earlier regime had not existed. Consequently, Barker (1971) could argue:

> Your Zulu goes to the medicine man because our understanding is too small. We have failed to answer his unspoken question, we have not helped him at a level where our help is seen to *be* help ... If we learn anything

> from this 'reversion' (as we so hatefully style it) to the medicine man, it is that physical healing is not considered enough in Zulu society ... Our Zulu patients do not just ask the ordinary question 'how?' – which we are expert at answering with our detailed knowledge of microbiology and biochemistry – but they also ask a more metaphysical 'why?' We, of course, most often do not realize that we are being asked the question at all, and almost never do we attempt to answer it. (Barker 1971: 559)

Indirectly through the intermediary of the African traditional healer, the gaze of the Bantu clinic had thus begun to engage with a new problem: that of the socio-cultural matrix which informed the African patient's view of illness and attitudes to western medicine.

The consequence of this was a bifurcation in the discourse of the clinic. On the one hand, recognition of the traditional healer's influence over the African's experience of illness encouraged research devoted to the scrutiny of traditional healing practices and illness beliefs. On the other hand, recognition of the African patient as a feeling person with psycho-social needs demanded a reorientation on the part of western doctors to accommodate these in the clinical context. This bifurcation formulated a new object of clinical knowledge – the African as a dichotomous patient produced at the confluence of western and traditional practices – who would remain a central figure in the eye of clinical medicine until the 1990s.

A dichotomous patient The old regime's triangulation method had linked signs and symptoms to locate the pathology in a unitary body. Conscription of the traditional healer into the diagnostic and therapeutic process overlayed this with a triangulation involving the pathology, the doctor and the traditional healer. Signs and symptoms were still important, but their significance now lay in revealing how the disease pattern reflected the play of traditional healing, as did a 1972 study correlating pathology in rural Africans with 'religion', 'education', 'witch-doctor attendance' and 'the wearing of shoes' (Edginton et al. 1972: 969). Now that illness was interdependent with the fabric of traditional illness beliefs, Watts could in 1972 conceive of illness reactions among urban Africans as a sequence of 'separate steps' (such as visiting a hospital, consulting an 'inyanga', and sacrificing a goat), with an 'average' African patient taking '2,5 steps'. Because these steps invariably led between western and traditional practices, the doctor should always 'obtain insight into the traditional world-views and practices of their typical patients and ... how ... to modify patients' attitudes and behaviour when this is essential' (Watts 1980: 591).

Affirming an African patient that was the intersection of a triangular relationship between it and the western and traditional practices now isolated for clinical surveillance, Ingle (1973) argued that 'it is axiomatic to start where people are and with what they believe' (Ingle 1973: 333), while Jansen's (1973) *The Doctor–Patient Relationship in an African Tribal Society* probed 'Bomvanaland' to explore the meaning of physical contact and the use of instruments during the examination of rural Africans:

> Taking the medical history, the doctor communicates with his patient in his role of interviewer and presents himself as the one who must ask before knowing. As soon as he takes the role of examiner, he has a less dependent position towards his patient. In stead [*sic*] of standing in front of the patient with empty hands, now as examiner he operates with several kinds of instruments: stethoscope, reflexhammer [*sic*], sphygmomanometer, etc. No doubt this contributes to the status of the white doctor. When the examination is extended to the taking of X-ray films, the prestige of the doctor reaches its peak in the eyes of the patient. This modern apparatus contributes highly to the image of a powerful man who has mysterious methods to 'see' the diseased parts inside the body. The Bomvana call the X-ray the *u-Gesi*, a term used both for electrical instruments and for electrical light. (Jansen 1973: 109)

By 1974, Barker could castigate western doctors for having 'been blind for so long that almost none of us know what this Black patient is thinking' (Barker 1974: 34), while writers such as Manganyi (1974), Mgobozi (1974), Mutwa (1974) and Ngubane (1977) elevated African medical traditions to the status of a systematically structured cosmology that was one side of a culturally relativistic coin. African 'traditions and customs' (Gumede 1974) were now a barrier to the advancement of medicine only when despised and neglected, whereas if incorporated into clinical care they were valuable diagnostic and therapeutic tools: 'Unless we see Africans as they see themselves in disease not only as the western doctor sees them, these cultural traditional practices will continue to block development. Yet with better understanding they could be utilised to act as catalysts in promoting change' (Gumede 1974: 35).

In producing the African as a dichotomous patient whose emotional needs were met by traditional practices while western medicine treated only the body, a self-reflexive element entered the gaze of the Bantu clinic to problematize its failure in this regard. In 1975 Stott asked: 'Do we identify our patient's needs?' Drawing upon Rogerian psycho-therapeutic principles, he advocated procedures for doctors in cross-cultural clinical encounters to monitor how their own attitudes and communicative tendencies might block rapport, and hear beyond what the patient said to the subjectivity that these words might conceal. For what the patient said was now only one aspect of the patient's view, and in certain cases might 'be no more than an excuse to see and assess the doctor', or a method of entering the surgery as a prelude to revealing 'something ... difficult to verbalise' (Stott 1975: 33). In effect, the roles of patient and doctor were now reversible, demanding that just as doctors be comfortable assessing the patient, so should they accept it when 'the patient becomes judge/assessor' (Stott 1975: 34).

This recursive analysis by which clinical medicine problematized its own role in relation to the African patient extended well beyond individual clinical encounters to embrace the whole discipline, and in 1978 *The Leech* devoted an edition to 'The Role and Place of the Traditional Medicine Man and "Witchdoctor" in African Health Care'. Where nineteen years earlier Gelfand's (1947) evaluation of 'witchcraft and medicine' as 'enemies to the sick African's peace of mind' (Gelfand 1947: 4) reflected general opinion, it could now be said of the doctor who devalued traditional healing that he 'is certainly entitled to his opinion, but it is important to remember that there is more than one way of throwing the bones' (Dick and Murray 1978: 312). In place of the old medicine as an absolute technology, was now a 'western medicine ... [with] its own cultural relativity', which made it possible both to see the traditional healer and transform this practitioner from a threat to African clinical care into 'the best person to assist' the western doctor (Dick and Murray 1978: 312).

A flurry of work from here into the late 1980s extended the cross-cultural clinical gaze to solidify the African patient as the simultaneous product of western and traditional medicine. For some, this reflected the all-determining influence of culture and acculturation (e.g. Cheetham and Griffiths 1982; De Villiers 1985; Farrand 1984); for others the possibility of an agentic patient whose choice of healer was determined by income and access to health care (e.g. Boonzaier 1985; Buchanan et al. 1979; Heap 1985); and for others a template by which western doctors could reproduce in clinical practice the function of the traditional healer by answering the questions 'Why am I ill?' and 'Who made me ill?' (Daynes and Msengi 1979). Perhaps epitomizing this was Segal and Ou Tim's (1979) work on 'the witchdoctor and the bowel'. This integrated the ideas of urbanization, choice of healer and traditional healing to argue for a system that could draw 'the traditional practitioner into the structure of the health services' (Segal and Ou Tim 1979: 310), both to police any possible harmful practices (e.g. Buchanan and Cane 1976; Kiernan 1978), and confirm the role of 'psychologist, psychiatrist, marriage counsellor and healer' in which 'the vast majority of Blacks believe in and consult the witchdoctor' (Segal and Ou Tim 1979: 310).

The 'quest for wholeness' and a subjective patient

The analyses that produced the relationship between clinical medicine, the African patient, and the traditional healer reconfigured the boundaries of the clinical encounter. For pathological medicine these had been restricted to the gaze of a solitary doctor and the isolated body of a single patient. Acknowledgement of the interrelationship between symptoms and feelings had brought the patient's immediate relationships to family, society and culture into the consulting room, but only as adjuncts to a process over which the doctor retained control through astute monitoring of the relationship between doctor, witch doctor and patient. By 1990, however, even the idea of the 'doctor–patient relationship' was an inadequate code for construing the psychological and socio-cultural forces at play, as the Bantu clinic began to fade under the close attention of sociologists, psychologists and anthropologists.

Thus, while somewhat paradoxically offering itself as a text devoted to 'whole-person care', *Clinical Health Psychology: A Behavioural Medicine Perspective* (Schlebusch 1990) argued for the untenability of distinguishing separate experiential realms for doctor and patient. Instead, the doctor, the patient, the disease, the illness and all interactions between them were now perceptually defined punctuations within an 'energy system … seen as a collection of parts secured by some type of interaction or interdependence':

> [E]ach person is comprised of systems which in turn are part of bigger external systems: while individuals are composed of molecules, cells and organs, they belong to families, communities, cultures, nature and the world. The biological, psychological and social structures of each individual are affected by other levels of system and *vica versa*. (Schlebusch 1990: 14–15)

Because it was the perceptual configuration of the observer rather than the object of observation that was now the crucial determinant of the clinical encounter, the patient's subjectivity could emerge as a focal object of clinical concern. Drawing on Eisenberg and Kleinman (1981), and McHugh and Vallis' (1986) work on 'illness behaviour', this 'bio-psychosocial' model constructed the patient as suffering not only from disease but also 'illness':

> A subjective, psychological and social experience which is therefore open to interpretation by both patients and the society in which they live, and

> may in fact occur in the absence of disease ... It has idiosyncratic elements and is oriented towards problems of existence and coping so that its measurement ... must be orientated towards the viewpoint of the patient. (Schlebusch 1990: 41)

Some sixty years after the African patient first entered the Bantu clinic as a passive corporeal container of pathology, the codes of medical perception had mutated to invert the relative importance of what was seen and what was heard. Then, all that was heard was that which assisted the eye to see since disease was coterminous with the body; now illness could not be separated from the viewpoint of the patient since what was said was the illness.

Accordingly, Simon (1988) could argue that in 'ignoring' the patient's view bio-medicine was 'mechanistic' and, alongside analyses that explained African disease and the distribution of health care from a Marxist framework, authoritarian: 'The medical practitioner and the political economist are alike: both diagnose from a position of authority and control without much knowledge of what it is the patient or subject sees and experiences, wants and desires' (Simon 1988: 11). To counter this, it was now important that the doctor engage in 'the study of patients' perceptions and how they act on these' (Simon 1988: 182). Similarly, Heap and Ramphele (1991) characterized the earlier analysis of the clinic and traditional healer as 'essentially a debate among professionals based on their perceptions'; criticized it for failing to obtain 'any significant input from the "patients" who are the objects of their concerns'; and invited the reader to contemplate precisely these sub-jectivities as they shaped 'perceptions of illness and sickness' among African hostel dwellers (Heap and Ramphele 1991: 117–20).

'The quest for wholeness' (Heap and Ramphele 1991) informing these approaches to ascertaining the patients's view thus concealed in its concern with freeing what was previously trapped the more pervasive disciplinary operation of contemporary clinical perception. For they create the possibility of evaluating as 'reductionistic' (Rogers 1992: 5) and as 'illogically and deleteriously' dividing of the patient (Schlebusch 1990: 14), all methods of clinical medicine that produce anything less than the 'whole person', to thereby invent precisely the 'whole' and subjective patient they claim to have discovered.

Bodies and voices

The changes traced here in the discourse of the Bantu clinic reflect a shift from the tangible yet silent and passive body, to a loquacious and subjectified 'whole person'. As a manifestation of power, how is this change to be understood?

From the Marxist and liberal-humanist view of sovereign power that in the 1970s began constituting the entire enterprise of South African medicine as a dehumanizing regime (see Dowling 1973; Medical Association of South Africa 1974), thoughts are freely spoken unless forcibly suppressed. The failure of clinical medicine until the 1980s to elicit 'the patient's view' and see the African patient only as a passive container of pathology is from this perspective evidence for a repressive regime in which the vociferous African was an immanent danger to be forcefully silenced. But in the Foucauldean schema silence is less a marker of repression than of discipline at play in the capillary complex of relationships uniting dominator, dominated and liberator. For, in this system,

> There is no binary division to be made between what one says and what one does not say ... Silence itself – the thing one declines to say or is forbidden to name, the discretion that is required between different speakers – is less the absolute limit of discourse, the other side from which it is separated by a strict boundary, than an element that functions alongside the things said, with them and in relation to them. (Foucault 1979: 27)

The absence from secular clinical discourse until the 1930s, and the reconfirmation from then until 1960 of the African patient as a mute body in the Bantu clinic, cannot be simplistically regarded as evidence for the stifling power of oppression. Similarly, the 1960s' appearance of a speaking patient whose feelings were increasingly counted in the clinical procedure is not to be seen merely as the eventual liberation of an African voice for so long barred from speech. Rather, this arc from silence to speech maps no more than the functioning of a productive power which at certain points manufactures silence and at others a provocation to discourse. For far from unique to African genealogy of clinical perception, an equivalent sequence from the mute body of the passive patient to the loquacious voice of the 'whole person' is apparent in the discourse of the British clinic (Armstrong 1982, 1984).

These convergences notwithstanding, it is true that the African patient had to wait some ninety years longer than its European counterpart to possess a 'Bantu anatomy' equivalent to Gray's, and some twenty years longer to be heard as a subjective being. It is also true that the utility of Bantu anatomy as an object by which the apartheid state in part found its conditions of possibility meant it would deliquesce as the discourse of liberal-humanism arose in the 1980s to invent the universal body and authentic person it claimed to 'liberate'.

The social science challenge that medicine engage with the authenticity of suffering in the words of the sick is therefore only a shift in disciplinary emphasis from the technology of seeing to that of hearing. For the tactical effect of this challenge is to install the confession, through which the most confidential ideas of everyone are amplified to audibility and lifted into socio-medical space as devices of disciplinary subjectification.

Notes

This chapter is adapted from an earlier version appearing in *Culture, Medicine and Psychiatry*, Vol. 21, no. 4, as 'The Bantu clinic: a genealogy of the African patient as object and effect of South African clinical medicine, 1930–1990', copyright 1997, with kind permission from Kluwer Academic Publishers, Spuiboulevard 50, PO Box 17, 3300 AA Dordrecht, The Netherlands.

1. Reviewers in 1944 of 'this pioneer attempt at filling the breach which has so long hampered South African medicine' (N.V.S. and P.K. 1944: 37) were critical of the generalizations made concerning disease distribution across the continent, but unequivocal in their support of its chapters on the patient and the examination, stating that 'the book is essentially clinical and should be in the hands of every medical practitioner dealing with the Bantu' (N.V.S. and P.K. 1944: 39).

2. This new concern with language and communication was operationalized in Campbell and Lugg's *Handbook to Aid in the Treatment of Zulu Patients* (1958). This was produced for use by European doctors in the non-European wards of Durban's King Edward VIII Hospital, and provided a compendium of instructions and diagnostic questions in English and their Zulu equivalents concerning everything from the routine physical examination, invasive instrumental investigations such as 'sigmoidoscopy', advice on home sanitation and the importance of always carrying a 'pass book'.

CHAPTER 10

Postscript: On the Anatomy of Power

Bound by liberal-Marxist conventions and all they imply in respect of the ahistorical human subject and an economist notion of power, conventional analyses of the socio-medical sciences proceed as if they were a species of judicial inquisition into the phenomena examined. They are therefore bound in their conclusions to offer a judgement of the case and recommendations concerning a course of retribution or rehabilitation that will guide the future actions of concerned individuals in the direction of a better practice characterized by greater equity, justice and so on.

Marks and Andersson, for example, concluded their study of typhus by noting that 'the true violence of South Africa' lies not in 'the infectious diseases which are defined by the Department of Health as "epidemics" – but TB, measles, and malnutrition and malnutrition-related diseases' (Marks and Andersson 1988: 278). Similarly, Packard ended his history of the political economy of tuberculosis in South Africa by noting:

> A new resurgence of TB is surfacing in the urban areas of the country as thousands of workers and their families attempt to escape the poverty of the Bantustans. Once again, industrial capital and the state have combined to lay the groundwork for a major upsurge in urban-based TB. The question that remains is whether the state and/or local authorities will also once again apply their time-honored policies of exclusion to solve this growing problem, perhaps in conjunction with new promises about the virtues of chemoprophylaxis. Or will they at last recognize the futility of this policy and begin to deal with the underlying causes of TB? (Packard 1989: 318–19)

As a final example, Zwi and Ugalde (1989) concluded their paper on an epidemiology of political violence with a reminder that 'researchers should strive to ensure that their work, can, in some small way, be used in the promotion of peace, the promotion of broader levels of democracy and participation, and the achievement of liberation for the oppressed' (Zwi and Ugalde 1989: 641). These conventional histories thus conform to the Marxist dictate that the human sciences should aim not simply to study the world but rather to change it. They therefore epitomize the confidence characteristic of the modern subject as an autonomous individual who through careful analysis gains access to the political control panel and there takes control over the design, direction and delivery of power.

From the Foucauldean perspective, this imperative to engage in therapeutic action is clearly ironic. For the dual structure of all power relations as 'strategic yet without a strategist' (Dreyfus and Rabinow 1983: 187) means that in recruiting socio-medical scientists to serve in a task of liberation these observers themselves participate in a regime of power, their claims to discern a repressive force which is lifted concealing a positive power which creates. In contrast, it is the aim of this postscript not to speculate on how the anatomy of power and the African body that is its object and effect might be changed, but to do no more than study it.

Rewriting the African subject

The African body¹ fabricated here in just some of the fantastic, geometric, pitiable, docile, dangerous, risky, anatomically dissected and subjectified configurations that have comprised its shifting truth within socio-medical discourse, this study offers a radical challenge to conventional histories of the socio-medical sciences. For it effaces the conventional notion that power and the body can be separated, 'that under power with its acts of violence and its artifice, we should be able to rediscover the things themselves in their primitive vivacity' (Foucault, in Kritzman 1988: 119). Instead, it does precisely the reverse, turning these 'things themselves' on their head by demonstrating how the body of the African as a pre-existing entity is in fact no more than an artefact of conventional accounts, an effect sustained only by elaborate efforts to rewrite history in a manner that produces the African as an unequivocal and subjective body.

Accordingly, there can be little doubt that the study will not be easily read for what it says by those with an investment in liberal-humanism and Marxism, and may even be interpreted as a reactionary text, a scandalous denial of what every historian knows to be the 'truth' of how the 'authentic' African was savagely mutilated by the unmitigated sovereignty of colonialism. However, to question the activities of socio-medical scientists, whether from the right or the left of the political spectrum, is not the same as being reactionary. For, open to an analysis of its own productive force, this study installs within socio-medical discourse a dispassionate gaze to the problem of the African body and socio-medical power. This is a gaze that does not seek solace behind the crash barriers of ideology and their implications that in the absence of ideology's distorting and perverting consequences colonialism and apartheid might never have occurred. By the same token, it is a gaze that is not compelled to repeat indefinitely, and with no effect other than a shifting of players' positions on a stage whose limits are already fixed, the refrain of the anti-repressive anthem: 'power is bad, ugly, poor, sterile, monotonous and dead; and what power is exercised upon is right, good and rich' (Foucault, in Kritzman 1988: 120).

Neither denying nor affirming either of these perspectives, this study fabricates a new, trans-humanist mode of strategic interrogation, by which the tactical integration of the socio-medical sciences within present-day programmes of disciplinary power may be studied and invested with a new relevance. This is a relevance that issues not from what they do, but from 'the power over life' (Atterton 1994) produced by the performance of these practices, through which the individual and the social are continuously invented, sustained and transformed as calculable and manageable entities in the very act of analysing them. For, since power relations are always 'both intentional and non-subjective' (Foucault 1979: 94), what is done by the doing of the socio-medical sciences is equally always of a dual character; this reassessment of power and knowledge itself both revealing the limitations of conventional approaches and actively inventing the genealogical perspective it sustains.

Why then has this not been recognized before within colonial and specifically African contexts of western socio-medical enterprise? What lines of force have until recently ensured that not even a single study has inverted the analytic codes of sovereign power and so moved beyond the space of progressive humanism to a point where the African body could be discerned as fabricated not found, and colonial socio-medical power as productive rather than merely destructive? An answer to these questions is suggested by exploring how the socio-medical sciences in South Africa have fabricated the Foucauldean notion of power, and how, in their failure to recognize its rejection of a transcendental subject, they are themselves the most obvious evidence for what it is that these disciplines do within the strategic space of contemporary society.

Foucault and the South African socio-medical sciences The Foucault schema is now over thirty years old, dating back to the 1961 publication of *Histoire de la Folie*, and of *Naissance de la Clinique* in 1963. English translations of the main texts drawn upon to inform the analytic and methodological basis of this study – *The Order of Things* (1973), *The*

Birth of the Clinic (1976), *Discipline and Punish* (1977) and C. Gordon's *Power/knowledge* (1980) – have been available since the mid-1970s, and by the early 1980s there were already a number of British and American studies that deployed Foucault to delineate the political anatomy of the European and American body.

In the decade since the mid-1980s it was therefore conceivable that equivalent explorations of socio-medical power in South Africa (which surely counts as one of the more startling examples of how power produces the body), could have been conducted. Yet by 1995 the only study to draw on this perspective was that by the English historian Megan Vaughan (1991) which, rather than deploying the Foucault schema as a new approach to power and challenging the anatomy of the African body in its own right, pressed Foucault into the service of what Gerhardt (1989: xxvi) characterized as the Marxist or 'conflict paradigm' in medical sociology. This reticence to embrace in its full implications the Foucualdean theory of power and knowledge is even more apparent when the work of South African scholars is surveyed with a view to establishing how this has invented Foucault.

In 1985 Muller published a book review of *Changing the Subject* (Henriques et al. 1984). This was titled 'The End of Psychology', and correctly identified the disciplinary essence of Foucault's notion that power is 'the vital current that animates the micro-circuits of human commerce and sociality. It enables as much as it constrains. It is explicitly against a Marxist notion of power as "the power to exploit"' (Muller 1985: 34). In another setting Muller's recognition of the Foucauldean insight into power might have marked the beginning of a novel and reflexive strand in analyses of the socio-medical sciences as the disciplinary side of sovereign power in South Africa. Yet, over the decade since Muller's review, an accurate reading of Foucault has been conspicuous only by its absence from South African socio-medical discourse. Instead, and on the few occasions where local scholars have deployed Foucault, the central thesis concerning the contingent status of the body has been systematically reversed to invent Foucault as yet another weapon in the armoury of Marxist class struggle or laissez-faire liberalism.

For example, in what appears to be the only instance where Foucault was deployed by a South African scholar in relation to contemporary medical practice, Pitfield characterized Foucault as an agent of the 'anti-medical' critique of bio-medicine: 'Foucault's basic argument is that the State upholds and promotes certain systems which appear to be aimed at caring for people, but which actually restrict peoples' rights in line with a dominant ideology' (Pitfield 1995: 248). By presenting 'the State' as the monolithic source of force and reversing the Foucauldean thesis concerning the productive power of the medical gaze, Pitfield cemented a vision of power as that which is held and wielded, her description of disciplinary power at work itself serving as a disciplinary conduit by confirming the individual as a pre-given entity:

> The ingrained desire of human beings to strive for optimum health and long life provides for a potential area of power domination within the medical model. Our subconscious accepts this desire as a norm ... Foucault suggests that power in these terms does not operate through coercion, but rather through an infiltration of the subconscious mind. (Pitfield 1995: 249)

In relation to the social sciences, a similar reading of Foucault characterized Webster's critique of them as 'the servants of apartheid'. Here, Webster cited Foucault's *The Order of Things* – 'the historical emergence of the human sciences was occasioned by a problem, a requirement, an obstacle of a theoretical or practical nature' (Foucault, in Webster 1986: 8) – not to demonstrate how the micro-powers of observation and recording enable the great shifts in political and economic manipulation by providing the human objects which these require to take hold, but instead to show the reverse. Thus: '[T]he structural transformation of the South African economy, particularly the challenge of Black labour, is the occasion for the emergence and growth of social research into industry' (Webster 1986: 16); and: 'faced by the crisis of the 1970s, the apartheid state is finding it increasingly necessary to mobilise social scientists to serve apartheid' (Webster 1986: 26). Webster's view suggests that for Foucault power is something to be grasped and wielded, that its locus resides in political life, when in fact for Foucault 'power is neither there, nor is that how it functions. The relations of power are perhaps among the best hidden things in the social body' (Foucault, in Kritzman 1988: 118).

Confirming this trend by which South African social scientists have deployed Foucault not to study power's productivity but rather to highlight the repressive hypothesis Foucault was preoccupied with dispelling, Dawes (1986) at once concealed the creativity of the psychological sciences by demonstrating their 'unresponsiveness' to the 'African context and to the needs of the majority of its citizens', and interpolated Foucault into a machinery that could free the African from entrapment and distortion:

> It is based on a range of largely Marxian studies developed in Europe as exemplified by Foucault (1970), Seve (1978), Althusser (1971) and others. While not a coherent group, psychologists of this persuasion are concerned to question the very basic assumptions of the discipline and how its knowledge

and practices have developed ... In so doing they expose this (unitary) subject as a product of deeply embedded ideological notions regarding the nature of 'man' inherent in natural science and capitalist social formations. (Dawes 1986: 33–4)

By conflating Foucault with Marxist ideologists, Dawes implies that the power Foucault discerned is the sovereign power of concealment and distortion, an ideological screen which ensures that what is seen is something less than the real and objectively given object of perception. Accordingly, Dawes responded only to the sovereign side of South African psychology, his critique of its 'unresponsiveness' to the needs of Africans obscuring the fact that as a component of disciplinary power it is precisely through the socio-medical sciences that the 'African context and the needs of the majority of its citizens' exist at all. In the Foucault schema, all human and social objects of knowledge are never any more or any less than the end result of a productive power. This includes the concept of ideology itself, which every time it is invoked serves further to crystallize the liberal-Marxist belief in an external reality that exists independently of power (Foucault, in C. Gordon 1980: 102).

As another example of how the discourse of conventional South African socio-medical science has fabricated Foucault, Nell (1991) drew upon a quotation concerning the correlative nature of power and knowledge – 'We are subjected to the production of truth through power and we cannot exercise power except through the production of truth' (C. Gordon 1980: 93–4, in Nell 1991: 69) – as a reminder that:

> [I]n a society on the brink of transformation, in which a search ... is under way for a democratisation of knowledge, for a redistribution of resources, for a sharing of knowledge and power in our society for the greatest good and justice, we need to remember that governments ... function by the truths rendered to them by an intellectual elite. (Nell 1991: 69)

Where the Foucauldean schema as expressed in Foucault identifies power as a network of disciplinary force relations distributed everywhere and coursing through the bodies, behaviours, beliefs and words of everyone, Nell's invocation did precisely the opposite, localizing the power of knowledge to those formal centres of knowledge production that in the diagram of discipline are simply the points of concentration in a generalized force field.

From this review of how Foucault has been fabricated in the South African social sciences and medicine, it is clear that his famous claim 'we have yet to cut off the head of the king' applies with especial vigour to this society, its anatomy of power bending even the written lines of Foucauldean analysis themselves into evidence for the belief that power emanates from the top (the courts, the state, the academy), when in fact power comes from below.

There is therefore a geo-political gap in how Foucault is understood and applied, a conceptual membrane marked by the contrast between South African interpretations of Foucault as a champion of the liberal-Marxist position on power which he contested, and the work of scholars from outside South Africa who apply the notion of discipline as a way of deconstructing the subject and the body by showing them to be inventions of power rather than discoveries of knowledge. How is this to be understood and, more importantly, what power function may be served by this selective permeability of South African socio-medical discourse to Foucault?

On the failure of Foucault in South African socio-medical science At the most prosaic level of explanation, the failure of Foucault to take hold in the South African socio-medical sciences may reflect nothing more than an inability fully to appreciate the more elusive ramifications of his writings, a failure that can itself be located within a broader tradition of what Nettleton (1992) described as the 'perceived obscurity and inaccessibility' of Foucauldean ideas to scholars immersed in the philosophies of the English as opposed to the French-speaking world:

> Wittgenstein once said that if a lion could speak we wouldn't understand it. Be that as it may, it is certainly true that if Continental philosophers all spoke English, most British and American philosophers wouldn't have much idea what they were saying. The two traditions divided about a century ago, and have been moving steadily apart ever since. (Papineau 1991, in Nettleton 1992: 105)

The obvious difficulty is that this explanation produces the idea that knowledge is unrelated to power, that it exists out there waiting to be grasped, understood and applied to one or other problem. It leaves untouched therefore the strategic question as to what the socio-medical sciences in South Africa or anywhere else do by not doing Foucault.

The answer has already been repeated throughout this study, and is merely confirmed here by the recognition that counterpointing its imperviousness to the Foucault schema is the readiness of South African socio-medical discourse to embrace all theories, models and methods that may be deemed 'social constructivist', in that their aim is to expose how various types of interests (e.g. class, social, political, technical) distort or contribute to the creation of certain types of knowledge. Without listing the many Whig, Marxist, and liberal-humanist analyses that can be found on any library shelf, examples of the more 'radical'

approaches to have found favour in the South African setting of attention include: the medical anthropological models of Kleinman (1980)
and Scheper-Hughes (1990), which inform the work of local writers
such as Rogers (1992), Lerer and Scheper-Hughes (in press), and Swartz
(1985, 1988, 1991); the social constructionist approach of Berger and
Luckmann (1967), Gergen (1982), and Shotter (1984) as it informs the
works of Levett (1987), or Butchart and Seedat (1991); the method of
discourse analysis developed by Potter and Wetherell (1987) and applied
locally by Lerer et al. (1995), or Scrooby (1994); and Bulhan's (1985) neo-
Fanonian methodology for understanding the dynamics of colonial
domination and revolution (e.g. Nell and Butchart 1989; Seedat 1993).

While all of these social constructivist approaches are consonant
with the Foucauldean concern to see socio-medical knowledge as
produced, sustained and selected as an outcome of various social
processes, they at the same time share another premise that renders
them dissonant with the genealogical approach of Foucault. Following
Nettleton, this is that

> whilst knowledge is socially created there exists an underlying truth, a real
> external world which remains more or less disguised or more or less under-
> stood. For all these constructivists' knowledge of the world is constructed
> through the play of either interests, perceptions or language; the material
> world, however, exists as an external reality. (Nettleton 1992: 136)

Hence, as a tactical complex within the force field of disciplinary power,
the affinity of the South African socio-medical sciences with methods
devoted to stripping away veneers of interests, motives and ideologies
mutates into a machinery of production that sustains the material
matrix of the corporeal and the social as parts of an objectively given
external reality. Perhaps ironically, it is therefore in this failure to understand accurately and to embrace the Foucault schema that the present
methodological configuration of the socio-medical sciences confirms
the South African anatomy of power as a Foucauldean economy of
disciplinary forces, tactics, strategies and knowledges. Because, within
the genealogical gaze, the pejorative terms that are the bedrock of this
methodological configuration (objectification, reification, stereotyping,
prejudice, positivism, alienation and so on) are not the techniques
through which bodies are imprisoned, 'but the analyses through which
they are created. Discourses against positivism or against alienation
are, therefore, objectifying strategies themselves, a part of the whole
which they presume to criticise, devices for establishing the subject as
"object" of perception' (Armstrong 1985: 114–15).

The relevance of Foucault to socio-medical practice in the present

From these observations it is possible to see that the Foucauldean perspective offers new insights and new ways of thinking about the contemporary practice of the socio-medical sciences. For, while this study has deployed materials from the past as a means by which to make its point concerning the correlative relationship between power and socio-medical knowledges of the human body and the subject, its relevance can be only for the present in which it is written and of which it is a product.

The Foucauldean perspective suggests, for instance, that biology, the body and disease cannot be simplistically regarded as materially given processes and external realities, but rather as at one and the same time inherently social strategies of surveillance and visibility. Consequently, they fall squarely within the remit of social psychological and socio-logical study, with the effect that instead of continuing to operate as adjuncts to bio-medicine by assisting in the understanding of illness experiences or the identification of social factors in the aetiology of disease, these disciplines can now study disease in its own right, by asking how certain diseases are invented, what makes them possible, and what, in turn, they make possible.

Flowing from this recognition is the pertinence of the Foucauldean approach to the ongoing and fractious debate between medicine and the psychological sciences (e.g. Manganyi 1991; Miller and Swartz 1990; Swartz 1988; Swartz and Levett 1989). As Nell (1992) has articulated it from the side of psychology, the willingness of psychologists to sub-ordinate themselves to the medical profession perpetuates a medical hegemony that suppresses the psycho-social origins and the subjectivity of illness: '[T]he medical gaze is barren, and psychology's pathetic fate is that its seduction by the clinic is followed by its own impotence. Psychologists deluded by the medical gaze are made impotent by the company they must keep in the *klinikos* – a silent doctor, and a longing patient' (Nell 1992: 230). As a result, continues Nell, psychology is rendered powerless to make the 'significant contribution to human welfare and ... a just society' (p. 228) that it should be doing by rescuing the 'lay public' from 'the ways in which medical technology and medical information-giving ... disempower clients, rendering them passive and ... helpless recipients of medical care' (p. 237). Such an argument is a restatement of the medicalization thesis, through which writers such as Illich (1976), McKeown (1979) and M. Singer (1990) have drawn on various types of evidence to demonstrate how medicine has invaded and taken control over increasingly extensive areas of life. From the Foucauldean perspective, however, the currency of the medicalization thesis is severely devalued by the disciplinary recognition that instead of repressing the body and disease, medicine in fact invents these, and therefore that those who oppose the power of medicine with their calls for a humanist and psychologized alternative can at best triumph in a palace revolution only. For, since they are no more than diverse sides of a unitary apparatus for the invention of the body, the person and the social as their objects and effects, any such inversion of the hierarchical relationship between medicine and psychology would be no more than the exchange of one spurious monarchy for another, which through its promised emancipation would further conceal the already well hidden locus of power to produce the knowing and free subject as its target and its relay.

> This type of discourse is, indeed, a formidable tool of control and power. As always, it uses what people say, feel, and hope for. It exploits their temptation to believe that to be happy, it is enough to cross the threshold of discourse and to remove a few prohibitions. But in fact it ends up repressing and dispersing movements of revolt and liberation. (Foucault, in Kritzman 1988: 114)

As a final example of the relevance of Foucauldean theory to the practice of the socio-medical sciences in the present, it suggests a whole new angle of approach to the question of the 'relevance' of western psychological knowledges and techniques for Africans in an African context (e.g. Anonymous 1986; Asante 1990; Berger and Lazarus 1987; Bulhan 1990; Seedat 1993). Conventionally, it is argued that because these emerged in Europe and America they can at best be of only limited value in the 'alien' context of an African society upon which they have been imposed, and at worst constitute the source of a pernicious brand of neo-colonialism. As Seedat argued in relation to the psychological sciences:

> Liberatory psychology is centred ... around the organising principle that rejects the primacy of Euro-American values and philosophical assumptions about humankind. Liberatory psychology is oriented towards placing the experiences of those other-than-European in the centre of its discourse ... The commitment to centre the African or 'Third World' psychosocial experience heralds the articulation of a dynamic, formative agenda that is connected to progressive and democratic voices throughout the world. (Seedat 1993: 253)

Against this point of view, and because within the genealogical perspective knowledge is never independent of the objects that are its effects, there can be no possibility of one way of knowing being more or less 'relevant' than any other. This implies that in their haste to dismiss 'Euro-American' science as irrelevant to Africa and Africans, critical socio-medical scientists arguing from an Africanist framework may be throwing out not only the bath water of a colonial past and a neo-colonial present, but with it precisely the African body that in the absence of these 'irrelevant' approaches would, quite simply, cease to exist as a manageable object of socio-medical knowledge.

In all likelihood, it is of course true that the place of the western, bio-medical body would immediately be taken by a novel African body as the effect of an indigenous African knowledge. But would this provide the apparatus of the state and the machinery of industry with the individual, social and demographic objects that have for so long been, and continue to be, the prerequisites for their functioning? While a study of indigenous African knowledge from the Foucauldean perspective has yet to be performed to answer this question, it probably would not. Hence the debate over relevance studiously avoids problematizing all those micro-powers that produce these essential objects (such as the clinical examination, the epidemiological survey or the participatory research interview) in favour of such epiphenomenal questions as those around notions like cosmology, epistemology, ideology and cultural imperialism.

The relevance of Foucault to the present lies therefore not in the possibility of Foucault bringing some kind of therapeutic leverage to bear on what the socio-medical sciences do, but simply in providing a method of analysis that permits of a perpetual monitoring not only of what these disciplines do, but of what it is that is done by their performance.

Afterword

Arguing from a feminist perspective, Nancy Harstock (1990: 166) wrote: 'reading Foucault persuades me that Foucault's world is not my world'. Along with other critics such as Bury (1986), Walzer (1986) and Dews (1987), she considers the genealogical aspiration to a non-interventive analytical neutrality as Foucault's greatest failing, the 'catastrophic weakness of his political theory' (Walzer 1986: 67). For, they argue, Foucault's formulation of power as omnipresent and obedient to only its own rules of ordering offers no hope for the future. If power is 'always-already present, constituting the very thing which one attempts to counter it with' (Paternek 1987: 111), there can be no escape and no progress, all phenomena continuously suspended in the ever-presence of the present. However, whether or not one agrees with Taylor's (1984) view that this is a spurious objection since the very neutrality it critiques is itself derived from an evaluative reason for this non-evaluative stance, it by no means removes the Foucauldean analysis from a participant position in the ongoing fabrication and re-creation of reality. On the contrary, precisely because knowledge produces power and power produces knowledge, the knowledge of genealogy and the genealogy of knowledge are always actively creating the world and so are far more than mechanisms by which it is simply studied.

What these critics therefore reveal in their preoccupation with the Foucauldean failure to provide any guidance for action is the 'assumption that there must be action and progress, a non-relativist way forward that has been defined by a western tradition in the sciences of man' (Armstrong 1987: 74). They thus fail to recognize that the Foucauldean analysis formulates its questions and performs its studies from a plane of analysis independent of this liberal-Marxist perspective, a plane that because it is independent of any humanist assumptions is neither for nor against humanism. Accordingly, Foucault is able to remind us that there is likely to be a completely different way of knowing and seeing our world, a way so different as to be incommensurable with and unrecognizable from our late-twentieth-century perspective. As Rorty (1986) has noted, Foucault thus succeeds in doing what philosophers are supposed to do, 'reaching for speculative possibilities that exceed our present grasp, but may nevertheless be our future' (Rorty 1986: 48).

Because this study is itself a component of the Foucauldean discourse that makes such an exercise possible, it cannot be viewed as independent of the domain it has analysed. Indeed, precisely because there can be no objects of knowledge in the absence of methods for their production, this study is itself a productive component in the discursive context of Foucauldean scholarship. As such, it can make no claims about being more correct than alternative explorations for thinking about thinking in the socio-medical sciences, and its strategy of assuming a 'true' reading of Foucault from which South African scholars have deviated must be read as a tactic of provocation rather than a claim to absolute certainty in respect of its readings of misreadings of Foucault. What is hoped, however, is that its analysis of Foucault's reception in African socio-medical science has gone some way to destabilizing what otherwise is experienced as certainty, and to bringing about some appreciation of how, while we can never be outside the loop of power, we can at the very least observe its operation and in this way appreciate that while sovereign power cannot easily be grasped by everyone, disciplinary power is within the grip of us all. Seeing and caring for the objects of our day-to-day experience is one thing, but only if we can also appreciate their origins as in part the outcome of what we do can we understand our place in the order of things.

Note

1. This study is no more than an invitation to contemplate the problem of the African body and an overview of the anatomy of power. It is an invitation because as well as being limited in its geographical focus on the unwinding of power and the corporeal in South Africa, it does not even attempt to explore the power implications of the indigenous practices and knowledges that counterpoint the western systems it investigates. It is an overview because each substantive chapter could itself be the subject of a full-length genealogy, and because in between the objects of knowledge they pick out lie great fields of socio-medical micro-power that this book ignores or only barely touches upon. For instance, the body of the African woman and the techniques of gynaecology; blood; the invention of infant mortality and the emergence of forensic pathology with its changing fabrications of death; the science of demography and the strategy of population; dentistry and the African mouth with teeth, or the discipline of nutritional science and its problematization of mastication, digestion, excretion and growth of the body.

Bibliography

Abramson, J. H. (1960) 'The Doctor as Teacher – His Practical Problems', *South African Medical Journal*, Vol. 34, 364–8.

Abramson, J. H., F. G. H. Mayet and C. C. Majola (1961) 'What is Wrong with Me? A Study of the Views of African and Indian Patients in a Durban Hospital', *South African Medical Journal*, Vol. 35, 690–4.

Achterberg, N. D. (1935) 'A Fresh Field of Research', *The Leech*, Vol. 6, no. 2, 8–10.

A. C. J. (1934/1906) 'Early Experiences of a Missionary Doctor (from a letter dated 12th February, 1906)', *The Leech*, Vol. 5, no. 2, 33–4.

Ackernecht, E. (1967) *Medicine at the Paris Hospitals 1774–1848*, Johns Hopkins University Press, Baltimore.

Aitken, R. D. (1944) *Who is My Neighbour? The Story of a Mission Hospital in South Africa*, Lovedale Press, Lovedale.

Albertyn, J. R. (1932) *The Poor White Problem in South Africa. Report of the Carnegie Commission. Part V: Sociological Report*, Pro-Ecclesia, Stellenbosch.

Anning, C. C. P. (1937) 'Native Health Assistants in Urban Areas', *Public Health (Johannesburg)*, Vol. 2, no. 3, 5–11.

— (1938) 'To-morrow We Die', *The Leech*, Vol. 9, no. 2, 7–11.

Anon. (1858) 'Book Review. Missionary Travels and Researches in South Africa. By Dr. David Livingstone', *British Medical Journal*, Vol. for 1858, no. LV, 52–3.

— (1894) 'News of the Month', *South African Medical Journal*, Vol. 2, 82.

— (1896) 'A Black Woman's Description of a Missionary's Work', *Medical Missions at Home and Abroad*, Vol. 6, 209.

Anonymous (1986) 'Some Thoughts on a More Relevant or Indigenous Counselling Psychology in South Africa, Discovering the Socio-political Context of Oppression', *Psychology in Society*, Vol. 5, 81–9.

Appel, S. (1989) 'Eugenics in South Africa, 1920–1932, A Historical Note', *South African Journal of Science*, Vol. 85, 612.

Armstrong, D. (1982) 'The Doctor–patient Relationship, 1930–1980', in D. Wright and A. Treacher (eds), *The Problem of Medical Knowledge*, Edinburgh University Press, Edinburgh.

— (1983) *Political Anatomy of the Body: Medical Knowledge in Britain in the Twentieth Century*, Cambridge University Press, Cambridge.

— (1984) 'The Patient's View', *Social Science and Medicine*, Vol. 18, 737–44.

— (1985) 'Review Essay, The Subject and the Social in Medicine, An Appreciation of Michel Foucault', *Sociology of Health and Illness*, Vol. 7, 108–17.

— (1987) 'Foucault and the Problem of Human Anatomy', in G. Scambler (ed.), *Sociology Theory and Medical Sociology* (59–76), Tavistock, London.

— (1990) 'Use of the Genealogical Method in the Exploration of Chronic Illness', *Social Science and Medicine*, Vol. 30, 1225–7.

— (1993) 'Public Health Spaces and the Fabrication of Identity', *Sociology*, Vol. 27, 393–410.

— (1995) 'The Rise of Surveillance Medicine', *Sociology of Health and Illness*, Vol. 17, 393–404.

Arney, R. W. (1982) *Power and the Profession of Obstetrics*, University of Chicago Press, Chicago.

Arney, R. W. and B. J. Bergen, (1983) 'The Anomaly, the Chronic Patient, and the Play of Medical Power', *Sociology of Health and Illness*, Vol. 5, no. 1, 1–24.

— (1984) *Medicine and the Management of the Living*, University of Chicago Press, Chicago.

Arnold, D. (ed.) (1988) *Imperial Medicine and Indigenous Societies*, Manchester University Press, New York.

Asante, M. K. (1990) *Kemet, Afrocentricity and Knowledge*, Africa World Press, New Jersey.

Atterton, P. (1994) 'Power's Blind Struggle for Existence: Foucault, Genealogy and Darwinism', *History of the Human Sciences*, Vol. 7, no. 4, 1–20.

Baran, S. (1971) *Development and Validation of a TAT-type Projective Test for Use among Bantu-speaking People*, National Institute for Personnel Research, Johannesburg.

Barker, A. (1959) *The Man Next To Me: An Adventure in African Medical Practice*, Harper and Brothers, New York.

— (1971) 'New, Good Doctors for an Altered Society', *South African Medical Journal*, Vol. 45, 558–61.

— (1974) 'The Social Fabric, Language and Prejudice', *The Leech*, Vol. 44, no. 2, 33–4.

Barlow, M. R. (1971) 'That Forgotten Human Being – The Patient', *South African Medical Journal*, Vol. 45, 925–6.

Barnes, J./Aristotle (1984) *Aristotle, The Complete Works*, Vol. 1. Princeton University Press, Princeton, NJ.

Barrow, J. (1801) *An Account of Travels into the Interior of Southern Africa, in the Years 1797 and 1798*, T. Cadell Jun. and W. Davies, London.

Batman, S. (1582) *Uppon Bartholome. His Book de Propretatibus Rerum, Newly Corrected, Enlarged and Amended, with such Additions as are Required, into Every Useful Book*, Thomas East, London.

Becklake, M. R. (1943) 'A Health Survey of 156 African Children in the Dikonyaneng Nursery School, Orlando', *The Leech*, Vol. 14, no. 2, 29–31.

Bedaux Company for Africa (1939) *Diet in Relation to Physical Efficiency with Particular Reference to African Mine Natives*, Bedaux Company for Africa, Johannesburg.

Berger, P. and T. Luckmann (1967) *The Social Construction of Reality*, Tavistock, London.

Berger, S. and S. Lazarus (1987) 'The Views of Community Organisers on the Relevance of Psychological Practice in South Africa', *Psychology in Society*, Vol. 7, 6–23.

Bernstein, R. E. (1938) 'The Student's Attitude to the Bantu Problem', *The Leech*, Vol. 9, no. 1, 28–31.

Bhaba, H. (1986) 'The Other Question: Difference, Discrimination and the Discourse of Colonialism', in F. Barker, P. Hulme, M. Iversen and D. Loxley (eds), *Literature, Politics and Theory* (148–72), Macmillan, London.

Biesheuvel, S. (1953) 'A Technique for Measuring Attitudes of Educated Africans', *Proceedings of the South African Psychological Association*, Vol. 4, 13–20.

— (1955) 'The Measurement of African Attitudes Towards European Ethical Concepts, Customs, Laws and Administration of Justice', *Journal of the National Institute for Personnel Research*, Vol. 6, no. 1, 5–17.

— (1957) 'The Influence of Social Circumstances on the Attitudes of Educated Africans', *South African Journal of Science*, Vol. 53, 309–14.

— (1959) 'Further Studies on the Measurement of Attitudes Towards Western Ethical Concepts', *Journal of the National Institute for Personnel Research*, Vol. 10, 1–18.

Biko, S. (1988/1970a) 'We Blacks', in A. Stubbs (ed.), *I Write What I Like* (41–6), Penguin Books, Harmondsworth.

— (1988/1970b) 'Black Souls in White Skins?', in A. Stubbs (ed.), *I Write What I Like* (33–40), Penguin Books, Harmondsworth.

— (1988/1972) 'White Racism and Black Consciousness', in A. Stubbs (ed.), *I Write What I Like* (75–86), Penguin Books, Harmondsworth.

Bloom, L. (1960) 'Self Concepts and Social Status in South Africa: A Preliminary Cross-cultural Analysis', *Journal of Social Psychology*, Vol. 51, 103–12.

Boehmke, M. (1928) 'Some Social Implications of the Poor White Problem', *South African Journal of Science*, Vol. 25, 82–8.

Boonzaier, E. (1985) 'Choice of Healer: An Important Area of Interest for General Practitioners', *South African Family Practice*, Vol. 6, 368–73.

Boshoff, P. H. (1935) 'A Note on an Abnormality in the Thigh Musculature of a Bantu', *The Leech*, Vol. 6, no. 2, 49.

Bouchard, D. R. (ed.) (1977) *Michel Foucault, Language, Counter Memory and Practice: Selected Essays and Interviews*, Cornell University Press, Ithaca, NY.

Bourne, W. (1578) *A Booke called The Treasure for Traveilers, Divided into Five Bookes or Partes, Contayning very Necessary Matters, for all Sortes of Travailers, eyther by Sea or by Lande*, Thomas Woodcock, London.

Brantlinger, P. (1985) 'Victorians and Africans: The Genealogy of the Myth of the Dark Continent', *Critical Inquiry*, Vol. 12, 116–203.

Brebner, I. W. (1950) 'Surgery in the Bantu', *The Leech*, Vol. 21, no. 1, 47–8.

Brink, A. J. (1959) 'Coronary Arteries of the Bantu Heart', *South African Medical Journal*, Vol. 33, 407–8.

— (ed.) (1988) *South African Medical Research: Twenty Years of Growth*, Owen Burgess, Pinetown.

Brodie, W. and W. Rogers (1894) 'Acute Specific Rhinitis', *South African Medical Journal*, Vol. 2, 7–8.

Broomberg, A. (1935) 'An Institute for the Study of Medical Conditions among the Bantu in Natal', *The Leech*, Vol. 6, no. 2, 10–12.

— (1936) 'An Investigation into the Incidence of High Blood Pressure in the Native', *The Leech*, Vol. 7, no. 2, 30–4.

Bruce Bays, J. (1908) 'The Injurious Effects of Civilization Upon the Physical Condition of the Native Races of South Africa', in *Report of the South African Association for the Advancement of Science, 6th Meeting, Grahamstown, 1908* (253–62), African Book Co., Grahamstown.

Bruwer, J., J. Grobbelaar and H. van Zyl (1958) *Race Studies (differentiated syllabus) for Std VI*, Voortrekkerpers Beperk, Johannesburg.

Buchanan, N. and R. D. Cane (1976) 'Poisoning Associated with Witchdoctor Attendance', *South African Medical Journal*, Vol. 50, 1138–40.

Buchanan, N., E. Shuenyane, S. Mashigo, P. Mtangai and B. Unterhalter (1979) 'Factors Influencing Compliance in Ambulatory Black Urban Patients', *South African Medical Journal*, Vol. 55, 368–73.

Bulhan, H. A. (1981) 'Psychological Research in Africa: Genesis and Function', *Race and Class*, Vol. 23, no. 1, 25–41.

— (1985) *Frantz Fanon and the Psychology of Oppression*, Plenum, New York.

— (1990) 'Afrocentric Psychology: Perspectives and Practice', in L. J. Nicholas and S. Cooper (eds), *Psychology and Apartheid* (67–78), Vision Publications, Johannesburg.

Burns Thomson, W. (1854) *Medical Missions. A Prize Essay*, Johnstone and Hunter, Edinburgh.

Burrows, E. (1958) *A History of Medicine in South Africa up to the End of the Nineteenth Century*, A. A. Balkema, Cape Town.

Bury, M. C. (1986) 'Social Constructionism and the Development of Medical Sociology', *Sociology of Health and Illness*, Vol. 8, 137–69.

Butchart, A. (1996) 'The Industrial Panopticon: Mining and the Medical Construction of Migrant African Labour in South Africa, 1900–1950', *Social Science and Medicine*, Vol. 42, 185–97.

— (1997) 'The "Bantu Clinic": A Genealogy of the African Patient as Object and Effect of South African Clinical Medicine, 1930–1990', *Culture, Medicine and Psychiatry*, Vol. 21.

Butchart, A. and D. S. O. Brown (1991) 'Interpersonal Violence in Johannesburg-Soweto: Incidence, Determinants and Consequences', *Forensic Science International*, Vol. 52, 35–51.

Butchart, A. and M. Seedat (1991) 'Within and Without: Images of Community and Implications for South African Psychology', *Social Science and Medicine*, Vol. 31, 1093–102.

Campbell, G. D. (1961) 'The Language of the Patient', *South African Medical Journal*, Vol. 35, 1000.

Campbell, G. D. and H. C. Lugg (1958) *A Handbook to Aid in the Treatment of Zulu Patients*, University of Natal Press, Durban.

Cape Of Good Hope (1880a) *Report of the Commission Appointed to Inquire Into, and Report Upon, the Best Means of Moving the Asylum at Robben Island to the Mainland (Vol. 1: Report)*, Saul Solomon and Co., Cape Town.

— (1880b) *Report of the Commission Appointed to Inquire Into, and Report Upon, the Best Means of Moving the Asylum at Robben Island to the Mainland (Vol. 2: Evidence)*, Saul Solomon and Co., Cape Town.

Carnegie Commission (1932) *Joint Findings. The Poor White Problem in South Africa*, Pro-Ecclesia, Stellenbosch.

Cartwright, A. (1971) *Doctors of the Mines*, Purnell, Cape Town.

Cassell, J. (1962) 'Cultural Factors in the Interpretation of Illness', in S. L. Kark and G. W. Steuart (eds), *A Practice of Social Medicine* (233–44), E. and S. Livingstone, London.

Casualty Officer S. S. (1934) 'A Day in non-European Casualty', *The Leech*, Vol. 5, no. 2, 36–8.

Chamberlain, E. N. and C. M. Ogilvie (1967) *Symptoms and Signs in Clinical Medicine* (8th edn), John Wright and Sons, Bristol.

Chamber of Mines Archives, 2325/713. Gold Producer's Committee. Circular no. 7/23. *Report of the Sub-committee of the Transvaal Mine Medical Officers' Association on Tuberculosis among Mine Natives*, 23 February 1923.

— 2309/F1806. Tuberculosis Research Committee, *Comments on Preliminary Statement by Chairman of the Tuberculosis Research Committee on Prevention of Tuberculosis*, May 1925.

— 2309/1777. Tuberculosis Research Committee, *Statement on Prevention of Tuberculosis (Made by W. Watkins-Pitchford)*, 17 June 1925.

— 2308/1544. Tuberculosis Research Committee, *Eighth Progress Report of Dr Peter Allan's Investigation of Tuberculosis in the Ciskeian and Transkeian Territories (by P. Allan)*, 16 July 1928.

— 1898/3642. Witwatersrand Native Labour Association Ltd, Johannesburg, *Comments on Movements of Natives Through the Johannesburg Compound and Hospital (Prepared by Production Engineering SA Ltd)*, 10 May 1951.

Charlewood, G. P. (1956) *Bantu Gynaecology*, University of the Witwatersrand Press, Johannesburg.

Cheetham, R. W. S. and J. A. Griffiths (1982) 'Sickness and Medicine – an African Paradigm', *South African Medical Journal*, Vol. 62, 954–6.

Church Missionary Society (1902) *Typical Work in a Medical Mission. No. 4. Pioneer Work*, Church Missionary Society, London.

Cluver, E. H. (1934) *Public Health in South Africa* (1st edn), Central News Agency, Johannesburg.

Collard, R. F. (1900) 'The Zambesi. The Doctor's Work', *Medical Missions at Home and Abroad*, Vol. 8, 218.

Collender, K. G. (1945) 'Mass Miniature Radiography', *The Leech*, Vol. 16, no. 1, 36–9.

Colonial Secretary (1910) *Control and Treatment of Syphylitic Natives* (circular no. 1, CSO 3/18524), Colonial Secretary's Office, Pretoria.

Conroy, J. (1907) 'Insanity Among Natives in Cape Colony', *South African Medical Record*, Vol. 5, 33–6.

Cory Library (PR 3624) 'The Fitzgerald letter-book'. Unpublished archival material, Cory Library, Grahamstown.

Couve, C. (1986) 'Psychology and Politics in Manganyi's Work: A Materialist Critique', *Psychology in Society*, Vol. 5, 90–130.

Crowhurst-Archer, B. (1960) 'A Psychiatric Approach to Tuberculosis', *South African Medical Journal*, Vol. 34, 242–3.

— (1965) 'The Role of Psychiatry in the Medical Curriculum', *South African Medical Journal*, Vol. 39, 635–6.

Crush, J. (1992a) 'The Genealogy of the Compound'. Paper presented to the Eighth International Conference of Historical Geographers, Vancouver, 16–21 August.

— (1992b) 'Power and Surveillance on the South African Gold Mines', *Journal of Southern African Studies*, Vol. 18, 825–44.

Crush, J., A. Jeeves and D. Yudelman (1991) *South Africa's Labour Empire: A History of Black Migrancy to the Gold Mines*, David Phillip, Cape Town.

Cummins, S. L. (1929) 'Virgin soil – and After. A Working Conception of Tuberculosis in Children, Adolescents and Aborigines', *British Medical Journal*, Vol. 2, 39–41.

Dapper, O. (1970/1668) 'Kaffraria or Land of the Kaffirs, also named Hottentots', in I. Schapera and B. Farrington (eds), *The Early Cape Hottentots Described in the Writings of Olfert Dapper (1668), Willem Ten Rhyne (1686) and Johanus Gulielmus de Grevenbroek (1695)*, Negro Universities Press, Westport, CT.

Dart, R. (1937) 'Racial Origins', in I. Schapera (ed.), *The Bantu-speaking Tribes of South Africa* (95–126), George Routledge, London.

Dawes, A. (1986) 'The Notion of Relevant Psychology with Particular Reference to Africanist Pragmatic Initiatives', *Psychology in Society*, Vol. 5, 28–48.

Daynes, G. and N. P. Msengi (1979) '"Why am I ill? Who made me ill?" The

Relevance of Western Psychiatry in Tanskei', *South African Medical Journal*, Vol. 59, 307–8.

De Beer, C. (1984) *The South African Disease: Apartheid, Health and Health Services*, South African Research Services, Johannesburg.

— (1990) 'A Brief History of Divisions in Health Care', *The Leech*, Vol. 59, no. 1, 7–8.

De Kock, V. (1950) *Those in Bondage*, Allen and Unwin, London.

De Ridder, J. (1961) *The Personality of the Urban African in South Africa (A Thematic Apperception Test Study)*, Routledge and Kegan Paul, London.

De Villiers, S. (1985) '(Consideration of) Illness Causation among some Xhosa-speaking People', *South African Journal of Ethnology*, Vol. 8, no. 2, 48–52.

Devisse, J. (1979) *The Image of the Black in Western Art (Vol. 2)*, William Morrow, New York.

Dews, P. (1987) *Logics of Disintegration: Post-structuralist Thought and the Claims of Critical Theory*, Verso, London.

Dick, B. and P. J. Murray (1978) 'Traditional Healers and the Medical Profession', *South African Medical Journal*, Vol. 53, 311–12.

Dietrich, K. (1993) 'Of Salvation and Civilization: The Image of Indigenous South Africans in European Travel Illustrations from the Sixteenth to the Nineteenth Centuries'. Unpublished D Litt et Phil thesis, University of South Africa.

Doell, E. W. (1955) *Doctor against Witchdoctor*, Christopher Johnson, London.

— (1960) *A Mission Doctor Sees the Winds of Change*, Christopher Johnson, London.

Douglas, M. (1966) *Purity and Danger*, Routledge and Kegan Paul, London.

Dowie Dunn, D. (1939) 'Medical Practice among Natives', *South African Medical Journal*, Vol. 13, 51–3.

Dowling, S. (1973) 'Medicine in South Africa', *Proceedings of the Medical Association for the Prevention of War*, Vol. 2, no. 8, 225–57.

Dreosti, A. O. (1935) 'The Measurement of Heat Susceptibility of Native Mine Workers of the Witwatersrand'. Unpublished MD thesis, University of the Witwatersrand.

— (1936) 'Industrial Medicine in the Witwatersrand', *The Leech*, Vol. 7, no. 2, 5–11.

— (1937) 'Pathological Reactions Produced by Work in Hot and Humid Environments in the Witwatersrand Gold Mines', *South African Journal of Medical Sciences*, Vol. 2, 29–36.

Drewe, F. S. (1925) 'The Dawn of a New Hope in Pondoland', *Conquest by Healing*, Vol. 2, no. 2, 39–41.

Dreyfus, H. C. and P. Rabinow (1983) *Michel Foucault: Beyond Structuralism and Hermeneutics* (2nd edn), University of Chicago Press, Chicago.

Dubow, S. (1987) 'Race, Civilization and Culture: The Elaboration of Segregationist Discourse in the Inter-war Years', in S. Marks and S. Trapido (eds), *The Politics of Race, Class and Nationalism in Twentieth Century South Africa* (71–94), Longman, Harlow.

Dugard, J. H. (1944) 'Health Education in the Rural Native School', *South African Medical Journal*, Vol. 18, 417–18.

Dyke, R. H. (1898) 'Light and Shadows in Basutoland', *Medical Missions at Home and Abroad*, Vol. 8, 218.

Edginton, M. E., T. Hodkinson and H. C. Seftel (1972) 'Disease Patterns in a South African Rural Bantu Population', *South African Medical Journal*, Vol. 46, 968–76.

Editorial (1904) 'The Sanitary Whipping Boy', *South African Medical Record*, Vol. 2, 70–1.

— (1911) 'Centralized Public Health Administration', *South African Medical Record*, Vol. 9, 129–30.

— (1912) 'An Urgent Question of Sociology', *South African Medical Record*, Vol. 10, 201–3.

— (1913) 'Comparisons in Native Mine Mortality', *South African Medical Record*, Vol. 11, 253–4.

— (1914) 'Infectious Diseases Legislation', *South African Medical Record*, Vol. 12, 121–3.

— (1919) 'The Hand of God in the Direction and Development of Modern Medical Missions', *Medical Missions at Home and Abroad*, Vol. 17, 269–72.

— (1935) 'The Native in Health and Disease', *The Leech*, Vol. 6, no. 1, 3–4.

— (1939) 'Medical History', *The Leech*, Vol. 10, no. 2, 6–7.

— (1961) 'The Language of the Patient', *South African Medical Journal*, Vol. 35, 985–6.

— (1967a) 'Health Promotion in a Multiracial Community', *South African Medical Journal*, Vol. 41, 662.

— (1967b) 'A Cross-cultural Outlook in Medicine', *South African Medical Journal*, Vol. 41, 818.

— (1975) 'Recognition of Community Medicine', *South African Medical Journal*, Vol. 49, 32.

— (1978) 'Lifestyle and Health', *South African Medical Journal*, Vol. 53, 733.

— (1986) 'Psychology in Society', *Psychology in Society*, Vol. 5, 1–3.

Egan, C. J. (1877) 'Statistics on Disease in King William's Town, British Kaffraria', *Medical Times and Gazette*, 4 August, 112.

Eiselen, W. (1929) *Die Naturelle Vraagstuk*, Cape Town.

Eisenberg, L. and A. Kleinman (eds) (1981) *The Relevance of Social Science for Medicine*, Reidel, Dordrecht.

Elliot, G. A. (1953) 'Coronary Arteries and their Diseases in the Bantu', *The Leech*, Vol. 23, no. 1, 25–9.

— (1964) 'The Integration of Medicine with Mental Health Activities', *South African Medical Journal*, Vol. 38, 148–51.

Erasmus, P. F. (1975) *Thematic Apperception Test (TAT-Z)*, Institute for Psychological and Edumetric Research, Human Sciences Research Council, Pretoria.

— (1984) *Manual for the Thematic Apperception Test (Zulu) (TAT-Z)*, Human Sciences Research Council, Pretoria.

Fanon, F. (1967) *Black Skin, White Masks*, Grove Press, New York.

— (1978) 'Medicine and Colonialism', in J. Ehrenreich (ed.), *The Cultural Crisis of Modern Medicine* (229–51), Monthly Review Press, New York.

Farrand, D. (1984) 'Is a Combined Western and Traditional Health Service for Black Patients Desirable?', *South African Medical Journal*, Vol. 66, 779–80.

Fick, M. L. (1927) 'The Value of Mental Tests. II. Application to Economic, Educational, and Colour Problems', *Social and Industrial Review*, Vol. 3, 223–6.

— (1929) 'South African Intelligence Tests: Comparison of Various Racial Groups, *Social and Industrial Review*, Vol. 8, 701–5.

Findlay, R. A. (1960) 'The Emotional Pattern of the Tribal Zulu as it Affects Pre-anaesthetic Assessment and Management', *South African Medical Journal*, Vol. 34, 854–5.

Fischer, W. O. A. (1929) 'A Preliminary Report on 1,402 Consecutive Autopsies on Native Mine Workers', *South African Medical Journal*, Vol. 3, 511–16.

— (1932) 'Record of 561 Consecutive Autopsies on Native Mine Workers', *South African Medical Journal*, Vol. 6, 359–61.

Fitzgerald, J. P. (1888) *A Short History of the Grey Hospital, Together with an Essay on Improved Sanitation*, S. E. Rowles and Co., King William's Town.

Flint, V. J. (1992) *The Imaginative Landscape of Christopher Columbus*, Princeton University Press, Princeton, NJ.

Flint, W. (1919) 'Race-consciousness and the Scientific Spirit', *South African Journal of Science*, Vol. 16, 1–16.

Foster, D. (1986) 'The South African Crisis of 1985', *Psychology in Society*, Vol. 5, 49–65.

— (1990) 'Historical and Legal Traces, 1800–1900', in S. Lea and D. Foster (eds), *Perspectives on Mental Handicap in South Africa*, Butterworths, Durban.

Foster, D. and D. Skinner (1990) 'Detention and Violence: Beyond Victimology', in N. C. Manganyi and A. Du Toit (eds), *Political Violence and the Struggle in South Africa* (205–33), Southern Book Publishers, Halfway House.

Foucault, M. (1972) *The Archaeology of Knowledge*, Tavistock, London.

— (1973) *The Order of Things*, Random House, New York.

— (1976) *The Birth of the Clinic: An Archaeology of Medical Perception*, London, Routledge.

— (1977) *Discipline and Punish*, Pantheon, New York.

— (1979) *The History of Sexuality*, Vol. 1, Allen Lane, London.

Fox, F. and D. Back (1938) *A Preliminary Survey of the Agricultural and Nutritional Problems of the Ciskei and Transkeian Territories*, Transvaal Chamber of Mines, Johannesburg.

Friedlander, F. C. (1974) 'Grey's Hospital: The Oldest Hospital on its Original Site in the Republic', *South African Medical Journal*, Vol. 48, 187–92.

Friedman, J. (1981) *The Monstrous Races in Medieval Thought and Art*, Harvard University Press, Cambridge, MA.

Fuller, E. (1897) 'Public Health Notes', *South African Medical Journal*, Vol. 5, 42–6.

Gale, G. W. (1938) *A Suggested Approach to the Health Needs of the Native Rural Areas of South Africa*, Record Printing Co., Benoni.

— (1943) *Doctor or Witchdoctor?*, South African Institute of Race Relations, Johannesburg.

Galloway, A. (1941) 'Palatal Measurement of Negro and Other Crania', *South African Journal of Science*, Vol. 37, 285–92.

Gear, H. S. (1938) 'The Field for Vital Statistics and Epidemiological Studies in Municipal Health Services', *The Leech*, Vol. 9, no. 2, 77–81.

G. E. F. M. (1898) *Medical Missions*, Simpkin, Marshall, Hamilton, Kent and Co., London.

Gelfand, M. (1943) *The Sick African: A Clinical Study* (1st edn), Stewart Printing Company, Cape Town.

— (1947) *The Sick African: A Clinical Study* (2nd edn), Stewart Printing Company, Cape Town.

— (1957) *The Sick African: A Clinical Study* (3rd edn), Juta and Co., Cape Town.

— (1984) *Christian Doctor and Nurse (The History of Medical Missions in South Africa from 1799–1976)*, Marrianhill Mission Press, Marrianhill.

Gergen, K. J. (1982) *Toward Transformation in Social Knowledge*, Springer-Verlag, New York.

Gerhardt, U. (1989) *Ideas about Illness: An Intellectual and Political History of Medical Sociology*, Macmillan, Basingstoke.

Gilman, S. (1985) *Difference and Pathology: Stereotypes of Sexuality, Race, and Madness*, Cornell University Press, Ithaca, NY.

Goddard, J. E. (1957) 'Health Visiting Among the Urban African', *Public Health* (Johannesburg), Vol. 17, no. 12, 533–6.

Goldberg, S. (1941) 'The Origin of the Lumbrical Muscles in the Hand of the South African Native', *The Leech*, Vol. 12, no. 2, 35–7.

Goldstein, S. (1993) 'Tracing the Health Promotion Movement', in M. Westaway (ed.), *Health Promotion – Proceedings of Six One-day Workshops held in Cape Town, Durban, Bloemfontein, Pietersburg and Port Elizabeth, 1–12 November 1993*, Medical Research Council, Pretoria.

Gordon, A. (1935) 'Mine Hygiene', *Public Health* (Johannesburg), Vol. 2, no. 5, 3–10.

Gordon, C. (ed.) (1980) *Power/knowledge: Selected Interviews and Other Writings 1972–1977 by Michel Foucault*, Harvester Press, Brighton.

Gorgas, W. (1914) *Recommendations as to Sanitation Concerning Employees on the Mines on the Rand*, Argus Printing and Publishing Company, Cape Town.

Grafton, A. (1992) *New Worlds, Ancient Texts: The Power of Tradition and Shock of Discovery*, Belknap Press of Harvard University Press, Cambridge, MA.

Greenblatt, S. (1992) *Marvellous Possessions*, Oxford University Press, Oxford.

Greenlees, D. (1895) 'Insanity Among the Natives of South Africa', *Journal of Mental Science*, Vol. 41, 71–7.

Grevenbroek, J. (1970/1695) 'An Elegant and Accurate Account of the African Race living round the Cape of Good Hope Commonly called Hottentots', in I. Schapera and B. Farrington (eds), *The Early Cape Hottentots Described in the Writings of Olfert Dapper (1668), Willem Ten Rhyne (1686) and Johanus Gulielmus de Grevenbroek (1695)*, Negro Universities Press, Westport, CT.

Grist, F. (1924) 'A Dream Come True. Medical Missionary Work in Pondoland, South Africa', *Medical Missions at Home and Abroad*, Vol. 20, 6–10.

Grobbelaar, F. P. (1934) 'Random Jottings of a Country Practitioner', *The Leech*, Vol. 5, no. 2, 13–14.

Gumede, M. V. (1974) 'Traditions and Customs', *The Leech*, Vol. 44, no. 2, 35–8.

Harstock, N. (1990) 'Foucault on Power: A Theory for Women?', in L. Nicholson (ed.), *Feminism/postmodernism* (157–76), Routledge and Kegan Paul, London.

Hattersley, A. F. (1955) *A Hospital Century. Grey's Hospital, Pietermaritzburg 1855–1955*, A. A. Balkema, Cape Town.

Hayes, G. (1993) 'Finding Spaces for Critical Thought'. Unpublished paper presented to the Forum on 'The Role and Function of Psychology in a New South Africa', Johannesburg, 3 September.

Heap, M. (1985) 'Health and Disease in Two Villages in South Eastern Lesotho: A Social Anthropolgical Perspective'. Unpublished M Sc dissertation, University of Cape Town.

Heap, M. and M. Ramphele (1991) 'The Quest for Wholeness: Health Care Strategies Among the Residents of Council-built Hostels in Cape Town, *Social Science and Medicine*, Vol. 32, 117–26.

Henriques, T., W. Holloway, C. Urwin, C. Venn and V. Walkerdine (eds) (1984) *Changing the Subject: Psychology, Social Regulation and Subjectivity*, Methuen, London.

Hertslet, L. E. (1946) 'The New Vision of Health from Four Angles', *Public Health* (Johannesburg), Vol. 10, no. 7, 20–6.

Hicks, J. W. (1896) 'The Sacredness of the Medical Calling', *Medical Missions at Home and Abroad*, Vol. 6, 87–8.

Higginson, J., C. Isaacson and I. Simson (1960) 'The Pathology of Cryptogenic Heart Disease', *Archives of Pathology*, Vol. 70, 497–507.

Hill, E. (1904) *Report on the Plague in Natal 1902–3*, Cassell, London.

Hinkle, G. J. (1986) 'Foucault's Power/knowledge and American Sociological Theorizing', *Human Studies*, Vol. 10, 35–59.

Hirschberg, W. E. (1967) *Monumenta Ethnographia: Early Ethnographical Pictorial Documents. Vol. 1: Black Africa*, Akademische Druk, Graz, Austria.

Holden, W. (1963/1867) *The Past and Future of the Kafir Races*, C. Struik, Cape Town.

Holland, H. T. (1923) 'Surgery', in H. Martin and G. Weir (eds), *Medical Practice in Africa and the East*, Students' Christian Movement, London.

Humphreys, N. (1958) *Mission Stories*, Blackfriars, London.

Huntley, G. (n.d.) *Simple Games for the Physical Education Lesson and for Social Occasions*, Juta and Co., Cape Town.

Illich, I. (1976) *Medical Nemesis*, Random House, New York.

Impey, S. P. (1896) *A Handbook of Leprosy*, J. and A. Churchill, London.

Ingle, R. F. (1963) *Doctor's Note*, Society for the Propagation of the Gospel, London.

— (1973) 'An Experience of Amagquira', *South African Medical Journal*, Vol. 47, 333–4.

Irvine, I. G. and D. Macauley (1905) 'The Life History of the Native Labourer', *Proceedings of the 75th meeting of the South African Association for the Advancement of Science*, Vol. III (342–67), South African Association for the Advancement of Science, Johannesburg.

Ivey, G. (1986) 'Elements of a Critical Psychology', *Psychology in Society*, Vol. 5, 4–27.

James, T. (1975) 'The First Fifty – A Review of the South African Medical Congresses', *South African Medical Journal*, Vol. 49, 1313–16.

Jansen, G. (1973) *The Doctor–Patient Relationship in an African Tribal Society*, Van Gorkum and Co., Assen.

Jansen van Rensburg, J. A. (1938) 'The Learning Ability of the South African Native Compared with that of the European', *Research Series No. 5*, South African Council for Educational and Social Research, Pretoria.

Jokl, E. (1935) 'Aortic Failure and Physical Activity', *The Leech*, Vol. 6, 35–6.

Kark, S. L. (1934a) 'The Economic Factor in the Health of the Bantu in South Africa', *The Leech*, Vol. 5, no. 2, 18–22.

— (1934b) 'The Society for the Study of Medical Conditions Among the Bantu', *The Leech*, Vol. 5, no. 2, 67–8.

— (1935) 'Problems of National Health', *The Leech*, Vol. 6, no. 2, 12–19.

— (1942) 'A Health Service Among the Rural Bantu', *South African Medical Journal*, Vol. 16, 197–8.

— (1944) 'A Health Unit as Family Doctor and Health Advisor', *South African Medical Journal*, Vol. 18, 39–46.

Kark, S.L. and J. Cassell (1952) 'The Pholela Health Centre. A Progress Report', *South African Medical Journal*, Vol. 26, 101–4, 131–6.

Kark, S. L. and E. Kark (1962) 'A Practice of Social Medicine', in S. L. Kark and G. W. Steuart (eds), *A Practice of Social Medicine* (3–40), E. and S. Livingstone, London.

Kark, S. L. and H. Le Riche (1944) 'A Health Study of South African Bantu School-children', *South African Medical Journal*, Vol. 18, 100–3.

Kark, S. L. and Steuart, G. W. (1957) 'Health Education and Neighbourhood Family Practice', *Health Education Journal*, Vol. 15, 1–10.

Kay, S. (1834) *Travels and Researches in Caffraria, Describing the Character, Customs, and Moral Condition of the Tribes Inhabiting that Portion of Southern Africa*, Harper and Row, New York.

Keen, P. (1948) 'A Psychological Approach to Bantu Medicine', *The Leech*, Vol. 19, no. 1, 6–9.

Kiernan, J. P. (1978) 'Is the Witchdoctor Medically Competent?', *South African Medical Journal*, Vol. 53, 1072–3.

Kjome, J. (1963) *Back of Beyond. Bush Nurse in South Africa*, Augsburg Publishing House, Minneapolis.

Kleinman, A. (1980) *Patients and Healers in the Context of Culture*, University of California Press, Berkeley.

Kloppers, P. J. (1973) 'The Aims of the Transkei and Ciskei Research Society', *South African Medical Journal*, Vol. 47, 287–98.

Kolben, P. (1731) *The Present State of the Cape of Good Hope, or, A Particular Account of the Several Nations of the Hottenots, Volumes 1 and 2* (trans. G. Medley), W. Innys, London.

Krige, P. E. (1939) 'The March of Medicine: A Brief Biographical History', *The Leech*, Vol. 10, no. 1, 63–73.

Kritzman, L. D. (ed.) (1988) *Michel Foucault: Politics, Philosophy, Culture: Interviews and Other Writings, 1977–1984*, Routledge, New York.

Kuper, H. (1947) 'The Concept of Social Medicine Applied to some Bantu-speaking Tribes', *The Leech*, Vol. 18, no. 1, 55–8, 66.

Laidler, P. W. (1937) 'Medical Establishments and Institutions at the Cape During the Opening Years of the Nineteenth Century', *South African Medical Journal*, Vol. 11, 481–6.

— (1938) 'Medical Establishments and Institutions at the Cape. VI. Dr J. Atherstone and the Introduction of Anaesthetics', *South African Medical Journal*, Vol. 12, 453–6.

— (1939) 'Medical Establishments and Institutions at the Cape. VIII. Through Epidemics to Reform', *South African Medical Journal*, Vol. 13, 223–9.

Laidler, P. W. and M. Gelfand (1971) *South Africa: Its Medical History 1652–1898*, C. Struik, Cape Town.

Lambley, P. (1980) *The Psychology of Apartheid*, Secker and Warburg, London.

Lapping, D. J. (1961) 'Polela Health Centre (a letter)', *South African Medical Journal*, Vol. 35, 39.

Laubscher, B. J. F. (1937) *Sex, Custom and Psychopathology: A Study of South African Pagan Natives*, George Routledge and Sons, London.

La Vaillant, M. (1796) *Travels Into the Interior Parts of Africa. By the Way of the Cape of Good Hope; in the Years 1780, 81, 82, 83, 84, and 85.* Vols 1 and 2 (2nd edn), G. G. and J. Robinson, London.

Lee, S. G. (1950) 'A Preliminary Investigation of the Personality of the Educated African by Means of a Projective Technique'. Unpublished MA dissertation, University of Natal, Pietermaritzburg.

Leech, The (1978) 'The Role and Place of the Traditional Medicine Man and "Witchdoctor" in African Health Care', *The Leech*, Vol. 48, no. 2.

Leibbrandt, H. C. V. (1901) *Precis of the Archives of the Cape of Good Hope. Journal, 1662 – 1670*, W. A. Richards and Sons, Cape Town.

Lemert, C. C. and G. Gillan (1982) *Michel Foucault: Social Theory as Transgression*, Columbia University Press, New York.

Lerer, L. B., A. Butchart and M. Terre Blanche (1995) '"A Bothersome Death" – Narrative Accounts of Infant Mortality in Cape Town, South Africa', *Social Science and Medicine*, Vol. 40, 945–53.

Lerer, L. B. and N. Scheper-Hughes (in press) 'Who is the Rogue? Hunger, Death and Circumstance in John Mampe Square', in N. Scheper-Hughes (ed.), *Mothers and Children at Risk*, University of California Press, Berkeley.

Le Riche, H. (1938) 'A Short Review of Some Recent Work in Nutrition', *The Leech*, Vol. 9, no. 2, 45–9.

Letlhaku, L. L. M. (1961) 'A Postmortem Examination of the South African Health-centre Service Experiment', *South African Medical Journal*, Vol. 35, 917–19.

Letts, M. (1949) *Sir John Mandeville*, Batchworth, London.

Levett, A. (1987) 'Childhood Sexual Abuse: Event, Fact or Structure?', *Psychology in Society*, Vol. 8, 79–100.

Lichtenstein, H. (1812) *Travels in Southern Africa in the Years 1803, 1804, 1805 and 1806* (trans. A. Plumptre), Henry Colburn, London.

Linnaeus, C. (Carl von Linne) (1735) *Systema Naturae, sive regna tria naturae systematice proposita per classes, ordines, genera, & species*, Theodorum Haak, Leyden.

Lipsius, J. (1592) *A Direction for Travaillers*, C. Bubie, London.

Liston, J. (1944) 'Health Officials', *Public Health* (Johannesburg), Vol. 8, no. 4, 9–15.

Loram, C. T. (1922) 'The Claims of the Native Question upon Scientists', *South African Journal of Science*, Vol. 18, 99–109.

Lowe, J. (1886) *Medical Missions. Their Place and Power*, Fisher Unwin, London.

Lynch, F. P. (1900) 'A Cure and its Results', *Medical Missions at Home and Abroad*, Vol. 8, 297.

McCord, J. B. (1926) 'Native Witch Doctors and Healers', *South African Medical Record*, Vol. 24, 195–205.

— (1951) *My Patients were Zulus*, Rinehart, New York.

McCulloch, J. (1995) *Colonial Psychiatry and the 'African Mind'*, Cambridge University Press, Cambridge.

McGregor, M. (1944) 'Health Education for Rural Bantu Children', *South African Medical Journal*, Vol. 18, 418–19.

McHugh, S. and T. M. Vallis (eds) (1986) *Illness Behaviour: A Multidisciplinary Model*, Plenum, New York.

McKeown, T. (1979) *The Role of Medicine: Dream, Mirage or Nemesis*, Basil Blackwell, Oxford.

McVicar, N. (1908) 'Health Training in Schools, with Special Reference to Native Schools', in *Report of the South African Association for the Advancement of Science, 6th Meeting, Grahamstown, 1908* (309–14), African Book Co., Grahamstown.

Malan, M. (1988) *In Quest of Health*, Lowry Publishers, Johannesburg.

Malefijt, A. (1968) 'Homo Monstrosus', *Scientific American*, Vol. 219, 112–18.

Malherbe, J. (1934) 'A Rare Congenital Abnormality of the Heart (bilocular heart)', *The Leech*, Vol. 5, no. 3, 22–4.

Manganyi, N. C. (1973) *Being-Black-in-the-World*, Ravan Press, Johannesburg.

— (1974) 'Health and Disease: Some Topical Problems of Socio-cultural Transition', *South African Medical Journal*, Vol. 48, 922–4.

— (1977) *Mashangu's Reverie*, Ravan Press, Johannesburg.

— (1991) *Treachery and Innocence: Psychology and Racial Difference in South Africa*, Ravan Press, Johannesburg.

Marks, S. and N. Andersson (1988) 'Typhus and Social Control in South Africa, 1917–1950', in R. Macleod and M. Lewis (eds), *Disease, Medicine and Empire* (257–83), Routledge, London.

Marley, R. (1860) *Medical Missionaries; or Medical Agency Co-operative with Christian Mission to the Heathen*, James Blackwood, London.

Martin, H. and H. Weir (eds) (1923) *Medical Practice in Africa and the East*, Students' Christian Movement, London.

Marwick, J. S. (1918) 'The Natives in the Larger Towns', *South African Journal of Science*, Vol. 15, 590–610.

Maynard, G. (1913) *An Enquiry into the Etiology, Manifestations and Prevention of Pneumonia amongst Natives on the Rand, Recruited from Tropical Areas*, South African Institute for Medical Research (publication no. 2), Johannesburg.

Maynard, G. and G. Turner (1914) *Anthropological Notes on Bantu Natives from Portuguese East Africa*, South African Institute for Medical Research (publication no. 4), Johannesburg.

Mead, R. (1748) *A Discourse on the Small Pox and the Measles*, John Brindley, London.

Medical Association of South Africa (1974) 'The True Facts About Medicine in South Africa', *South African Medical Journal* (supplement), Vol. 48, 1–7.

Meirus, A. (1587) *Certaine Briefe, and Speciall Instructions for Gentlemen, Merchants, Students, Souldiers, Mariners, and c. Employed in Services Abrode, or Anie Way Occassioned to Converse in the Kingdomes and Governements of Forren Princes*, John Woolf, London.

Menko, H. (1954) *Contributions of the Netherlands to the Development of South African Medicine (1652–1902)*, H.A.U.M., Cape Town.

Mentzel, O. F. (1921/1785) *A Complete and Authentic Geographical and Topographical Description of the Famous (and all things considered remarkable) African Cape of Good Hope* (in three parts, trans. H. J. Mandelbrote), Van Riebeeck Society, Cape Town.

Mercury, The (1959) '100 Years of Service to Humanity: Centenary of the Grey Hospital', *The Mercury* (supplement), 11 June.

Messum, G. B. (1895) 'Presidential Address to the South African Republic Medical Association', *South African Medical Journal*, Vol. 2, 267–9.

Meyer, E. T. (1941) 'Studies on Physical Measurements of Bantu School Children', *The Leech*, Vol. 11, no. 2, 37–39.

Mfenyana, K. (1988) 'Attitudes of Rural African Patients Toward the Use of Drugs as Prescribed by Doctors, *South African Family Practitioner*, Vol. 9, no. 4, 137–42.

Mgobozi, P. M. (1974) 'The Problem of Tuberculosis among Africans', *The Leech*, Vol. 44, no. 2, 45, 56.

Miller, J. (1849) *Medical Missions. An Address to Students*, Simpkin Marshall and Co., London.

Miller, T. and L. Swartz (1990) 'Clinical Psychology in General Hospital Settings: Issues in Interprofessional Relationships', *Professional Psychology*, Vol. 21, 48–53.

Minde, M. (1956) 'Early Psychiatry in Natal', *South African Medical Journal*, Vol. 30, 287–91.

Minnaar, G. G. (1975) 'Die Invloed van Verwestering op die Persoonlikheid van 'n Groep Zoeloemans'. Unpublished Ph D thesis, University of Pretoria.

Mirvish, L. (1962) 'Psycho-somatic Aspects of Gastro-intestinal Diseases', *South African Medical Journal*, Vol. 36, 210–12.

Mitchell, J. A. (1908) 'The Growth of the Native Races of the Cape Colony and Some Factors Affecting It', in *Report of the South African Association for the Advancement of Science, 6th Meeting, Grahamstown, 1908*, African Book Co., Grahamstown.

Mokhobo, K. P. (1971) 'Medical History-taking among the Bantu Tribes of South Africa', *South African Medical Journal*, Vol. 45, 111–14.

M.O.M. (1894) 'Climate and Venereal Disease', *South African Medical Journal*, Vol. 11, 154.

Moodie, D. E. (1960) *The Record, or a Series of Official Papers Relative to the Condition and Treatment of the Native Tribes of South Africa: Part III*, A. A. Balkema, Cape Town.

Moodie, D. (1976) *The Perception and Behaviour Patterns of Black Mineworkers on a Group Gold Mine*, Anglo American Corporation, Johannesburg.

Moorshead, F. (1922) 'The Evangelistic Function of Medical Missions, *Medical Missions at Home and Abroad*, Vol. 19, 17–19.

Moorshead, R. F. (1926) *The Way of the Doctor: A Study in Medical Missions*, Carey Press, London.

Movsowitz, L. (1971) 'Some Thoughts on Medical Training from a Morbidity Survey in General Practice in Uppington', *South African Medical Journal*, Vol. 45, 133–5.

Muller, J. (1985) 'The End of Psychology: Review Essay of "Changing the Subject"', *Psychology in Society*, Vol. 3, 33–42.

Muller, J. and N. Cloete (1987) 'The "White Hands": Academic Social Scientists, Engagement and the Struggle in South Africa', *Social Epistemology*, Vol. 1, 141–54.

Munster, S. (1550) *Cosmographiae Universalis Libri vi*, Basel.

Murray, J. F. (1963) 'History of the South African Institute for Medical Research', *South African Medical Journal*, Vol. 37, 389–95.

Murray, W. A. (1932) *The Poor White Problem in South Africa. Report of the Carnegie Commission, Part IV: Health Report*, Pro-Ecclesia, Stellenbosch.

Mutwa, C. (1974) 'The Role of the Medicine-man in Black Society', *The Leech*, Vol. 44, no. 2, 79–81.

National Health Services Commission (1944) *Minutes of Evidence: Vol. 8. 135th sitting, Polela, 3 August 1943 (8647–70)*, Government Printer, Cape Town.

Native Recruting Corporation Ltd (1928) 'Suggestions Relating to the Medical Examination of Native Mine Labourers', *Proceedings of the Transvaal Mine Medical Officers' Association*, Vol. 8, 7–8.

Nell, V. (1991) 'PINS: That Trashy, Trashing Journal', *Psychology in Society*, Vol. 15, 67–70.

— (1992) 'The Case for an Independent Licensing Board for Psychology', *South African Journal of Psychology*, Vol. 18, 17–20.

Nell, V. and A. Butchart (1989) 'Studying Violence in a South African City', *Critical Health*, Vol. 28, 44–9.

Nettleton, S. (1992) *Power, Pain and Dentistry*, Open University Press, Buckingham.

Newton, A. (1950). '"Traveller's" Tales of Wonder and Imagination', in A. Newton (ed.), *Travel and Travellers of the Middle Ages* (159–73), A. Knopf, New York.

Ngubane, H. (1977) *Body and Mind in Zulu Medicine*, Academic Press, New York.

N.V.S. and P.K. (1944) 'Book Review. The Sick African', *The Leech*, Vol. 15, no. 2, 37–9.

Orenstein, A. (1922) 'Compound Sanitation', *Proceedings of the Transvaal Mine Medical Officers' Association*, Vol. 2, no. 5, 1–15.

Orford, M. (1935) 'Bodily Habitus in the Bantu', *The Leech*, Vol. 6, no. 1, 41–3.

Orwell, G. (1949) 'Nineteen Eighty-four', Secker and Warburg, London.

Packard, R. (1989) *White Plague, Black Labour*, University of Natal Press, Pietermaritzburg.

Park-Ross, G. A. (1937) 'Tropical Sanitation and its Application to Native Reserves', *Public Health* (Johannesburg), Vol. 2, no. 4, 27–32.

Parry, C. D. H., J. Tibbs, G. Cummins, H. Brice, E. Angellos, F. Thompson, C. Stretch and B. Stoppe (1994) 'A Study of the Knowledge, Attitudes, Perceptions and Awareness of Youth towards Alcohol and Alcohol Advertising', *Urbanisation and Health Newsletter*, Vol. 21, 43–50.

Paternek, M. (1987) 'Norms and Normalization: Michel Foucault's Over-extended Panoptic Machine', *Human Studies*, Vol. 10, 97–121.

Paterson, R. L. (1950) 'Rural and Mission Hospitals in Relation to Disease and Health in the Bantu', *The Leech*, Vol. 21, no. 1, 90–4.

Pearson, A. and R. Mouchet (1923) *Practical Hygiene of Native Compounds in Tropical Africa*, Bailliere, Tindall and Cox, London.

Phillips, H. (1990) *Black October*, The Government Printer, Pretoria.

Phillips, R. E. (1948) *The Bantu in the City. A Study of Cultural Adjustment on the Witwatersrand*, Lovedale Press, Lovedale.

Pitfield, D. (1995) 'Medicalization and Medical Intervention: What Does it Mean in Practice?', in C. Allais (ed.), *Sociology in Health and Illness*, Lexicon, Isando.

Pliny (1938) *Natural History. With an English Translation in Ten Volumes.* Vol. 1 (trans. H. Rackham), Heinemann, London.

Posel, D. (1991) *The Making of Apartheid 1948–1961*, Clarendon Press, Oxford.

Poster, M. (1990) *The Mode of Information*, University of Chicago Press, Chicago.

Potter, J. and M. Wetherell (1987) *Discourse and Social Psychology: Beyond Attitudes and Behaviour*, Sage, London.

Power, D. J. and H. De V. Heese (1978) 'The Role of Community Paediatrics in South Africa', *South African Medical Journal*, Vol. 53, 408–10.

Pratt, M. L. (1985) 'Scratches on the Face of the Country; or, What Mr. Barrow Saw in the Land of the Bushmen', *Critical Inquiry*, Vol. 12, 119–43.

— (1992) *Imperial Eyes: Travel Writing and Transculturation*, Routledge, London.

Pretorius, C. C. (1977) 'A Comparative Study of Tswana Schizophrenic Patients and "Normal" Tswana Subjects by Means of the TAT-Z Test'. Unpublished MA dissertation, University of South Africa.

Public Health Notes (1894) 'Public Health, Cape Town', *South African Medical Journal*, Vol. 2, 75.

Purchas, S. (1619) *Microcosmus, or the Historie of Man*, London.

Radcliffe-Brown, A. R. (1923) 'The Methods of Ethnology and Social Anthropology', *South African Journal of Science*, Vol. 20, 124–47.

Raven-Hart, R. (1967) *Before van Riebeeck: Callers at South Africa from 1488 to 1652*, C. Struik, Cape Town.

— (1971) *Cape of Good Hope 1652–1702: The First Fifty Years of Dutch Colonisation as Seen by Callers* (Vol. 1), A. A. Balkema, Cape Town.

Ravenstein, E. E. (1898) *A Journal of the First Voyage of Vasco da Gama 1497–99*, Hakluyt Society, London.

Reader, D. H. (1963) 'African and Afro-European Research: A Summary of Previously Unpublished Findings in the National Institute for Personnel Research', *Psychologia Africana*, Vol. 10, 1–18.

Reid, A. (1927) *Sanitation and Public Health* (2nd edn), Juta and Co., Cape Town.

Rheinallt-Jones, J. D. (1926) 'The Need of a Scientific Basis for South African Native Policy', *South African Journal of Science*, Vol. 23, 79–91.

Rogers, P. (1992) 'Explanatory Models of Illness Amongst Primary Health Care Users in Mamre'. Unpublished MA dissertation, University of Cape Town.

Rorty, R. (1986) 'Foucault and Epistemology', in D. C. Hoy (ed.), *Foucault: A Critical Reader*, Basil Blackwell, Oxford.

Rose, N. (1985) *The Psychological Complex: Psychology, Politics and Society in England, 1869–1939*, Routledge and Kegan Paul, London.

— (1988) 'Calculable Minds and Manageable Individuals', *History of the Human Sciences*, Vol. 1, no. 2, 179–200.

Royal Society (1665–66) *Philosophical Transactions, Giving some Accompt of the Present Undertakings, Studies, and Labours of the Ingenious in Many Considerable Parts of the World*, John Mortyn and James Allestrey, London.

Sachs, S. B. (1959) 'The Meadowlands Method, An Experiment in an Integrated Curative Service', *South African Medical Journal*, 33, 781–4.

Sachs, W. (1937) *Black Hamlet: The Mind of an African Negro as Revealed by Psychoanalysis*, Geoffrey Bles, London.

— (1996) *Black Hamlet* (with introductory essays by S. Dubow and J. Rose), Witwatersrand University Press, Johannesburg.

Sandeman, J. C. (1965) 'The Thoracic Azygos Venous System in the Bantu', *The Leech*, Vol. 35, no. 1, 17–18.

Schaap, M. E. (1953) 'Health Visiting Among the Urban Bantu', *Public Health* (Johannesburg), Vol. 17, no. 12, 533–6.

Schapera, I. (ed.) (1959) *David Livingstone. Family Letters 1841–1856* (Vol. 1), Chatto and Windus, London.

— (ed) (1961) *Livingstone's Missionary Correspondence, 1841–1856*, Chatto and Windus, London.

Schedel, H. (1493) *Liber chronicarum*, Nuremburg.

Scheper-Hughes, N. (1990) 'Three Propositions for a Critically Applied Medical Anthropology', *Social Science and Medicine*, Vol. 30, 189–97.

Schimlek, C. (1950) *Medicine versus Witchcraft*, Marrianhill Mission Press, Marrianhill.

Schlebusch, L. (1990) 'An Overview of Bridging the Mind–Body Dichotomy Within the Health Care System', in L. Schlebusch (ed.), *Clinical Health*

Psychology: A Behavioural Medicine Perspective (3–23), Southern Books, Halfway House.

Scrooby, C. (1994) 'Illness Experience and Brain Damage: A Narrative Window on Stroke and Alzheimer's Disease'. Unpublished MA dissertation, University of South Africa.

Seager, J. (1993) 'Addressing the Impact of Urbanisation on Health in South Africa', in D. Yach and G. Martin (eds), *Building a Healthy Nation Through Research* (73–85), Medical Research Council, Cape Town.

Seedat, M. A. (1993) 'Topics, Trends and Silences in South African Psychology 1948–1988'. Unpublished Ph D thesis, University of the Western Cape.

Seftel, H. C. (1964) 'Diabetes in the Johannesburg African', *The Leech*, Vol. 34, no. 4, 82–7.

Segal, I. and L. Ou Tim (1979) 'The Witchdoctor and the Bowel', *South African Medical Journal*, Vol. 56, 308–10.

Seymour, M. C./Mandeville (1967) *Mandeville's Travels*, Clarendon Press, Oxford.

Sharpe, W. D./Isidore (1964) 'Isidore of Seville. The Medical Writings. An English Translation with an Introduction and Commentary', *Transactions of the American Philosophical Society*, Vol. 54, no. 2, 1–75.

Shearer, O. L. (1938) 'A National Physical and Health Education Scheme', *Public Health* (Johannesburg), Vol. 3, no. 3, 13–20.

Sherwood, E. T. (1957) 'On the Designing of TAT Pictures, with Special Reference to a Set for an African People Assimilating Western Culture', *Journal of Social Psychology*, Vol. 45, 161–90.

Sherwood, R. (1958) 'The Bantu Clerk: A Study of Role Expectations', *Journal of Social Psychology*, Vol. 47, 285–316.

Shotter, J. (1984) *Social Accountability and Selfhood*, Basil Blackwell, Oxford.

Silbert, M. V. (1970) 'The Cape Morbidity Survey and its Significance in the Training for General Practice', *South African Medical Journal* (supplement), Vol. 44, 1–28.

Silove, D. (1990) 'Doctors and the State: Lessons from the Biko Case', *Social Science and Medicine*, Vol. 30, 417–29.

Simon, C. M. (1988) 'Dealing with Distress: A Medical Anthropological Analysis of the Search for Health in a Rural Transkeian Village'. Unpublished MA dissertation, Rhodes University.

Singer, M. (1990) 'Reinventing Medical Anthropology: Toward a Critical Re-alignement', *Social Science and Medicine*, Vol. 30, 179–87.

Singer, R. (1959) 'The Coronary Arteries of the Bantu Heart', *South African Medical Journal*, Vol. 33, 310–15.

Siraisi, N. G. (1990) *Medieval and Early Renaissance Medicine*, University of Chicago Press, Chicago.

Skaife, W. (1925) 'Discussion on Tuberculosis Detection and Prevention of Tuberculosis During Work Period', *Proceedings of the Transvaal Mine Medical Officers' Association*, Vol. 5, no. 5, 1–8.

South African Native Affairs Commission (1905) *Report and Minutes of Evidence*, Government Printer, Cape Town.

Sparrman, A. (1786) *A Voyage to the Cape of Good Hope, Towards the Antarctic Polar Circle, and Round the World, but Chiefly into the Country of the Hottenots and Caffres, From the Year 1772 to 1776. Volumes 1 and 2* (2nd edn), J. and J. Robinson, London.

Spencer, I. F. (1975) 'Postgraduate Training and Qualification in Community Medicine in South Africa', *South African Medical Journal*, Vol. 49, 35–43.

Stavorinus, J.S. (1798) *Voyages to the East Indies. The Whole Comprising a Full and Accurate Account of all the Late Posessions of the Dutch in India, and at the Cape of Good Hope* (Vols. 1, 2 and 3), G. G. and J. Robinson, London.

Steele, R./Anglicus (ed.) (1893) *Medieval Lore: An Epitome of the Science, Geography, Animal and Plant Folk Lore and Myth of the Middle Age, Being Classified Gleanings from the Encyclopaedia of Bartholomew Anglicus On the Properties of Things*, Elliot Stock, London.

Steinberg, M. (1993) 'Halting the Spread of AIDS in South Africa: The MRC's Strategy', in D. Yach and G. Martin (eds), *Building a Healthy Nation Through Research* (89–99), Medical Research Council, Cape Town.

Steuart, G. W. (1962) 'Community Health Education', in S. L. Kark and G. W. Steuart (eds), *A Practice of Social Medicine* (65–92), E. and S. Livingstone, London.

Steyn, K. (1993) 'Chronic Diseases of Lifestyle: A Threat to All South Africans', in D. Yach and G. Martin (eds), *Addressing the Impact of Urbanisation on Health in South Africa: The Medical Research Council's Response*, Medical Research Council, Cape Town.

Stoney, M. (1923) 'The Use of a Breathing Screen in the Examination of Natives', *Proceedings of the Transvaal Mine Medical Officers' Association*, Vol. 3, no. 8, 4.

Storr, N. V. (1950) 'Medical Diseases in the Bantu', *The Leech*, Vol. 21, no. 1, 49–51.

Stott, N. G. H. (1975) 'Do We Identify our Patients' Needs?', *The Leech*, Vol. 45, no. 3/4, 33–4.

Sutherland-Strachan, A. (1932) 'Haemosiderosis', *The Leech*, Vol. 4, no. 1, 29–31.

Swanson, M. (1977) 'The Sanitation Syndrome: Bubonic Plague and Urban Native Policy in the Cape Colony, 1900–1909', *Journal of African History*, Vol. 18, 387–410.

Swartz, L. (1985) 'Issues for Cross-cultural Psychiatric Research in South Africa', *Culture, Medicine and Psychiatry*, Vol. 9, 59–74.

— (1988) 'Some Comments on the Draft Ethical Code for South African Psychologists', *South African Journal of Psychology*, Vol. 22, 228–39.

— (1991) 'The Politics of Black Patients' Identity: Ward Rounds on the "Black Side" of a South African Psychiatric Hospital', *Culture, Medicine and Psychiatry*, Vol. 15, 217–44.

Swartz, L. and A. Levett (1989) 'Political Repression and Children in South Africa: The Social Construction of Damaging Effects', *Social Science and Medicine*, Vol. 28, 741–50.

Taylor, C. (1984) 'Foucault on Freedom and Truth', *Political Theory*, Vol. 12, no. 2, 152–83.

TBRC (Tuberculosis Research Committee) (1932) *Tuberculosis in South African Natives with Special Reference to the Disease among Mine Labourers on the Witwatersrand*, South African Institute for Medial Research (publication no. 30), Johannesburg.

Ten Rhyne, W. (1970/1686) 'A Short Account of the Cape of Good Hope and of the Hottentots Who Inhabit That Region', in I. Schapera and B. Farrington (eds), *The Early Cape Hottentots Described in the Writings of Olfert Dapper (1668), Willem Ten Rhyne (1686) and Johanus Gulielmus de Grevenbroek (1695)*, Negro Universities Press, Westport, CT.

Thompson, G. (1827) *Travels and Adventures in Southern Africa*, Henry Colburn, London.

Thompson, H. P. (1932) *Medical Missions at Work*, Society for the Propagation of the Gospel in Foreign Parts, London.

Tilsley, G. E. (1924) 'The Careless Ethiopian', *Conquest by Healing*, Vol. 1, no. 2, 43–7.

Tobias, P. V. (1947) 'Studies in Bantu Anatomy. Introduction', *The Leech*, Vol. 17, no. 1, 17–30.

— (1978) 'Reflections on Anatomy and Physical Anthropology', *South African Medical Journal*, Vol. 53, 1066–71.

Tobias, B. and P. Reddy (1993) 'Tracing the Health Promotion Movement', in M. Westaway (ed.), *Health Promotion – Proceedings of Six One-day Workshops held in Cape Town, Durban, Bloemfontein, Pietersburg and Port Elizabeth, 1–12 November 1993*, Medical Research Council, Pretoria.

Transvaal, The (1904) *Report of the Transvaal Labour Commission, Minutes of Proceedings and Evidence*, His Majesty's Stationery Office, London.

— (1905) *Report of the Coloured Labour Compound Commission*, Government Printer, Pretoria.

Transvaal Archives Depot, AG 202/10 LD 1786. Dr J. G. Visser, *Re Liberation of Native Lunatics from the Lunatic Asylum.* February–March 1910.

— CS 863/14966. *Lunacy Amendment Act, 1908.*

— SNA 162/275/02. Secretary for Native Affairs to Chief Labour Inspector, 'Mine natives', *Emaciated Condition of,* 4 February 1902.

— FLD 15 147/57. *Notes of a Meeting Held in Pretoria Between His Excellency the Lieutenant Governor and a Deputation from the Chamber of Mines in Regard to the Air Space Provided in Chinese Compounds,* 8 July 1904.

— GNLB 5/2910. *Medical Examination of Native Labourers Before Leaving the Transvaal* (correspondence between G.H. Coke, assistant medical officer of

Government Native Labour Bureau compound, compound manager and Secretary for Native Affairs), August–September, 1909.

— GNLB 211/29151. *Medical Dispute re Condition of Native Nontswaku*, December 1920.

Transvaal Chamber of Mines (1903) *Report to the Commissioner for Native Affairs on the Mortality Amongst Natives on the Mines of the Witwatersrand*, Transvaal Chamber of Mines, Johannesburg.

Turler, J. (1575) *The Traveiler of Jerome Turler, Divided into Two Bookes. The First Containing a Notable Discourse of the Manner, and Order of Traveiling Oversea, or Into Straunge and Forrein Countreys. The Second Comprehending an Excellent Description of the Most Delicious Realm of Naples in Italy. A Worke Very Pleasaunt for all Persons to Reade, and Right Profitable and Necessarie unto All Such as are Minded to Traveyll*, Abraham Veale, London.

Turner, G. A. (1907) *Report on the Alleged Prevalence of Pulmonary Tuberculosis and on Some of the Principal Diseases Existing in the Kraals of the Natives in Portuguese East African Territory*, Hayne and Gibson, Johannesburg.

— (1911) 'Some of the Tribal Marks of the South African Native Races', *Transvaal Medical Journal*, 11 February, 12–15.

Turvey, M. (1951) *Waiting for Health at Mkambati. An Account of the Leper Settlement*, Society for the Propagation of the Gospel in Foreign Parts, London.

Union of South Africa (1914) *Report of the Tuberculosis Commission (U.G. 34–14)*, Cape Times Ltd, Government Printer, Cape Town.

— (1916) *General Report of the Miners' Phthisis Prevention Committee*, Government Printing and Stationery Office, Pretoria.

— (1919) *Report of the Influenza Commission*, Government Printer, Cape Town.

— (1928) *Department of Public Health. Report for the Year Ended 30th June, 1928*, Government Printer, Pretoria.

— (1929) *Department of Public Health. Report for the Year Ended 30th June, 1929*, Government Printer, Pretoria.

— (1930) *Department of Public Health. Report for the Year Ended 30th June, 1930*, Government Printer, Pretoria.

— (1935) *Department of Public Health. Report for the Year Ended 30th June, 1935*, Government Printer, Pretoria.

— (1937) *Department of Public Health. Report for the Year Ended 30th June, 1937*, Government Printer, Pretoria.

— (1940) *Department of Public Health. Report for the Year Ended 30th June, 1940*, Government Printer, Pretoria.

— (1941) *Department of Public Health. Report for the Year Ended 30th June, 1941*, Government Printer, Pretoria.

— (1945) *Department of Public Health. Report for the Year Ended 30th June, 1945*, Government Printer, Pretoria.

— (1947) *Department of Public Health. Report for the Year Ended 30th June, 1947*, Government Printer, Pretoria.

Van Heyningen, E. (1989) 'Public Health and Society in Cape Town 1880–1910'. Unpublished Ph D thesis, University of Cape Town.

Van Onselen, C. (1980) *Chibaro: African Mine Labour in Southern Rhodesia*, Ravan Press, Johannesburg.

—(1982) *Studies in the Social and Economic History of the Witwatersrand. Vol. 2: New Nineveh*, Ravan Press, Johannesburg.

Van Velden, D. D. (1943) 'A Case of Developmental Malposition of the Intestine', *The Leech*, Vol. 14, no. 2, 33–4.

Van Wyk, C. W. (1970) 'Mouth Pigmentation Patterns in a Group of Healthy South African Bantu', *South African Medical Journal*, Vol. 44, 177–86.

Vaughan, M. (1991) *Curing their Ills: Colonial Power and African Illness*, Polity Press, Cambridge.

Walzer, M. (1986) 'The Politics of Michel Foucault', in D. C. Hoy (ed.), *Foucault, A Critical Reader*, Basil Blackwell, Oxford.

Wasserman, H. P. and T. Heyl (1968) 'Quantitative Data on Skin Pigmentation in South African Races', *South African Journal of Clinical and Laboratory Medicine*, Vol. 8, 98–101.

Watkins-Pitchford, W. (1908) 'Hygiene in South Africa', *Transvaal Medical Journal*, Vol. 4, 67–75.

Watts, H. L. (1980) 'Some Reactions to Illness of Urban Black and Indian Families in Durban', *South African Medical Journal*, Vol. 57, 589–91.

Webster, E. (1986) 'Excerpt from "Servants of Apartheid"', *Psychology in Society*, Vol. 6, 6–28.

Wells, L. H. (1933) 'The More Important Dimensions of the Bony Pelvis in the Native Races of South Africa', *The Leech*, Vol. 19, no. 3, 1–6.

— (1949) 'The Possible Field of Anatomical Research in South Africa', *South African Journal of Science*, Vol. 42, 78–89.

WHO (World Health Organisation) (1983) *Apartheid and Health*, WHO, Geneva.

Wilcocks, R. W. (1932) *The Poor White Problem in South Africa. Report of the Carnegie Commission. Part II: Psychological Report, The Poor White*, Pro-Ecclesia, Stellenbosch.

Williams, H. (1887) 'First Experiences in the Kuruman District', *The Chronicle of the Church Missionary Society for the year 1887*, Church Missionary Society, London.

Yach, D. and S. Tollman (1993) 'Public Health Initiatives in South Africa in the 1940s and 1950s: Lessons for a Post-apartheid Era', *American Journal of Public Health*, Vol. 83, 1043–50.

Zwi, A. B. (1987) 'The Political Abuse of Medicine and the Challenge of Opposing It', *Social Science and Medicine*, Vol. 25, 649–57.

Zwi, A. B. and A. Ugalde (1989) 'Towards an Epidemiology of Political Violence in the Third World', *Social Science and Medicine*, Vol. 28, 633–42.

Index